BETWEEN MOON

ROBERT GRAVES

BETWEEN MOON AND MOON

SELECTED CORRESPONDENCE

Edited with a commentary by
Paul O'Prey

MOYER BELL LIMITED
MOUNT KISCO, NEW YORK & LONDON

Published by Moyer Bell Limited

First American Edition, 1990

**LIBRARY OF CONGRESS
CATALOGING-IN-PUBLICATION DATA**

Graves, Robert, 1895–1985
Between moon and moon : selected letters of Robert Graves, 1946–1972 / edited with commentary and notes by Paul O'Prey. —1st ed.
    p. cm.
    Includes index.

ISBN 1–55921–031–1 Pb
    1. Graves, Robert, 1895–1985—Correspondence.   2. Authors, English—20th century—Correspondence.   I. O'Prey, Paul, 1956–
II. Title.

PR6013.R35Z48   1990
821'.912—dc20   90–37414
[B]   CIP

Printed in the United States of America
Distributed by Rizzoli

CONTENTS

Introduction   9
Acknowledgements   11
Correspondents   13
Biographical Notes   17

Part One   1946–1951   21
Part Two   1951–1957   99
Part Three 1957–1963   169
Part Four   1964–1972   229

Appendix   'Summary of Critical Principles'
from *The Nazarene Gospel Restored*   289

Notes   295
Index   318

INTRODUCTION

Robert Graves has always been an extraordinarily prolific letter writer, answering every letter he received – often as many as twenty a day – usually by return of post, and has always attached great importance to his correspondence with both friends and colleagues. This selection is only a very small percentage of the total number of letters he wrote between 1946 and 1972, and in choosing I have tried to find those letters which give the clearest and most honest impression of Graves's character, and which, when linked together, form a sort of 'spontaneous autobiography' to be put alongside what he himself calls the 'spiritual autobiography' of his *Collected Poems*.

As in the first volume* I have limited the number of correspondents so as to avoid giving too diffuse or blurred an impression and have not included any of the great quantity of letters he wrote in reply to strangers who had written to him – academics, fellow writers, aspiring poets, enthusiastic readers or 'reverend mothers' of American churches devoted to Goddess worship who consider Graves to be a prophet – so as not to distract from the main currents of his life.

Most of his close friends are included here, with the notable exceptions of Alastair Reid, the Scottish poet, translator and journalist, and Graves's four 'Muses'. Reid has not kept any of the letters he received from Graves, and I have rejected *Quoz*, a collection of letters they exchanged in the fifties with the intention of publishing them, because although they remain unpublished they are not genuine, spontaneous letters but carefully considered and revised interchanges of opinions on various subjects. (On the other hand, I have included two letters to the press which, although not 'genuine' letters, seemed directly relevant to other letters in the book.) As for the letters to the four 'Muses', it will not be possible to publish them for many years; some, over four hundred letters to Aemilia Laraçuen,

In Broken Images: Selected Letters of Robert Graves, 1914–1946, edited by Paul O'Prey (Hutchinson, 1982).

are in a university special collection in Canada, inaccessible until ten years after the death of Graves or of his wife, whichever is the later.

As before, my commentary and notes have been restricted to a minimum, so as not to take away valuable space from the letters themselves, though I hope they are sufficient for a reader with little knowledge of Graves's life to have a full appreciation of the correspondence.

Other editorial practices have also remained the same as in the first volume. I have silently altered a few slips of the pen, when what is meant is obvious. Where the reading of a word is in doubt it is given in square brackets. Dates at the head of letters have been standardized and addresses given only where a change is indicated, except in Part Two when Graves was alternating between Deyá and Palma; in this case I have put at the top of each letter the place from which it was written, if known. In a few instances I have omitted a tiresome repetition or a short passage which might be unduly offensive to someone still alive; these omissions are marked by a row of four dots on a separate line.

Paul O'Prey
Granada, December 1983

ACKNOWLEDGEMENTS

Robert and Beryl Graves and I wish to thank the following people and institutions for their cooperation in supplying copies of letters in their possession, and for their patience in checking illegible passages in the copies against the originals: the Poetry/Rare Book Collection of the University Libraries, the State University of New York at Buffalo (for letters to Alan Hodge and Lynette Roberts); Valerie Eliot; Ruth Fainlight and Alan Sillitoe; Terence Hards; the Liddell Hart Centre for Military Archives at the University of London, King's College; the Lilly Library, Indiana University (for letters to Karl Gay); T. S. Matthews; Michael Podro and Fanny Podro; the Richard A. Gleeson Library, University of San Francisco (for letters to James Reeves); Derek Savage; Idries Shah; Joanna Simon; the Humanities Research Center, the University of Texas at Austin (for letters to James Reeves and Martin Seymour-Smith); the Special Collection of the University Library, the University of Victoria, BC (for letters to Selwyn Jepson and James Reeves) and R. Gordon Wasson. And to Cassell & Co. for permission to reproduce poems by Graves, and to Penguin Books Ltd for permission to quote from *The Greek Myths*.

I personally owe thanks to a number of people who have helped me in various ways. In particular I would like to acknowledge the help of: Richard and Ann Billows and Graeme Fife, for checking classical references; Nicholas Drake, for his assistance and helpful reactions to early drafts; Karl and Rene Gay, for answering a number of questions; Lucia Graves; Michael and Stella Irwin; the London Library and the London Library Trust; Martin Seymour-Smith, for his continued and invaluable help and advice; Michael Sofroniou; and Ronnie and Asta Wathen.

I also wish to thank the Southern Arts Association for a bursary to help with the costs involved in the production of the book; my parents, for further 'bursaries' and for their support throughout; my wife, Pilar Garcia, for her practical assistance, her ideas and her untiring enthusiasm; and once again, Robert and Beryl Graves, who have helped so much but who have insisted on my having a completely free hand in saying and including what I liked.

CORRESPONDENTS

For earlier letters to T. S. Eliot, K. C. Gay, Alan Hodge, Basil Liddell Hart, T. S. Matthews and Lynette Roberts, see *In Broken Images: Selected Letters of Robert Graves 1914–1946* (Hutchinson, 1982).

T. S. Eliot (1888–1965). Major American poet, critic and playwright. Graves first corresponded with Eliot when the latter was editor of *Criterion* in the 1920s, and again when Eliot, a director of the publishing firm of Faber and Faber Ltd, published Graves's *The White Goddess* in the 1940s.

Ruth Fainlight (born 1931). American poet, playwright and short-story writer. Publications of her poems include *To Set the Matter More Clearly and Other Poems* (1968), *Poems* (1971; with Ted Hughes and Alan Sillitoe), *Twenty-one Poems* (1973) and *Sybils and Other Poems* (1980).

K. C. Gay (born Karl Goldschmidt, 1912). Private secretary to Graves and Laura Riding, 1934–39. As a German Jew he was a refugee in England at the outbreak of the Second World War, but then served in the Pioneer Corps and the Royal Navy. In 1947, after obtaining British citizenship, he returned to Mallorca to work with Graves until 1965, when he became Curator of the Poetry Collection in the Lockwood Memorial Library at the State University of New York at Buffalo. He is now retired and lives in Palma de Mallorca.

Terence Hards (born 1929). Graves published Hards's sole book of poetry, *As It Was*, as a Seizin Press book in 1964. *Visitors*, Hards's play for radio, was broadcast by the BBC in 1984.

Captain Sir Basil Liddell Hart (1895–1970). English military

13

historian and writer. His many books include studies of the theory and strategy of war; several biographies (including *T. E. Lawrence: In Arabia and After*) and several military histories which are now established classics, such as his histories of the two world wars. In 1965 he published his *Memoirs* in two volumes.

Alan Hodge (1915–79). English writer and historian. He collaborated with Graves on three books: *The Long Week-End: A Social History of Great Britain 1918–1939*, *The Reader Over Your Shoulder: A Handbook for Writers of English Prose*, and *Work in Hand*, a volume of poems (with Norman Cameron). After the Second World War, during which he was assistant private secretary to the Minister of Information, Brendan Bracken, he worked for Hamish Hamilton, the publisher, and co-founded and co-edited with Peter Quennell the magazine *History Today*.

Selwyn Jepson (born 1899). English thriller writer and 'financial adviser' to Graves. His books include *Keep Murder Quiet* (1940), *Man Running* (1948), *The Hungry Spider* (1950), *The Black Italian* (1954), *A Noise in the Night* (1957) and *Fear in the Wind* (1964).

T. S. Matthews (born 1901). American journalist, who became managing editor of *Time* magazine. His book of memoirs about Graves, Laura Riding, Schuyler Jackson and others of his friends, *Jacks or Better* (retitled *Under the Influence* for publication in Britain) was published in 1977.

Joshua Podro (1895–1962). Polish-Jewish (originally Podrovsky) writer and businessman who fought in France in the First World War; later he was a well-known Yiddish journalist in New York, then founded the International Press Cutting Bureau in Britain. During the Second World War the bureau was evacuated from London to Paignton and he and Graves met as neighbours; Graves was writing *King Jesus* at this time. Podro was also a dedicated scholar of Judaism, and his historical investigations brought him to conclusions similar to Graves's, whom he influenced a good deal with his ideas. They collaborated on *The Nazarene Gospel Restored* (1953) and *Jesus in Rome* (1957). Podro also wrote *Nuremberg, the Unholy City*, a comparative study of modern and medieval persecution in Germany, and *The Last Pharisee* (1959), a biography of Rabbi Joshua ben Hananyali, the last of a generation of Pharisees that witnessed the destruction of Jerusalem and the rise of Christianity.

James Reeves (1909–1978). English poet, critic and schoolteacher. His first book of poems, *The Natural Need*, was published in 1936 by Graves and Riding as a Seizin Press book (with an introduction by Riding). His books include: *The Complete Poems for Children*, *A Short History of English Poetry*, *Commitment to Poetry*, *The Critical Sense*, *Inside Poetry*, *Selected Poetry and Prose of Robert Graves* (1961, for schools). His many editions in the Heinemann Poetry Bookshelf Series, of which he was general editor, include selections of the poetry of John Clare, S. T. Coleridge, G. M. Hopkins and Emily Dickinson. His *Collected Poems* were published in 1974.

Lynette Roberts (born 1909). Welsh poet. Her books include *Poems* (1944), *Gods with Stainless Ears* (1951) and a book about Captain Cook's journey to Australia, called *The Endeavour*.

Derek Savage (born 1917). English poet and critic, whose books include *Hamlet and the Pirates* and *The Withered Branch*.

Martin Seymour-Smith (born 1928). English poet and critic. He lived in Palma with Graves from 1951 to 1954, as tutor to Graves's son William. His books include the first old-spelling edition of Shakespeare's *Sonnets*, *Poets through Their Letters*, *Guide to Modern World Literature* and *Robert Graves: His Life and Work* (Hutchinson, 1982), the first biography of Graves.

Idries Shah (born 1924). Born in Simla, India, of a family of Afghan origin. Writer of many books, particularly about the thought and study of Sufism, of which he is generally considered to be the foremost (if somewhat controversial) international authority. He is of the Naqshabandiyya order and often referred to as 'King of the Sufis'. The central books in his 'Sufi-studies' are *The Sufis* (1964, with an introduction by Graves), *The Way of the Sufi*, *Tales of the Dervishes* (with an introduction by Graves), *Learning How to Learn*, *The Perfumed Scorpion*, *Seeker after Truth* and *The Magic Monas-*

tery. Other works include *Oriental Magic, Caravan of Dreams*, the three *Mulla Nasrudin* books and *The Dermis Probe*.

Alan Sillitoe (born 1928). English poet and novelist. The best known of his books include *Saturday Night and Sunday Morning* (1958), *The Loneliness of the Long Distance Runner* (1959), *The Rats* (1960, poems), *The Ragman's Daughter* (1963), *Road to Volgograd* (1964) and *Guzman Go Home* (1968). Graves's letters are usually addressed to both Sillitoe and his wife, Ruth Fainlight.

Dr George Simon (1902–77). Celebrated radiologist and teacher (at St Bartholomew's Hospital and the Brompton Chest Hospital) and author of various books on radiology.

John Wain (born 1925). Poet, novelist and critic. Professor of Poetry at Oxford; his many books include *Hurry on Down, Strike the Father Dead, The Pardoner's Tale* (novels), *Professing Poetry* (Oxford lectures) and *Poems 1949–1979*.

R. Gordon Wasson (born 1898). American banker and ethnomycologist. He began his career as a journalist, became a Wall St reporter, joined the bank J. P. Morgan and Co. as press agent and later rose to be vice-president of the company. With his Russian wife, Valentina, a paediatrician, he dedicated all free time to the study of mushrooms in history and religion (and was helped considerably by Graves); their discovery of sacred mushroom-eating cults in Mexico became famous. His books include *Mushrooms, Russia and History* (Pantheon Books, New York, 1957; with Dr Valentina Wasson), *Les Champignons Hallucigènes de Mexique* (Paris, 1958; with Professor Roger Heim) and *Soma: Divine Mushroom of Immortality* (New York, 1969).

BIOGRAPHICAL NOTES
1946–1982, including principal publications

May 1946	Returns to Deyá, Mallorca with his wife Beryl and their three small children. Graves had left Deyá, where he had been living with the American poet Laura Riding, in July 1936, at the outbreak of the Spanish Civil War.
September 1946	*King Jesus* published.
May 1948	*The White Goddess* published.
September 1949	*The Common Asphodel* (collected essays on poetry) published.
November 1949	*The Islands of Unwisdom* published in USA.
April 1950	*The Golden Ass* (translation of Apuleius) published.
November 1951	*Poems and Satires* published.
October 1953	*The Nazarene Gospel Restored* (with Joshua Podro) published.
1954–55	Clark Lectures at Cambridge.
February 1955	*Homer's Daughter* and *The Greek Myths* published.
June 1955	*Collected Poems 1955* published.
September 1955	*The Crowning Privilege* (Clark Lectures) published.
February 1956	First of several lecture tours to the USA (lectures at Mount Holyoke College, Massachusetts).
April 1957	*Jesus in Rome* (with Joshua Podro) published.
May 1957	*They Hanged My Saintly Billy* published.
March 1958	*5 Pens in Hand* (lectures, essays, 'historical anomalies', stories and poems) published.
January 1959	Visits Israel at the invitation of the government.
April 1959	*Collected Poems 1959* published.
February-March 1959	Musical *Song of Solomon* written, with his daughter Jenny Nicholson; unperformed.
November 1959	*The Anger of Achilles* (translation of Homer's *Iliad*) published.

May 1960	*Food for Centaurs* published.
January 1961	First meets Idries Shah, in Mallorca.
February 1961	Elected Professor of Poetry at Oxford.
May 1961	*More Poems* published.
April 1962	*Oxford Addresses on Poetry.*
August 1963	*New Poems 1962* published.
March 1964	*The Hebrew Myths* (with Raphael Patai) published.
April 1964	*Man Does, Woman Is* (poems) published.
March 1965	*Mammon and the Black Goddess* published.
July 1965	*Love Respelt* (poems) published.
September 1965	*Collected Poems 1965* published.
1966	*Seventeen Poems Missing from Love Respelt* published.
1967	*Poetic Craft and Principle* (lectures) published.
October 1967	Visits his daughter Catherine in Australia.
1967	*The Rubaiyyat of Omar Khayaam* (a new translation, with critical commentaries, with Omar Ali-Shah) published.
May 1968	Visits Hungary and the Soviet Union.
July 1968	Made Adoptive Son of Deyá.
September 1968	Awarded a gold medal for poetry at the Cultural Olympics at Mexico.
December 1968	Awarded the Queen's Gold Medal for Poetry.
1969	*The Crane Bag, and Other Disputed Subjects* published.
1969	*Poems About Love* published.
May 1970	At the invitation of the PEN Club visits Hungary, where he establishes the Robert Graves Prize for Poetry.
May 1971	Visits Hungary again.
1971	*The Green-Sailed Vessel* (poems) published.
1972	*Difficult Questions, Easy Answers* (essays) published.
1973	*Timeless Meeting* (poems) published.
October 1973	Visits Poland and Hungary.
1974	*At the Gate* (poems) published.
July 1975	Eightieth birthday.
July 1976	Visits Poland.
1978	Last visit to London.

PART ONE

1946–1951

Having left Deyá, Mallorca, where he was living with the American poet Laura Riding and their German secretary Karl Gay, at the outbreak of the Spanish Civil War in 1936, and having subsequently broken with Riding in 1939, Robert Graves spent the war years living in Galmpton, Devon, with his second wife Beryl and their three young children: William (aged six), Lucia (aged three), and eighteen-month-old Juan.

As soon as the war was over, however, Graves was very anxious to return to Deyá. In February 1946, his eldest daughter (from his marriage to Nancy Nicholson), Jenny Nicholson – a young journalist who had made her name as a war correspondent – visited Spain for the *Sunday Dispatch*. Graves asked her to go to Mallorca, if she could, and find out what condition his two houses were in and whether the local political situation made a return there feasible. Jenny reported that Canelluñ, the house Graves and Riding had left at four and a half hours' notice and with one suitcase each ten years previously, was in excellent condition, untouched by war and carefully looked after by Juan Gelat and other friends in the village; in her letter to him she wrote that she had found his straw hat 'lying on the hall table where you chucked it down in haste ten years ago – but carefully dusted . . . and a half-written letter beginning "Dearest Jenny" on your writing desk . . .' She also reported that the political situation was peaceful and food plentiful.

Overjoyed at this news, Graves hastily made all preparations necessary and on 15 May he and the family set off in a chartered air taxi, stopping at Rennes to see Majorcan friends living there, and at Toulouse and Barcelona.

One of the first letters Graves wrote after his return to Deyá was to James Reeves, with whom he was collaborating on an anthology of poetry for schoolchildren. Graves first met Reeves in 1935, after

23

Reeves had sent some of his poems to Riding, which both she and Graves liked very much; Reeves, then a twenty-eight-year-old Cambridge graduate with a schoolmaster's job, was soon incorporated into the Riding–Graves circle, becoming a contributor to *Focus* and *Epilogue* (periodicals edited by Riding and Graves; see *In Broken Images*, pp. 242 and 245); in 1936 his first book of poems, *The Natural Need*, was published by them as a Seizin Press book, with an introduction by Riding. At that time W. B. Yeats was compiling his edition of *The Oxford Book of Modern Verse* and asked Graves to contribute; Graves deferred his consent, however, until Yeats gave his opinion of *The Natural Need*, a copy of which was sent to him by Riding. Yeats replied (23 May 1936):

Dear Miss Riding

Too reasonable, too truthful. We poets should be good liars, remembering always that the muses are women and prefer the embrace of gay warty lads. Yet [there] are fine things in him – 'Thoughts and Memories', the end of 'The Place', 'His going in the morning a song for swallows'. Much else. I wish I had met with his work some weeks ago.

Consequently, Graves refused to contribute to the anthology and always later referred to this as an example of Yeats's 'fraudulence' as a poet.

Though Graves admitted that the quality of James Reeves's poetry was very uneven, Reeves was one of the very few contemporary British poets whom he admired. In a BBC Radio review of Reeves's *Collected Poems 1929–59* he said, 'I know no living English poet who can touch him.' He also recalled how W. H. Davies (1871–1940) had kept a list of poets, whom he struck off one by one whenever they said or did anything unethical (until there were only two names left: Graves's and his own – though Graves did not mention this point in the review); Graves said, 'I keep a similar list. It has very few names left on it. I struck off Yeats when I got that letter. James Reeves is still there.'

During the war their friendship grew closer and included both their families (Reeves and his wife, Mary, had three children).

The first three paragraphs of the following letter are written (typed) by Beryl Graves, the rest by Graves himself.

No date   Canelluñ
                                                                Deyá
                                                              Mallorca

DEAR James,

WE have just recovered this vast old Underwood typewriter from
Palma and I am trying it out. Very strange feeling. We have just
received your letter dated June 20th today July 11th. With the
French frontier closed they take that time.

WELL here we are and everything is lovely, particularly in the
garden, weather perfect, veg and fruit wonderful. Prices terribly
high, rations wretched – we have to buy on the black market. We
have just run out of the sugar we saved up in England to bring
here, plus a small ration that has been distributed since we got
here. Our next pound will cost us around 15s. Luckily we don't
need much here as there is so much fruit. We are well in touch
with news as we have a wireless, also we get *The Times* air edition
which is expensive but worth it as it reaches us in 2 to 3 days.
Naturally we feel a bit isolated from people but what else can
one be if anywhere nice. It was lovely seeing Mary in London,
though I'm afraid we were rather distrait as we were still without
visas at that time.

It was a nice little aeroplane and would have been a nice flight
to anyone who liked flying. The children liked it but were sick – we
couldn't be sick as the paper bags people used to be sick into are
apparently not in production again yet and William and Lucia
used the available tumblers to capacity and sometimes more. It
was nice to be in France again though; I did wish we could have
stayed there longer, I had forgotten how much I liked Rennes. The
difference between France and Spain is so terrific. We got stuck
at Toulouse and at Barcelona. Toulouse was hopeless, no petrol
ready for us, nobody knew or cared but liked to look at the plane
and talk about the war. Eventually we had to fly to the nearby
civilian airfield where they actually did put in the petrol but with
about 6 chaps hanging round smoking cigarettes right over the
petrol frightened us out of our wits. At Barcelona we nearly
landed on a flock of sheep and then ran through a wire. We were
received with much politeness and everyone looked very smart and
efficient – though they weren't nearly as efficient as they pretended
to be, perhaps, here Robert continues the story, because they had
only recently opened the civil aviation port and we were the first

air-taxi to make the hop to Majorca which is a military zone. It needed 24 hours and the British Embassy at Madrid to straighten things out. It all turned out lucky in the end because the bad weather improved and we had a non-air-sick flight over the Foradada and Valldemosa and could see our house in the distance. The island looks wonderful from the air, the terraces and compact villages and everything was still very green because of late rains. At the airport Gelat and Juan[1] and [the] cars were waiting with much emotion. They haven't aged the appropriate ten years, nobody has really except the children who have grown up – the little Francisca of *Laura and Francisca*[2] is now a deep-bosomed strapping girl of, I suppose, 19, and Miguel the loutish Fonda boy is a Guardia Civil, very presentable, and married to the highly refined daughter of Juana Pescadora. Margarita of the café, she of the boss-eye and wicked tongue, is dead: God castigated her with cancer for her wicked denunciations of innocent people during the Troubles, and Jaime has married a woman from another village of the plain who seems an improvement. The wicked doctor[3] has had two strokes (God has been castigating to some purpose) and totters about, usually crying when addressed. All our friends are well and uncastigated, and the Gelat family send greetings. The grandchildren are sweet. Juan III is going to be just like his grandfather Gelat; and Catalina II just like Tia Maria, Gelat's sister.

No foreigners at all in the village except an old lame English spinster who paints flowers all day in a Bloomsbury attic she has made for herself at the Fonda, and it is sad to see so many unoccupied furnished houses.

The Cala[4] is just as before except that there is more sand now, at both ends of the beach. Wm can manage the climb without effort, Lucia with a little coaxing. She has her 3rd birthday on July 21 so that isn't bad, is it? in this weather. Alpargatas[5] are not what they were, they wear out in about ten days; and all the cars except the high-ups' run on 'Majorcan petrol' – gas made from almond kernels or olive pip charcoal – which stinks the interior out. We have been only once to Palma, leaving Juan at the Fabrica, but with Lucia shopping was difficult, though it was a relief not to have to think of points and coupons; so now we shop in Sóller which is very well stocked. I hope in about a month's time to have my books from England here and a complete library of the poets;

but will have to wait for Karl before getting down to the work of selecting our anthology. At present I am revising a whole lot of scattered literary essays of mine.[6] The children have had a brief illness of Spanish [tummy] cured by an M-&-B preparation; otherwise are fine. The two younger ones sleep in what was Laura's workroom; and Beryl has the press-room (we are going to sell the press)[7] as her study . . . We aren't allowed to send food parcels to you, unfortunately.

Now what about the Christmas holidays? Get your passports renewed, and then get the Spanish Consulate to give you the forms to fill in for a visa, and then two people from here will sponsor you. If we combine the visit with anthology decisions 'pleasure and interest will go hand in hand'.

Much love to you all   Robert

The people of Deyá were as delighted to see Graves as he was to see them; they saw his arrival as a hopeful sign of the reopening of the tourist trade and a return to political and economic stability. The family settled in quickly and the first job, he wrote to his friend Tom Matthews, was to 'convert' Canellun from 'a childless and carefully arranged museum place into a free-and-easy family one'. This involved disposing of all the papers Riding had left behind, which she had asked Graves to destroy; accordingly he sold several sackfuls of poetry and prose to a Palma wastepaper merchant: 'a pity, but they will make good cardboard and wrapping paper', he wrote to Karl Gay, who had remained in London, working for Joshua Podro's International Press Cutting Bureau (see page 14) until he received confirmation of his British naturalization and could rejoin Graves (which he did in 1947).

To Alan Hodge

No poems recently, but I found here what I think a very nice one[8] which I left behind in 1936, and have sent to the US *Nation* in answer to a request.

29 June 1946

Dearest Alan:

Thanks for your budget. Yes, we now have the air-mail *Times*, and a Phillips radio set which gets England rather more clearly than we got it down at Devon, so are *au courant* with all your latest climatic and dietetic disasters. And yes, there is such freedom of speech here and absence of any sense of constriction or restriction that I don't feel in the least cramped about writing to you. The Terror of the Civil War times is now ancient history, and there is general speculation about what will happen, if anything, in September; life is certainly very hard for the labouring classes, but no revolution is talked. They have had it.

Thank goodness the children go nicely brown instead of that horrid red, or freckling. They love the heat and have escaped new-arrival stomach, as Beryl has not. It laid her low on the very morning of San Juan[9] when the Fabrica feast of *arroz paella*, roast kid, *ensaimadas*, etc., had been spread with no unlavish hand. I count as an old-arrival and have been spared. The great thing is to be able to drink as much as I like of any drink I like except whisky (which I don't like) and of course vodka which I have never sampled. Pimientos and aubergines are now in the market, and this is when they catch *salmonetes*[10] – Beryl says they have too many bones.

Yes, I was so relieved about the *New Statesman* review,[11] having publicly said just before I left that if I have a good review there I would know that I was a failure and my friends would find me lying dead with a smoking revolver by my side in a public *pissoir* like the hero of a decadent French novel. *King Jesus* will be out in Sept. on both sides of the Atlantic and I am now revising my early essays on poetry. I am still in 1926 and the style doesn't mature until about 1934. We look forward very much to James's poems.

Gelat has undertaken that while there is any food left on the island we shall eat it: he and I are so mutually (or is it reciprocally?) grateful to each other for past services that it is almost uncomfortable. All the same we must devise a means of getting bacon and butter and coffee and so on. I am getting a private bank a/c in the US which should help a bit. My stock has gone up among the *señores* of the island since I have had my novels translated into Spanish: three more are being translated this year, but *not KJ*!

It is really hot at last, and when the flies encouraged by the recent unseasonable rains have died off all will be perfect; the breeze always blows off the sea and bulges the entrada curtain slightly.

Fulfilling Laura's behests I have destroyed all her loose writings
– several half-finished or ¼-finished books and bundles of scrawled
notes. She left a lot of unhappiness behind but we are clearing it
off gradually: unhappiness breeds clutter.

Love and success to Hamilton's[12] reprints.   – Robert –

Rations: We've had so far 1½ lb sugar, 1½ lb rice, 10 lbs
spuds, 1½ lb lard, 1½ lb barley, for the family in six weeks. The
spuds cost about 6d a lb which is modest in comparison with the
£2 10/- a lb which the local radio says they cost in London today.

In March 1943, Graves had met Martin Seymour-Smith, then a
fourteen-year-old schoolboy, whose librarian father, Frank Seymour-
Smith, used to obtain books for Graves during the war. Graves and
Beryl immediately liked Martin, who became a frequent visitor to
Galmpton, and Graves took a great interest in his poetry and
education.

25 July 1946

My dear Martin:
   I should have written before, but you know how it is when
broad seas flow between: it doesn't seem to matter much putting
off a letter for two or three days, or weeks, and soon it is months.
Well, we arrived very safely and everything was ten years older,
but just the same: for example, all my shirts and trousers and socks
wearable; and five jars of green tomato chutney eatable, and
cigarette tobacco in my tobacco jar smokeable. And the
Encyclopaedia Britannica and *Times Atlas* ten more years out of
date. But it is wonderful to be here and will be still more wonderful
when the traffic jam breaks and our friends can come out. Beryl and
I were talking about you this evening: wondering what has been
happening. Apart from the British Vice-Consul and his wife we
have seen no English-speaking people since we left. I am feeling
thoroughly relaxed now that Beryl is becoming acclimatized and
bolder with her Spanish and the children are able to cope a lot
better with the weather and change of food. (We are all very well
indeed and the heat is intense.) My first writing job here was to
make final amendments in *The White Goddess*, which are now being
typed by Karl and sent to Creative Age Press in US (they are
definitely publishing it; and will do it before Fabers). Then I set

myself to revise and see what was worth keeping of my early essays. They are very badly written and inaccurate, but I found that I had already in 1920 planned a line that I have been following ever since. I dare say they'll make a book if I'm ruthless enough. This last week, because Beryl teases me that I can't write modern fiction, I have written a 10,000 word story[13] for *Cosmopolitan* which offered me a large fee; the result is a bit prostitutish, but as the proceeds will be spent in the black market, she thinks this is excusable. (The Biblical text is in Amos, commented on by Jesus (see *King Jesus*) in the case of the High Priest's w.c.)[14] I found a lost poem of mine about the Bass Rock here among my papers, quite nice, and have sent it to the US *Nation* but not written anything new: not feeling settled enough yet for poems. That will come, I hope. There don't seem to be many, or indeed, any books that I feel I want to read; in US or England. I hope that this does not mean that I am getting stupid; it is more likely that nobody has much to say.

This is a wonderful land for people with money, and I feel a bit ashamed of ranking as such; but really it *is* nice not to worry about coupons and points and to be able to drink what one likes when one likes and not to have to fill in a single form.

Now waiting for September to know whether *King Jesus* is going to be a financial success, and to what degree. It doesn't really make much difference, because I will always work; except that it will determine what books I will be able to afford to write, and whether we can give ourselves a bit more liberty by getting a car, etc.

I was amused that I *did* get a nasty review in the *New Statesman* for my poems – you remember I prophesied awful things for myself if I got a good one! and may you always fare likewise!

The evening lizards are on the netting of our windows catching moths, so pretty to watch that it is difficult to work. I have not been to a bull-fight yet being perfectly content with bathing and picking greengages off the trees.

Love to Marjorie and yourself and respects to your father.

Yours ever,   Robert

Love from Beryl.
Tell us what's happening. Airmail (5d) saves 3 weeks.

In September 1946, *King Jesus* was published by Creative Age Press in the USA. Tom Matthews, the managing editor of *Time* magazine and a long-standing friend of Graves, read an advance copy and, as he and his wife Julie had recently become 'pious' (Graves's word – to Alan Hodge), he disliked the book and told Graves so, comparing the novel to George Moore's *The Brook Kerith* (1916). This was an unreasonable comment on what is one of Graves's best historical novels, though Graves was expecting a bad press ('never will a book have been so hard hit since Milton's day', he wrote to Gay).

29 August 1946

Dearest Tom:

I was touched to get a very long, very sweet, wholly autograph letter from you; especially as the letter I sent you from here by airmail some two months ago hasn't turned up yet at your office: perhaps it's the stamps that lure some philatelic office boy – letters from here always arrive in Britain, seldom in the US. I am now well posted in your family's doings again, after two years of silence. Good.

About *King Jesus*: your criticism interests me very much, especially as I know that it comes straight from your heart, and gives me a foretaste of the bludgeoning that the book will get from a large part of the solid core of educated Americans, especially in the Middle West. It is, however, an oversimplification of the case: I mean, the comparison with George Moore. Moore had no historical conscience and imposed a theme on the story rather than letting the story emerge logically from the historical data: and he scoffed at Jesus as a charlatan. Jesus was not a charlatan but true-born and perfectly uncompromising and knew his scriptures better than either George Moore or yourself: and it was not a simple faith, as you say, but a highly complex and esoteric one. By his failure to be the Jewish Messiah, he became the Christian God: which does not make Christianity or Judaism 'false', but merely proves their irreconcilability. The importance of the book will be apparent not only to scholars but to a very large number of people who have not managed to keep their childhood faith unspotted and are aware of four main *cruces* in the Gospels: 1) The Nativity story; 2) The baptism story; 3) The sudden change in Jesus's behaviour in the last 48 hours before the Cross; 4) The Resurrection. It would be easy to dismiss 1) and 2) as fairy tales if the early Christians had been wilful liars or romancers, but they weren't; 3) the cursing of the barren fig-tree, the riot on the Temple Hill, the calling for swords, the order to the disciples at the Last Supper to abandon their simple faith in Providence, were terrible occurrences and have been stumbling-blocks to all Christians ever since and could not have been wantonly invented by the early Christians; 4) there is a pagan reference to the Crucifixion (Thallus) which can be dated to AD 50 – which involves a resurrection sequel. The Gospel story as it stands simply does not add up unless one makes three assumptions:[15] that Jesus was actually King of the Jews crowned in the ancient formula (Psalm 2) which made him technically a 'Son of God'; that at the close he was literally carrying out the 'worthless shepherd' prophecy of Zechariah; that he survived the Crucifixion but then had to disappear, after having briefly returned, because he was legally accursed under the Deuteronomia law. (An example of G. Moore's complete ignorance of the set-up is that he makes J. go to the Essenes after the Crucifixion: the Essenes were the strictest of all the Pharisaic sects and could not possibly have admitted him after he had once hanged on a tree.) I am pretty well up in the *Lives* of Jesus and all the vast literature on the subject, and this is literally the first book to reconcile all the known historical data. About 'improving on the Gospels': if you read in the original Greek, or in translation, the other contemporary Gospels and Epistles which were suppressed for one reason or another, their unfamiliarity gives you a sense of disappointment, and you say 'How right to have suppressed them!' But the fact is that the 4 canonical Gospels are inconsistently contradictory, written in poor Greek and leave out, or gloze over, many points of greatest interest: and are libels both on the Jews and on Jesus himself who was true-ruled, perfectly uncompromising and completely loyal to the One Indivisible God of Israel. So if anyone talks of 'blasphemy' – you see, one has to accept blasphemy as a term that J. would himself have used, and he makes it quite clear (if you rule out the 2nd century Alexandrian additions to St John) that he is not God, and that God is alone and supreme.

Anyhow, if my version can be historically disproved on its main thesis, OK; but it has already convinced several scholars and even wrung an admission from a Catholic priest that it explains the story better than the Church herself does – he says he'll write to champion me if I get into too much trouble!

So, anyhow, there it is; and I have no doubt that your valuable journal will as usual find a smart reviewer with no historical education to oversimplify the argument for your teeming millions of readers, and it won't make the least difference to my affection for you and Julie and the family.

I have just given your message to Gelat who is delighted at the thought of seeing you again. Everything is just as it was, barring food shortages and a general stagnation due to Spain's being cut off from the rest of the world.

Your letter came by the same post as a most distressing letter from Jane Lye.[16] Who am I to cast stones? But Len has been very clumsy and cowardly too, I think. It looks as if she'll be left absolutely flat.

If you don't come here for the next couple of years, we may visit US first: that is, if there is money enough and if Betty and Ricardo[17] are true to their offer of entertainment on their Maryland farm.

It is nice that your boys are good at athletics, that makes all the difference at college and school – unfair, but there it is.

At the moment I am amusing myself by translating an early religious novel – Apuleius's *Golden Ass*[18] – which was last well translated in 1566.

The children go to school next month: William to the village boys' school, Lucia and Juan to the Nuns. They will teach them Spanish and Mallorquín. We have been having wonderful bathes and Beryl is ever so much better in health. If your gift parcels ever get through the greedy customs, I'll let you know gratefully.
Love   ·Robert·

Your letter (ordinary mail) took 5 weeks to arrive, Jane's (air mail) ten days. She tells me that your mother is ill. I am awfully sorry and hope it is nothing serious.

Matthews's wife Julie also wrote; she did not want to read *King Jesus* as she had also become a 'believer' and thought she would be offended by it.

5 September 1946

Dearest Julie:

Thanks ever so much for your whacking long letter which contained all the news that we have been wanting to hear and gave us a very good picture of how you are making out. It is nice to know that you and Tom have survived the first 21 years of marriage so successfully: it must be almost a record for the Eastern States except in the Catholic belt. That the Fitzgeralds are separated does not surprise me, that they are both RCs does not surprise me, but how come Bob is marrying again and that she continues with her second husband? – that doesn't make sense to me under Canon Law which is, or should be, the same everywhere from Rome to the Catholic Mission Centre in Japan. Another religious point that needs clearing up is what sort of a 'believer' Julie Matthews is: is 'Church' Episcopalian or Catholic or what? 'Confession' does not sound very Bishop Matthewsy.[19] Sorry you think *King Jesus* would offend: I want no 'millstone about my neck' as a punishment for doing anything of the sort. I conclude that it must be Anglo-Catholic that you have become, because the Catholics are very strong on Jesus being a figure in history as well as having been Son of God – a title which I historically concede him – and being also God, a title to which he has a *de facto* claim at least. On the whole, I think you are wise not to read the book; because my view is that if you believe implicitly in Jesus' doctrine as literally relevant today, the 'Christian life' would involve you in separating yourself from most of the things you most enjoy, in Judaizing yourself completely, and in embracing a sort of Stalinite communism laced with Seventh Day Adventism – and how awkward for your family that would be.

Beryl often wishes she were religious, in her low moments: this is a dreadful epoch, and religion seems to be the only thing to keep one going in bad weather of all sorts. I never have that wish; poetry has always supplied my religious needs. This may seem a stupid statement but I am realizing, have been realizing for the last three years, that real poetry, there is very little of it like the trace of gold when they wash gravel, is an epitome of the ancestral religion of Europe which made the Minoans what they were, and which was submerged by the Aryan invaders about 2000 BC and finally stamped out by the Christians – though a great deal of it has

34

infiltrated into later Catholicism. Catholicism is really an uneasy marriage of Pharisaic (in the good sense) ethics and monotheistic theory with the festival-year of the Old Religion which was dominated by the Virgin as Queen of Heaven. But if one wants to be in touch with as many people of religious life as possible, as you do, then Catholicism (or Anglo-Catholicism) is the only solution of the problem; and I should obviously become a Catholic, if I thought that it added up historically and was compatible with my poetic principles. It is just too bad.

At any rate I agree with you that these are times in which one is returned to first principles and in which 'the good life' as it is sometimes called, which you define as 'the Christian Life', is the only thing of any real interest, apart from family happenings. So don't think that I am anything but sincere in my pleasure that you have become a 'believer'.

Today we went in a motorboat to the Foradada with the children, after Juan had nearly got drowned in the Cala – he was noticed floating bottom-upwards out of his depth! – and saw an eagle's nest over the hole in the Foradada and a lot of wild duck and jelly fish. We have had three weeks of monstrous weather for this time of year – actually Sirocco alternating with storms which has a deadening effect on the mind and causes a crime wave in the cities, and being an ill-wind has the good effect of drying the washing instantly and bringing the thunder-fish to the coast – very tasty, few bones.

Now is the grape and fig season – grapes poor this year – and living is dreadfully expensive. Thanks ever so much for sending the parcels, but I doubt if they'll get through.

Gelat is now 65. He has to be careful of his heart and so avoids ever losing his temper. He is full of ripe wisdom and loves you and Tom dearly. His grandson and namesake is the spit and image of him; the intervening generation Juan is perfectly sweet and very talented but without G's genius. We don't worry about Russia. They are always dependably Russian whether White Red or post Rev.

God bless you all.   Robert

Much love to your mother. Mine is going very strong at 88. And to the boys. I am very pleased that Tommy is at Princeton. Sam[20] is very happy at Cambridge and may go on to Princeton for architecture. Catherine[21] is having another child – her third. So nice about Do and his family. To think of Charles a six-footer. He was tiny in 1939 – I liked him a lot, very plucky. No we never got the parcels Tom sent to England. Here nothing arrives unless registered.

King Jesus, however, proved to be extremely popular and did not receive such a hostile reception as Graves had expected; though there was certainly some controversy, it did not provoke the 'unintelligent bludgeoning' that his later and much more carefully researched and considered *Nazarene Gospel Restored* was to receive.

In a letter of 4 November he describes its reception in the USA to Basil Liddell Hart:

King Jesus is out in USA and has had a very uncoordinated press; on the whole remarkably favourable and very long and emotional. The historical criticisms raised have been minor and easily refuted, and what really pleases me is that the only man in the US who is a real authority on the subject, Dr Solomon Zeitlin, the Hebrew Dean of Dropsie College, Philadelphia, who edits the *Jewish Quarterly*, is very sympathetic towards the book and says (off record but never mind) that the facts are not historically disprovable.

The Christian theologians there are all very sore and ruffled, but that was to be expected. They are a conventional lot. It will be very interesting to see what the British press has to say. The book comes out in England on Nov. 24th or thereabouts; only 12,000 copies so it will be gone in a week.

At the end of the year Graves was correcting proofs of *The White Goddess*, which wasn't published, however, until May 1948. He wrote to T. S. Eliot at Faber, which was publishing the book in Britain.

10 December 1946

My dear Eliot:

Many thanks for your letter of 25th November, and for your promise of a copy of Sullivan's *Fibre*.[22]

Yes, thanks: comfortable and well fed, though (it seems) shortly to be without an Ambassador.

I have got two instalments of proof but will keep both here until I get the complete set, if you don't mind, because I may need to make changes in earlier chapters to tally with the later.

I should be disappointed if you couldn't use the cover which I designed for the book and which Kenneth Gay[23] executed. Is your decision final about this?

Perhaps the book will not have such a limited sale as I thought at first; because my *King Jesus* is arousing what is technically called a storm of controversy and in *The White Goddess* I justify all, or practically all, the mythological theory I introduced into it.

Along the road from my house here is the Arabic College where the Blessed Ramon Llull[24] (or Lullius) wrote most of his books. He was a very good chap, but too independent minded to make the grade to sainthood, despite a distinguished martyrdom. The trouble was, of course, that he was a poet.

Merry Christmas –
Yours ever
                                                          Robert Graves

In 1942 Graves had asked Lynette Roberts's husband Keidrych Rhys, the editor of *Wales*, if he knew of any interesting young poets. In answer to this, Rhys had urged Derek Savage to send his poems to Graves for comment. Graves then wrote back to Savage a detailed criticism of the poems, saying:

The poems were a pleasure. One day you'll discard a good many of them when you have ones to take their place which you'll like better. I hope the ones that go will be the ones that have the Cambridge-metaphysical touch, which derives from Milton's undergraduate ambitions for himself and which is what gives British Poets the charnel smell you complain of.

In December 1943, Savage sent Graves a small book of his poems, *A Time to Mourn*, just published (by Routledge); again Graves sent detailed notes on individual poems and at the end of the letter (7 December) told Savage of an idea at the back of his mind:

One day I hope to get all the poets together – the ones who are really heart and soul poets as I judge you to be – and persuade them to re-establish the broken basis on which poetry formerly was settled. I don't mean the establishment of an academy of poets, but only an agreed corpus of poetic meaning. 'Ixion', 'wild swan', 'metal men', should have precise mythical connotations as well as the personal associations that they may have for the particular poet. Similarly with metre: e.g. the sonnet should perhaps be reserved for a particular range of poetic experience. And the Shakespearean differentiated from the Petrarchan. And certain principles of good poetic manners would be informally agreed on. I mean nothing more frightening than the sort of experiences that used to be held in the Apollo room of the Devil in Fleet Street when Ben Jonson was about.

It was as a critic, however, that Graves came to value Savage most, and in June 1946 he sponsored him for an Atlantic Award in Literature (Savage's other sponsor was Herbert Read, his publisher at Routledge). Savage consequently received an award of £250.

16 December 1946

My dear Savage:

Now isn't that good? If my recommendation carried any weight I am very pleased; and glad that the decision was made before my *King Jesus* came out. I don't think I'm very popular now among the sort of tycoons who award scholarships.

Yes, it's a wonderful feeling to be master of one's own time – as much as anyone can be, that is, with a family – especially when one is doing anything so necessary and thankless as writing critical stuff.

I am having an enjoyable time now on proofs of my *White Goddess*, a sort of historical grammar to the language of poetic myth; a dreadful book to write because the subject had never been attempted – and my problem was like Jehovah's on the Sixth Day of Creation, how to forge a pair of tongs with which to hold the red-hot metal when one is forging a pair of tongs. In the end he created 'em; together with the Rainbow and other necessary odds and ends.

Good luck to your forge and rainbows. I look forward to the results of your freedom.

Yours v.s.,   Robert Graves

Savage was now able to give up his job as a market gardener at

Bromsash, though at this time the rented house he and his family lived in was sold and they had to find other accommodation. The 'gamekeeper's cottage road problem' in the following letter refers to an isolated cottage in Sussex which they intended to rent but whose surrounds became a sea of mud in winter. (In the end they did not live there but moved to another isolated cottage in Cornwall.)

17 January 1947

Dear Savage:

Many thanks for your letter of Jan. 2. Well, I hope now you'll be able to get the loam from under your fingernails for a while! The solution to the gamekeeper's cottage road problem is a brushwood causeway and a boyscout's hand-cart on ball-bearings. The baby should not be much trouble for the first nine months. Get as much as possible done before it gets to the troublesome age – advice from father of seven. Those early critical works of mine you mention were largely written with a baby on each knee and an elder child around my neck. I have been re-reading them again with the idea of rescuing what is good in them for a *Collected Essays*; I find that the general point of view was not so bad, but the details are very sketchy. I could not afford to buy books and it was impossible to get away to libraries. I have a small family again: 2, 3 and 6 years old. But now I can afford servants and books and people to do research for me; thank heavens.

Your plan of finding out what the writer's task is seems good to me. For myself I feel that writers want *grounding*, as my parents said when at last they consented to send me to a good preparatory school to prepare for a scholarship! Alan Hodge and I did some of it in *The Reader Over Your Shoulder*, trying to teach them the rudiments of prose-writing. In *The White Goddess* I am attempting the more difficult critical task: it is a sort of historic grammar of poetic myth, explaining: how the unicorn got its tail, why God created grass and trees before he created the heavenly bodies, what coffin King Arthur was buried in, what name Achilles assumed when he hid himself among women,* where is Wisdom to be found?† etc., etc.

Well, well! The sun is shining with all its might on the beanfield just outside my window and I must take this to the post. But I agree with you that critics are needed, and that to be a critic one must contrive to be independent, and that this is an almost impossible task. As soon as, for instance, one links oneself to a university or other educational system, one's liberty to think properly is impaired.

Yours v. sincerely   Robert Graves

* DROSOESSA, if you've always wanted to know.

† Under an appletree on a Wednesday in the apple month.

To T. S. Eliot

19 January 1947

My dear Eliot:

I have asked Creative Age to send you the cover design of *The White Goddess*, done by Kenneth Gay with me standing over him all the time. It shows the Goddess Carmenta giving Palaimedes [*sic*] the eye which enables him to understand the flight of the cranes which originated the alphabet. I hope you'll like it.

I have yielded to a poetic compulsion in *The White Goddess* proofs to answer Sir Thos. Browne's[25] 'puzzling questions not beyond all conjecture' about Achilles' assumed name among the women and what song the Sirens sang. The answer to the first is Drosoessa [*margin note*: The Demon of the Year becomes 'a woman called "Tear of the Sun" (dew) when he reaches the fourth month, being for a few days still a σκοτιος, a boy confined to the women's quarters, presided over by the Goddess Scotia']; this is got from Empedocles, the Cretans and the Irish. The answer to the second, a Hellenization of the corresponding early Irish addresses to heroes from priestesses of Avalon islands, makes it quite a nice poem. Well, I'll try to stop improving the book, but my mind gives me little peace.

Yours v. sincerely   Robert Graves

To Karl Gay

15 February 1947

Dearest Karl:

Thanks very much for the bodkins and the letter. The year is now well into Spring here, though the wind often blows cold from the Pyrenees, and Carnival is on, with the village children dressing up and collecting pesetas by dancing from Son to Can. Let's hope this will be the last really cold winter you ever have to face, at any rate without gas or coal or something. Various old people have died this last month including the old Bartolome of Son Bauza (who used to fish in his old age) and the old dame of Calabat from whom we used to get bitter oranges.

Expenses in ordinary living (but with two maids to feed) work out at about £1000 a year for us. Until there's a change of Govt or something it can't be reduced. So I'm hoping in the Lord Jesus. My article on the 'History and Logic of King Jesus' in the *New York Herald Tribune* was given a big spread (Feb. 4th) and prefaced by dear Tom with a [footling], patronizing, Goddish article about my 'taking the road to Damascus', but I was glad he did it. I have already had three or four mad air-mail letters from people who call me a lying hypocrite and threaten to pray for me; and I think the sales will be given a bit of a shove. I hope so, because they were a bit stationary. The book has now been sold to Sweden, Holland, Hungary, Czechoslovakia, Denmark and I forget where else.

You may have seen the cutting about the Bank of England director who claimed to have written a poem of mine 'Flying Crooked'; he is in a great state of distress because he got it by genuine inspiration (telepathy or something) and was rather proud of it. He wrote it in only a minute or two and it took me three days! Cassells are doing my *Collected Poems* this autumn, and will I think bring them up to date.

I am making only slow progress with *The Golden Ass*, because I keep tinkering with *The White Goddess*. I concealed from you that Eliot wanted a plain cover for the *Goddess*,* but I sent for yours from USA and I'm glad to say that he's all for using it. I have made various small confirmations of my argument lately; it really is quite impressive now, and nothing is *forced*. I restored the missing five-line ending of 'The Song of Amergin'[26] as follows:

A I am the womb of every holt,
O I am the blaze on every hill,
U I am the queen of every hive,
E I am the shield for every head,
I I am the grave for every hope.

Which was odd, because the succession of h's came without searching for them. I daresay it *did* go something like that.

Alan in his last letter didn't mention coming; perhaps it's off.

Laura has now given her signature for the 'sale' of these houses to me,[27] the fees will be about £50 but it will be good to have it settled in my name at last. And I've paid off the Ca'n Torrent mortgage.

. . . .

Falkland is a sodden old wretch; I hope he trips over his beard and breaks his gin-bottles into little pieces.

Beryl will write.

Love to you and Marie.   Robert

No word yet from Billy Philpot.
* All proofs are here up to Chap. 19.

To T. S. Eliot

23 March 1947

My dear Eliot

I have just about finished work on *The White Goddess* proofs, but since they are still in galley the index will have to wait for the page proofs. I will send them to you by ordinary post, or in someone's luggage if that is quicker. But I feel very bad about the present increase in the length of the book I have made as a result of getting back here to my library and being able to make good the sketchier parts of the argument. I have, for example, added what amounts to a whole chapter at the end to explain the historic steps by which Christian mysticism, with its opposition of ideal godhead to the material trinity of World, Flesh and Devil, developed as an improvement on the original Mother-and-Son Orphic mysteries concerned with the δαιμων ξνιαντος.[28] This is most important as allowing me to explain the exact difference between the God-worshipping mystic eulogized in Aldous's *Perennial Philosophy*[29] and the Goddess-worshipping poet – between whom stand many Catholic betwixt and betweens – but to reach that point I had to go into the question of why Iahu (Jehovah) was originally a title of Isis; and what the mystical meaning of the jewels of the High Priest's (and the King of Tyre's) breastplate, nearly all mistranslated in the Authorized Version,

42

was; and how they are related to the Sacred Grove sequence in the 'Wisdom' mystery of Proverbs. Deep waters! Deep, but pellucid.

So, as I say, the book grew, having already grown far beyond its original size and now I don't know what you'll say, about the extra 15,000 words!

There are two alternatives:

1) Print it as it stands and charge the public more; and if the public can't be made to pay enough to make the first edition an economical proposition, tell me that I must forfeit a part or all of my advance.

2) Break the book in two. It divides fairly well at the end of a chapter on galley 162, since the extra material is mostly at the end and the last galley 24 will have index tacked on it.
I would of course prefer the first solution.[30]

As a poet you'll sympathize with me for having felt obliged to pursue the argument to the finish; as a publisher-that-was I sympathize with you for having so unexpected and awkward a problem on your hands. So there's no question of any quarrel or lack of confidence between us; but what must be done will be done. Certainly the book is very much better now, and though I can't claim to have got everything right I have been able to check and cross-check all my phonier-seeming theories and there are not many important elements in the history of Western myth not examined.

Yours v. sincerely –   Robert Graves

To Karl Gay

2 April 1947

Dearest Karl

. . . .

I have at last got the *White Goddess* proofs back to Eliot. I don't know what the hell he'll say to the extra 15,000 words I added. I seem fated to project books of 60,000 words and find they work out to 150,000. And the most exacting books I write – *The Reader Over Your Shoulder* and *White Goddess* were worse than *King Jesus*, took twice as long – are the ones with least sales prospect. However, my last additions to the book have been the most interesting – especially the great joke that the Christian

43

Trinity doctrine is a *Hebrew* development of the Sacred Grove mystery. Of course, it should have struck me before that there are no *mysteries* without mystagogues, and the mystery is just legally announced in the Athanasian Creed without any mythic interpretation. My guess is that the Christians never really knew the explanation, but took the theory from the Jews.

Other joke: my brother Dick[31] is now Alcalde of Jerusalem, but refuses to use a swagger car – drives about in an antique fly with a veteran grey horse and a beribboned horsewhip.

Here the south wind continues to blow in a headachey way, drying up the gardens. We have had two rains with it, which streaked the house with mud – Algerian vineyard dust blown off and mixed with rain. Douglas and Jane[32] may be at the Posada this summer. There are three Germans in the village now, in a house on the Putsch[33] [*sic*]: they are all right, really . . .

More thanks and tears for your needles . . .

Jenny writes that her US tour is making her more and more pro-Russian. Alex's[34] Russian tour will probably have the opposite effect. He has just been made Director of the *Continental Daily Mail* and they have bought a medieval castle overlooking the Port of Porto Fino in the Gulf of Genoa. We have got to know the Gitteses.[35] Nice people, but returning to US in April or so. Their 12-year-old boy is a well-known local archaeologist and will find his American friends of the same age exactly 10 years below him in mental age. He has identified my bullfight brooch with the lancer on it as pre-Roman Iberian, not Visgothic as Schwarz[36] told me.

It should be a good year for fruit, but about olives one can't prophecy until summer. We have just hatched out some chicks and as it's the first time Beryl and the children are very excited.

Love – and to Marié   Robert

Graves met Joshua Podro in Devon during the war, when Podro's International Press Cutting Bureau had been temporarily evacuated to Paignton, near Galmpton. Though a businessman, Podro's spare time and energy were dedicated to the study of Jewish religious history; he knew the Hebrew, Aramaic and Syriac languages and had, it was said, the largest private library of Judaica in London. Podro was a Polish Jew, the same age as Graves and, like him, had received a strict religious upbringing, had fought in France as a Fusilier in the First World War and had ceased to hold orthodox religious beliefs. Podro, with his knowledge of Hebraeo-Aramaic history, was of great help to Graves when he was writing *King Jesus* and the men became close friends when they realized how intent they both were on wiping out the 'traditional misrepresentations' of Jesus and in finding out 'who and what had antagonized the two religions'.

25 April 1947

My dear Joshua:

I forget whether I answered your recent letter in which you were good enough to reassure me that my views on Numbers 23–27[37] are not necessarily nonsensical. As I see the case now, the Jews made the political mistake of formulating an altogether too holy and idealistic a God, and making a Pharisee of him, i.e. *separating* him from the material creation, and allowing him to delegate the supervision of human affairs to archangels – who were not equal to the task. Although Michael as Wednesday's angel claimed to have defeated Satan (formerly Nabu the wise serpent, who in the elder dispensation had been the god of Wednesday) this was an empty boast. Only a few devout Jews were capable of the purely mystic concept of Jehovah as Light, Peace and Life; Satan controlled the rest. The same thing of course happened with Christianity. Saints have been very few, ecclesiastics many.

The Jewish monthly *Commentary* of New York has sent me a very carelessly written and unfortunate review of *King Jesus* by Mordecai Chertoff. Heaven knows, I am not an authority on Jewish history, but I do know the elements of it; so E. E. Cohen the editor who invited me to reply now has a 'Megillah'[38] on the way. Chertoff said that I accused the Jews of killing Jesus! and (among other things) that 'the pious Jews of his day shunned Greek'! (Query: were the Sephiagint impious?)

I asked Karl if he could get me the cutting from the *Tablet* of March in which a letter of mine appeared which seems to have gone astray with one or two more; he referred me to you. Apparently, he has some trouble with you which prevents him from passing on the message but he didn't explain what. Really, I PLEASE am very sorry, Joshua. I know Karl well and am very fond of SAY NOTHING him; but I know how touchy he is and, as he would himself admit, OF ALL occasionally unreasonable. And I think I know you well enough, THIS TO HIM

45

too, to understand how impossible you must find it to make sense of him. I don't even know whether he has told you that he hopes soon to get his naturalization and end a very difficult situation in his private affairs – as opposed to his work with you – by going abroad and working for me again. *Tout savoir est tout pardonner*.[39] He has been having a wretched time. I don't know whether I should have told you even as much as this, but I feel so warmly towards you, and have felt Karl as my responsibility for so long, that it would be wrong not to mention it. Please don't let him know that I have written and accept my apologies on his behalf for any ungraciousness he has shown. I hope that he has been long enough with you to have made his stay worth the trouble of training him. I have no idea when he will give you notice to leave: or whether, indeed, he may change his mind and decide to stay because his private affairs have changed or because he can't get his naturalization or visa . . . Very few Jews, of course, are free of phobias of one sort or another, the result of the monstrous treatment they have received as a community; and as a Gentile of the British ex-governing classes [*margin note*: 'ex' is Beryl's critical gloss] I feel it my duty to take no offence when a Jew confuses me as an individual with my class – as in the case of Mordecai Chertoff with whom this letter began. What a world this is!

I have written a careful argument for the press summarizing all the relevant texts of the Pentateuch about God's promises to Abraham and Isaac and Moses about the Land of Canaan. It makes an interesting study of the legal aspects, which, so far as I know, have not been publicly summarized before; and I find that the Arabs have a better title to reside in the N. of Palestine than the Jews concede them though the Jews cannot be prevented from entering so long as they do not forcibly dispossess any peoples already there of their lands or claim sovereign rights, as in the South.

. . . .

Love to Fanny and yourself from us both   Robert

To T. S. Eliot

8 May 1947

My dear Eliot

I am just finishing a translation for Penguin Classics of Apuleius's *Golden Ass*; and finding that Aldington's lovely translation is full of mistakes. There is a particularly mischievous one in his account of the pageant of Isis at Corinth where he shows Mercury with a birchen wand, not an olive one. This has led me into an error in *White Goddess* Galley 96 last two lines, Galley 97 first nine lines as far as the words *Birth Goddess*. The whole passage should be removed except for the words on line 3 Galley 97:

The birch is the tree of inception.

If the printers have already made up the pages and don't want to lose the space, I can send them new material to fill up.

I am so sorry. *The Golden Ass* is a very much better book than I had suspected and the queer Latin is a deliberate joke, a parody of the high-faluting style of the popular story teller who liked to impress audiences at fairs and street corners. (Rabelais did the same in imitation of the same class of story tellers, Gargantua being a giant from popular Celtic mythology.)

Yours ever sincerely   Robert Graves

Graves met George and Joanna Simon in Brixham in 1942, and very soon a close friendship began which was to be maintained until Simon's death in 1977 and which is still maintained by his wife and children. Simon, an enthusiastic reader, was deeply interested in all of Graves's ideas and Graves frequently consulted Simon for medical evidence to support his historical theories (for example, Jesus's survival of his ordeal on the Cross). It was not so surprising, then, that Simon, a celebrated doctor, should turn to Graves for 'magical' advice when medical science failed him: in 1945 his wife had had a second miscarriage, and on 15 April 1946 Graves sent him instructions on what to do to achieve the Goddess's blessing, in order to avoid a further miscarriage:

Magical instructions. Clear out all rubbish from the house (backs of drawers, under stairs, etc., between May 14 and June 14) and burn it, unless classifiable as salvage, in the backyard. A bunch of

primroses would please the Goddess and, when nobody is
snooping, a handful of pearl barley laid on a raised stone. The
birds will eat it; but they belong to her. To show that you really
are cultivating her, not the Holy God of the immaterial universe,
the following charm will gratify her exceedingly. It is chockful of
astrological magic:

meaning: 'the five feasts are enough for us, Artemis of the Nut-
tree, when you are about' (i.e. the working week, excluding the
Sabbath and Sunday both of which Jehovah appropriated to
himself). The formula *S.T.C.D.Q.* can also be represented with
willow, holly, nut, oak, apple. The five-petalled primrose is an even
neater sign, as John Donne recognized.

> Live primrose, then, and thrive
> In your mysterious number five.

I think Wizard Graves has said enough for the present.

Oh: make no overconfident arrangements for the child's birth
and *if* it is born (here I am averting Nemesis) treat it with salutary
neglect and put it in a birchwood cradle; if obtainable. Most
Finnish furniture is birch, isn't it?

Love and nonsense   Robert

The Simons duly followed the instructions and, whether due to the
Goddess or not, on 27 June 1947 their first daughter, Helena, was
born. Graves heard about the birth of the child while he and the
family were on holiday in France, staying with their friends Ricardo
and Betty Sicre.

22 July 1947   Chez M. le Docteur Sicre
(till August 3)   La Bestide de Seron
                                                                Ariège
                                                                France

Dearest George and Joanna:

This is a large rambling dirty charming house where the parents
and sisters of our dear friends Ricardo and Betty Sicre live; Ricardo
was a Spanish Republican refugee (a battalion commander at 20)[40]
whom we befriended in England in 1939. Later he became a US
Army Intelligence Service captain, and married Betty who was a
flying-woman (Canadian) seconded to the same service; they have
a little boy now and are expecting another child next month. Their
adventures have been pure William Le Queux,[41] and yesterday
when Ricardo went to Andorra (where he's getting me 30 pesetas
for my US dollars instead of the official Spanish rate of 15!) the
great black market centre of W. Europe, as it was the great
espionage centre in the war, he heard from the local hotel
commissionaire the latest news of the Nazi spies he had succeeded
in arresting during the war. All were well and hearty in the
American zone and writing to Andorra for large packages of coffee
and sugar for which they were prepared to pay in dollars.

Since writing the above I have had the unusual and
mythologically interesting experience of being bitten in the heel
by a viper. Really it was very strange, because in my *White Goddess*
there is a whole chapter devoted to this. The God of the Year
used to end this way before being conducted to the Silver Island
of the dead. What was interesting was that my vision went all
blurred beginning with a 'megrim' pattern in silver like this:

which I suppose must have a connection with Silver Island. It
gradually spread from a small thing until it enclosed the whole
field of vision and then began turning round: which perhaps
explains why the Islands of the Dead were said to revolve. I still
can't walk for pins and needles; but feel all right otherwise.

We are still basking in the reflected happiness of your daughter's
birth. Dress her very plainly because she's going to be beautiful and
a danger to men, with a nativity so close to midsummer.

Wm has become an ardent fisherman, catches lots of tiddlers
which are fried for the children's tea. Lucia is interested only in
personal adornment and sewing: it was thoughtless of us to give
her the name of the patron saint of dress-makers!

Much love   Robert

Can't settle here to any work. No privacy, no ink, no thoughts
and a heat-wave, the worse for this valley being very green and
damp. Beryl is having too much work to do, for a real holiday,
because I can only hop at present and Juan needs a strong man to
cope with him. Also there's a deaf aunt here who acts as skivvy
and is very much shouted at, and retaliates by hiding everything
we need in odd corners and watching us search for them with
poker-faced glee.

To Joshua Podro, whose son David had recently been married.

15 December 1947 – My mother's birthday   Deyá

My dear Joshua:

I should have written to congratulate David on his marriage –
I'm sure it will be a success. Jews don't marry so lightheartedly and
foolishly as the *goyim*. I'd have loved to be present at the ceremony.

The stones flung in Jerusalem[42] did not hit me, thanks; and I'm
glad my brother Dick escaped. They say that if he survives until
May he'll be offered another job by the Jews who, as you say,
value him. At Christmas we are having Arnaldo and Ruth
Rosentingl and their boy to celebrate Jesus the prophet: I told you,
I think, what wonderfully good friends they were to Wm and us
in Barcelona.[43] (I hope they're not strictly *kosher*, because we rely
a lot on our annual pig sacrifice. However, we have a large bin
of olive oil and are getting a turkey, so they won't starve.)

I have been very busy on revised proofs of *The White Goddess*;
it is a pity that there's no room for a lot of new mythological
discoveries I have made; I'll have to print them one day as a
supplement. Today I found that the Anakim whom Caleb chased
from the Negeb are identical with the Sons of Anax (a mythical
Carian of Cretan stock, who was 10 cubits high) who were
apparently priests of the God Car, or Qaru, or Ker, or Q're, or
Huru, who was also Horus. As Q're is the Massoretic name for
Jehovah, and as Horus had the title Iahu, which Jehovah also had,

my view that the Jews adopted the God of Hebron when they captured the shrine has additional confirmation.

About Partition: speaking from the point of view of religious tradition, I should say that 'he who holds Hebron (rather than Jerusalem) holds Palestine'. I think it's a silly partition. The Jews should have all the South, including Jerusalem and Hebron, and share the North with the Arabs (also Sons of Abraham) if the 15 relevant texts in the (Pentateuch) Scriptures are to be fulfilled, as they have a habit of being in the long run. But better something than nothing.

In Jewish tradition are there 'Seven Ages of the World': from Adam to Noah, from Noah to Abraham, etc? Or is that a Christian invention? I ask because they are apparently based on the events of the 7 day Creation.

We are all well and working hard. I have about four books coming out next year, or supposed to be coming out. Love to Fanny, who's a bright memory to us; and to yourself.

Yours ever   Robert

I have just bought a remarkably clear and sensible and original book *Man and Temple* by Raphael Patai.[44] It is first class and I agree with almost every word.

In the New Year Honours list in January it was announced that T. S. Eliot had been made a member of the Order of Merit. Graves characteristically attributed this to his having accepted *The White Goddess* for publication (though he didn't say so to Eliot); he also attributed the misfortunes of certain other publishers to their having turned it down, as he explained to Alastair Reid in *Quoz*:

I sent it to two publishers [OUP and Macmillan] . . . One of these rejected it politely, saying that he would not venture to persuade his colleagues of its merit, though convinced himself. He died three weeks later. Another rejected it impolitely and almost at once was found hanging from a tree in his garden dressed in a skirt, blouse, nylon knickers and a brassière. I saw the White Goddess's terrible hand in that, but never found what sort of tree it was. Yew? Elder? Then Eliot accepted the book with enthusiasm and within the year had a Nobel Prize and an OM. 'Makes you think, doesn't it?'

8 January 1948

My dear Eliot:

Here's the index of the *White Goddess* with a few misspellings that the compilation revealed. At last.

I was very glad to read about your OM in *The Times* air-edition – glad that they didn't fob you off with a CH – it comes very early, you aren't an Old Man yet, but it shows a sensible appreciation by the Govt of how little work of real merit has been done by the generation above you.

Happy new year.

Yours ever   Robert Graves

In January 1949 Graves received a letter from Dr Valentina Wasson concerning the death of Claudius. Because of the pseudo-autobiographical technique Graves used in *I, Claudius* and *Claudius the God* the story was inevitably broken off just before Claudius's murder, which was engineered by his wife Agrippina. There are three main classical accounts of the crime, by Suetonius, Tacitus and Dio Cassius, all of which Graves quoted in full at the end of *Claudius the God*. All three say that Claudius was given a plate of poisoned mushrooms, and Suetonius and Tacitus go on to say that either by vomiting or by a great evacuation of the bowels he saved himself, but was then given a second poison by his physician Xenophon (as the accomplice of Agrippina), either by a gruel or enema (Suetonius) or by pretending to make him vomit again by putting a feather down his throat – only the feather was dipped in a quick poison (Tacitus). Dr Wasson, a Russian-born paediatrician then living in New York, was writing a book about mushrooms with her husband R. Gordon Wasson (vice-president of J. P. Morgan and Co., the Wall St Bank). (It was later published as *Mushrooms, Russia and History* (1957).) The Wassons were investigating Claudius's death from the mycological angle. The mushrooms he ate, nowhere described as poisonous, were, the Wassons suggested, those known as *Amanita caesarea*, a tasty, wholesome mushroom, though Locusta, the poisoner hired by Agrippina, slipped into the dish a mushroom of another variety, *Amanita phalloides*, equally tasty but deadly poisonous and causing very similar symptoms to the ones Claudius suffered. Dr Wasson asked Graves if he had any views on the subject.

In reply, Graves came up with a new theory on the second poison used: also at the end of *Claudius the God*, he quotes a satire by Seneca (Nero's tutor) called *The Apocolocyntosis of Claudius*. 'Apocolocyntosis' is a portmanteau word combining 'apotheosis' (deification) and '*colocynthos*' (pumpkin) and the previously agreed translation was 'The Pumpkinification of Claudius' – presumably because Seneca believed the emperor was a pumpkin-headed fool. At this point Graves realized that in Greek '*colocynthos*' also means the wild gourd, which, although a useful purge in minimal doses, is a powerful alkaline poison.

26 January 1949

Dear Dr Wasson:

You give me no information about your theory. The point of the word *Apocolocyntosis* (to me) is that it hints at the drug – the wild gourd or colocynth, famous for the 'O man of God there is death in the pot' story of Elijah. The accounts of his death all state that the poison was introduced into the mushrooms, not that the mushrooms were themselves poisonous. Seneca evidently knew a lot: the *vae me cacavi*[45] is characteristic of colocynth, so is the speechlessness. In my *King Jesus* I suggest the colocynth as the cause of Herod I's death too – see Josephus – it fits clinically like a glove. (Locusta would have had to get her colocynth from the Negeb or Transjordania.)

That's my view. I know of none others. What's yours? If I'd knew [*sic*] as much in 1934 as I do now I'd not have accepted the misleading translation 'Pumpkinification'. The colocynth was used in World War I in the famous laxative BEF 'no. 9 pill' and served to discourage malingerers, and a free translation of *Apocolocyntosis* would therefore be: 'No. 9'd to Glory'!

Yours sincerely   Robert Graves

They didn't have to be very subtle in those days: no chemical analysis of organs of the deceased.

Gordon Wasson replied to Graves's letter, saying he and his wife were both impressed by the wild gourd theory and thought it complementary to their own mushroom theory, which he explained in greater detail. Graves then set out to reconstruct the murder step by step.

6 March 1949

Dear Mr and Mrs Wasson:

Many thanks for your long and interesting letter. Now that I have re-read the documents with care and read up my handbook of *Edible Fungi* (by John Ramsbottom, Penguin Edition, London and New York, 1943) I can agree with your theory in all essentials. *Amanita phalloides* (R. says) which is much preyed upon by slugs, is responsible for ninety per cent of deaths by mushroom-poisoning; he blames the information given in the Press and taught in village schools that an 'edible fungus peels and does not turn silver black': superstitions that date from Diphilus (3rd century) and Nicander (4th century). But *A. phalloides* answers both these tests! So far as I can make out, *A. caesarea* is not native to Britain; yes, now I see Ramsbottom says it isn't. Anyhow, my *Companion to Latin Studies* (Cambridge University Press) is full of misinformation on the subject. It identifies *Boletus edulis* with *A. caesarea* and says that Claudius was poisoned with fly-agaric, another of the poisonous *Amanitae*. (As a boy I once touched fly-agaric with the tip of my tongue, to see what it tasted like. I was scared nearly out of my wits at the burst of fire that shot through me and at the swelling of my tongue!)

(By the way, Horace says:

. . . pratensibus optima fungis
Natura est; aliis male creditur . . .[46]

But that advice seems as unsound as Diphilus' and Nicander's.)

The account by Suetonius of the clyster seems to me the most reasonable; it would have disguised the bitterness of the colocynth, since you and I agreed that this may have been the second drug used. From his account only one night of sickness elapsed. Locusta's plan may have been merely to cause sufficient prostration to be able to finish him off by other means. I think you have overlooked a passage in the *Apocolocyntosis* in which Seneca says that Claudius began to bubble up the ghost between noon and one o'clock of *October 13th* (the second dose beginning to take effect) but couldn't manage to bring the matter to an end even then. If he followed the usual Roman customs, he would have eaten his *cena* between 3.45 and 6.45 on October 12th ('the ninth hour; for three hours'). If phallin latency is 10–12 hours, I don't

see why he should not have been taken sick early in the morning
of October 13th (say 5 o'clock) after a normal evening and night,
been prayed for by the Consuls and Senate about 10 o'clock, but
then shown signs of complete recovery: Locusta's dose being
sufficient for a lean, empty-bellied man but not for a fat, full-
bellied one, especially after he had vomited up (as Suetonius
suggests) the greater part of the meal. So they decided to finish
him off with a colocynth clyster. If Tacitus and Seneca were *both*
correct about times, Nero was proclaimed Emperor at noon, the
lucky hour predicted by the astrologers, *while Claudius was still
alive*; and Claudius, speechless and prostrate, was hastily covered
with clothes *not*, as Tacitus suggests, to pretend that he was still
alive and so delay matters until Nero could be proclaimed, but
to pretend to the comedians that he was already dead – though
(by a double bluff) they were told to continue with the show as
if he were alive. Perhaps he died smothered, like his immediate
predecessor!

Whether the *Vae me, puto concavavi me* was spoken from under
the bedclothes, or whether it greeted the earlier bowel-movement
to which Tacitus refers as having been 'of service to him', after
which he said no more, is doubtful; but I should say that the
comedians heard the rectal explosion and an inarticulate vocal
noise which (being comedians) they afterwards burlesqued –
probably imitating his stutter *concacacavi*, with the joke implied
that he really meant *concavi me* – 'I have hollowed myself out
by this terrific purgation.'

If you are writing a learned dissertation on the theme, please let
me see it. I suggest that you print the relevant texts in full. (There's
also an epigram by Martial on a glutton:

Boletum, qualem Claudius edit, edas.)[47]

If you care to make use of these letters of mine on the subject,
please do so, but I should like to see proofs, because I have kept no
copy of the first one.

Yours sincerely,   Robert Graves

P.S. If, as seems likely, the whole of *Apocolocyntosis* was in
verse originally, not merely *Jam Phoebus, Jam medium, Haec ait
et turpi* and the rest, we can restore the *vae me* verse as:

Claudius e lecto moribundis [*sic*] *verba suprema*
Effudit: 'O vae me, me-me, puto, concacacavi.'[48]

To James Reeves

24 March 1949

Dearest James

I answered you by return about 'He Fell among Thieves',[49] but my letter seems to have fallen among thieves, or stamp collectors – we have a new issue now. My theory was that what was wrong with the poem was that Newbolt was trying to show how much better Kipling would have written if he had been educated at Clifton and a major University instead of at the United Services College somewhere in Devon wasn't it? It is a show-off piece: insincere. The CH was invented because Robertson-Nicoll[50] [*sic*] wasn't good enough for the OM. Its second recipient was Newbolt: how he must have envied Kipling *his* OM. And how Alfred Noyes[51] must have envied Newbolt his CH.

O Lord, keep our souls pure!

We are very much exercised by the prospect of your joblessness in Sept. – I write this in Palma on a pouring wet day with a very loose café nib – and wonder whether there's any hope of your coming out to Deyá. We can let you have the Posada to live in rent free – it's furnished and quite big – and could help in lots of other ways – if you could write a book here, or something. It might be an easier life for Mary – but perhaps the problems of Stella's education, etc., etc. I don't know . . .; but we'd love to have you. I have quite a decent libary here, of course. ¿Perhaps for a year, as a try-out?

You know what things are like here: as they were, but a bit run-down. Same climate. Living costs much reduced since the £ has been quoted at 100 pesetas instead of 66. Karl and Rene live quite well with their child on £5 a week and Ca'n Torrent rent free. I don't know what your private income is, of course.

Anyhow, it may be worth considering.

Much love to you all   Robert

In April Reeves wrote to say he had found another teaching job, at the Training College, Weymouth, and therefore wouldn't be taking up the invitation to move to Deyá.

That spring Reeves published a small volume of poems, *The Imprisoned Sea*, and reviewers of the book drew attention to what they saw as a Gravesian influence on his poetry.

23 April I guess, 1949

Dearest James:

We are simply overjoyed to hear about your job; and where could be nicer than Weymouth?

Yes, I saw the Fraser[52] review because my name appeared in it:[53] it was very decent, but it hadn't occurred to him that Reeves might have influenced Graves at least as much as Graves, Reeves. Personally, I find no poem by either that is fundamentally characteristic of the other. (In the current *Horizon* Spender[54] does me the honour of copying my metrical forms and themes, and I can't say I like it, especially as I have never found anything of *his* worth copying.)

Robertson-Nicholl was a sort of 'Garvin'[55]: a dreary literary political.

. . . .

Kenneth and Stephanie Robinson, Colonial Office and Somerville friends of my niece Sally, have rented us a house off Vincent Square, Westminster, from July 1–29. Nice and central and has a back garden. Will be seeing you.

So sorry about Martin's malaria.

Love to all   Robert

My *Common Asphodel* should be out soon; will send you a copy.

Fraser is, I think, an intelligent and energetic Canadian who is married and up at Oxford. He wrote the first article on my novels, as such, that has ever appeared anywhere – if it's the same Fraser.

13 May 1949

Dearest James:

How's mumps? No *serious* symptoms we trust. Thanks very much for the poem and letter. We like the poem very much. If my eyes should fail me[56] I don't think I'd be capable of serious work: I still rewrite prose 4 times and poems 7 and my inner ear depends on my outer eye. Sorry about Watt's[57] mistake: I told him to send you only anthologies, but you know what girls in offices are.

We're coming to England, everything permitting, which is a large
order, by air via Valencia and Madrid direct to London and
returning, everything permitting, by the same route. It's damnably
expensive but we must get to London this year, and other ways
are impossible with the children (total £223!) and I expect it'll pay
in the end. Will be with my niece Sally (Chilver) at 108 Clifton Hill,
NW8 (near Alma Square) except for a week at Lowestoft with
Margaret and Berwyn Eastwood towards the end of July. Return:
Aug. 2nd. We dread travel in England during holiday time with
our three uncivilized children but we do want to see you so much
and it'll have to be arranged somehow.

Len has gone off to Reno and behaved so horribly to Jane that
she doesn't feel so bad as she might; he's said to be doing only
second-class work. Sad.

You'll remember Dorothy and Montague Simmons.[58] They sold
up and went to Florida at Laura and Schuyler's[59] invitation to
help with the citrus fruits. Montague had a £1500 a year job which
he liked and did well, but Dorothy was crazy about L. and S.
and so he resigned. (They have two children.) A frightful bust-up
ensued. Details aren't forthcoming, but so far as I can make out
Schuyler set them black-a-more tasks and treated them like dirt
[. . . .]; and that I imagine was Schuyler carrying on the Gujieff[60]
[*sic*] tradition – he'd been in that awful Gujieff Institute at Paris
[*sic*], where Katherine Mansfield[61] died, where Old Beelzebub as
he called himself tried to break his disciples' hearts for his own
good. She's now had to ask Papa to send her the return fare for
herself and children, while Montague washes dishes somewhere in
hopes of rejoining her. But will he get his job back? Margaret
Russell[62] told us of this.

What a world!

Tambimuttu[63] asked me to contribute homage to the poet Eliot
on his 60th birthday. Why 60th? Why Eliot? Why homage? *The
White Goddess*, true, is to come this month they say (25/-) from
his publishing firm; but he'll have his reward for that in Heaven
without my homage. I don't know when my *Essays on Poetry* will
appear. The contract's signed and Hamish Hamilton has the
typescript. Perhaps this autumn. Perhaps 1950. Heaven knows and
I don't ask. With Karl's help it's now in decent order. Karl's also
helping me get all my short stories, plays and miscellaneous essays
(of any interest) into form now: I don't know for whom or

when.[64] The Utopia possibly to be called 7 Days in New Crete is in the 5th day and four chapters or so from the end: a damned queer affair. I have had only the vaguest idea what was going to happen and left the logic of events to surprise me, chapter by chapter. It concerns the problem of evil: how much evil is needed to sustain 'the good life'.

When that's done I pick up my historical novel about the Solomon Islands and the Woman Admiral in 1595.[65] I'm also working on a mythical ballet with Joän Junyer[66] by correspondence: he wants to do the décor.

Juan is sickening for something, probably measles: hope the others get it over before we fly.

Gelat and the Madona send their sympathies about your eyes. He's been very ill: poisoned heart, but with Dios's help will live another few years. I wish his son was of a nobler and less penny-greedy nature; but the grandson now aged 11 promises to revert to type.

The weather here is absolutely awful – mist, rain and no really fine day for the last month. No bathing.

Poet's World[67] not yet arrived.

Wm won second prize in a boys' race – so his accident can now be forgotten.

Lucie's been ill with arthritis and a strained heart; John's[68] been painting very well and has now been forced to send to the RA by economic pressure.

Much love from us both to you all.   Robert

We listen to Jacob[69] on the wireless; he really thinks before he speaks and we like him, though he has a little pomposity to shed still.

That summer Graves, Beryl and the children went to England. Graves wrote to Karl Gay in Deyá.

14 July 1949

Dearest Karl and Rene

This is a scratch to tell you we're alive and kicking feebly. Too many people to see: talk, talk, talk all day. A frightful heatwave worse than any in Majorca because of the dirt and the impossibility of having sea-bathes or going about naked.

Eileen Garrett[70] was grand, and sent you both her love. She'll do *The Tap*,[71] I think. She read a few chapters the night before she left and liked it. Also *Occupation: Writer*.

We're bringing Martin back with us; he's been invaluable here. Probably arrive on the 12th.

My next book will be a hist. novel wished on me by Sally about the Weslyan [*sic*] wars in Tonga (1885–90) for which she has promised me full documentation, and Martin is getting me the outlying books. It is a sort of South Sea farce with a wicked missionary as the tragic figure.[72]

Saw Norman;[73] apparently the Life Insurance won't give him even a short term credit. High blood pressure. He's scared. Sally also is threatened with loss of a kidney. Me, I'm fine. Children all with coughs. Saw Hogben[74] and liked him; stopping with him on return from Wales.

Have got your radio from Oxford. What am I to do with it?

Nasty, complicated, silly letter from Laura. – Answered simply and ingenuously.

Am broadcasting on the Parable of the Talents; recording tomorrow; script approved. Also reading 7 of my poems. Don't know when it will be put on the air. Am completely and utterly confused by London; but still remember you both with affection.

Love   Robert

In 1939, when Graves and Riding ended their long literary partnership, Riding (who at the same time 'repudiated' poetry) verbally ceded to Graves all rights in their collaborative works, including *A Survey of Modernist Poetry* (1927), *A Pamphlet against Anthologies* (1928) and their joint work in *Epilogue* (1935–37). However, when Graves put extracts from these works (with full acknowledgements to Riding) into his collected essays volume, *The Common Asphodel*, Riding in effect prevented their republication in the USA. Hamish Hamilton published the book in Britain and Creative Age Press was keen to publish in America; Eileen Garrett, however, although recognizing that legally Graves had the right to republish the collaborative work, thought that Riding's 'ethical position' should be considered and therefore wrote to Riding in Florida and received in reply a strong letter of objection. Garrett suggested Graves himself write, which he did, and in return he received the letter he mentioned to Gay. Graves explained Riding's objections in a letter to Alan Hodge, who was then working for Hamilton.

No date

Dearest Alan:

Hamish offered sheets of the *Asphodel* to Creative Age Press and they refused them because of a wholly unnecessary fuss. Eileen Garrett (who runs the CAP), although the collaborative works of L. and me are free of copyright in USA because never published there, thought it 'morally right' to ask Laura if she minded, etc., and in reply Laura sent a long *megillah* – a good Jewish word for an immensely long tedious hair-splitting tract – saying that she wouldn't mind, if I used only excerpts from the books and printed them in an appendix in small print, with all sorts of promises and undertakings about copyright (which would have been invalid in any case). She said she did not recall what she had told me in the emotional stages of our personal leave-taking, but she remembered that she had been generous to me.

In England, the case is different. The two relevant books were published by Heinemann and Cape who have been served notice to reprint and duly declined; the copyright returns to Laura and me. As you may remember from those foul days, she verbally gave up to me all her rights in our collaborative work, which she rejected as a 'great mistake', on the understanding that I made way for Schuyler on the *Dictionary*,[75] which as you know I had been financing as well as working on, and left my 3000 dollars in the Nimrod house-building venture.[76] To show her further generosity, *after* the leave-taking, she pocketed my 2000 dollars advance on *Sergeant Lamb* (paid her in error) and said she was sorry but she couldn't return it. She left me flat.

It seems to me that since the collaborative books were offered as 'word by word collaborations', they cannot be decently cut up into extracts, and as Laura does not wish to revive the memory of her partnership with me, I am justified in standing by her verbal surrender of her rights and republishing them – as I am now doing – included in a volume of my own, explaining the case; the only legal question she could raise would be payment to her as co-author proportionate to page-length, and of course that could easily be settled. It would be a great help if you could remember her making the surrender; certainly you'll remember your being ousted from the *Dictionary* – you lost your hope of profit and a year's work, plus actual money invested in living.

But she hasn't yet been told of the English edition and I therefore propose to let sleeping dogs lie ... The pair of them are in very low water – the farm's up for sale and everyone there seems to hate them. They talk of taking up the pen again; but I fear they'll find the nib's crossed and the market dead.

Anyhow: reassure Hamish that everything's all right. Laura can't take any action: could not get an injunction against the book's publication even if she could afford a legal case. He is simply republishing copyright material, vested in me, which she has no desire to republish herself, or jointly, and in which she has verbally at least resigned her interest; and I make full acknowledgement of the collaboration. Fortunately Watt is still Laura's agent, and cross with her about the *Dictionary*'s delays; so he'll support me, as I know you will. (Old A.S. is dead, rest his soul.)

Love and haste – from usward to you-both-ward

Robert

Laura said it would be 'unseemly' for either of us to publish, in individual volumes, collaborative work even though acknowledged as such; alternatively, that she might one day be faced with the same problem as me. To this I answered that it was not considered unseemly to print Shakespeare's early collaborative plays in the main canon of his work, even though he later quarrelled with the collaborators; and that if she wished to print collaborative work of mine and hers in a volume of her own in US I would be glad to give her permission.

(The extracts from *Epilogue* are not long (only 21 pages) and as I wholly financed (and lost about £1000 over) the issues, I am entitled to reprint whatever I please, to recoup my losses.)

While in England Graves saw Joshua Podro again, now back in London from Paignton. Podro's criticisms of *King Jesus* originally suggested to them the idea of working out the 'real story' more exactly together; in London now they agreed to set to work on a collaborative analysis of Gospel discrepancies, Graves's task being to supply the Roman and early Christian background to the story, Podro's to supply that of first-century Judaism.

The result of their work was *The Nazarene Gospel Restored* (Cassell, 1953), the conclusion of which was, briefly, that Jesus had been a devout Jew, belonging to a small apocalyptic sect known as

Zophim, or 'Watchers for the Kingdom', and organized on Free Essene lines:

He took the contemporary Pharisaic attitude towards the Mosaic Law, making only minor reservations [see *The Nazarene Gospel Restored*, XLVIII. d, LXXX. *e* and CVI. *f*], never equated himself with God and, though he performed certain faith cures in God's name, neither did nor suffered anything that lay outside the sphere of natural human experience. Granted, he was set apart from his fellow-Israelites, because John the Baptist had chosen him as the person to whom the whole corpus of Messianic prophecies referred, and secretly annointed him King of Israel; yet his deference to the Great Sanhedrin's religious authority continued to be no less sincere than the devout Catholic's is to the Holy See today. [*The Nazarene Gospel Restored*, Foreword]

Jesus also, they believed, survived his ordeal on the Cross only to find that the Kingdom of Heaven had not come and that his sacrifice had been premature. (For a fuller explanation of their conclusions, see the Appendix.)

Apart from an initial meeting in July to agree on general principles, the collaboration was necessarily by letters, a great number of which passed between them, though here there is room for only a very few.

3 August 1949   Kneesworth Hall
                                                      Near Royston
                                                      Herts

My dear Joshua:

How busy you have been! The question of lay-out will settle itself I think; but if one treats opposite pages (e.g. 2 and 3, 4 and 5) of an octavo book as a single unit one can have four parallel columns, which should suffice; especially as the reconstructed Aramaic version could go as an appendix. May I keep your scheme?

Of course there are quotations from Lost Gospels, and the fragmentary 'Sayings Of' to include in the list, and even the bit from the Talmud about the High Priest's retiring room and the donation from the prostitute.[77]

(I wish I hadn't either sold or given away so many of my source books used when writing *King Jesus*.)

I think the Gospels all began with *Sayings* of Jesus, with slight explanations of the setting, and the Passion narrative. These were rounded off in different ways by different churches, according to local requirements. If Mark has 'miracles' in it, that simply means that it was needed to off-set the miracles of Apollonius of Tyana who had been to India and did a lot of Yogi magic. I assume that the original *Sayings* of Jesus were authentic and that so was the original Passion narrative, and that both can be recovered in great part by critical comparison with Hebrew parallels, and a knowledge of Gentile political and religious bias. Once it is accepted that he said: 'It is easier for Heaven and Earth to pass away than for one jot or tittle of the Law to pass away,' the task is fairly straightforward. All breaches of the First Commandment (his identification of himself with God) which abound in St John can be ruled out.

I don't know how our collaboration will work, but I'm sure that we'll come to firm conclusions on details since we agree in principle. This is a job that should have been undertaken long, long ago. If properly documented it is bound to make itself felt as an influence in separating the idea of Jesus from the idea of the Man-god – ethics, in fact, from myth. There is a place for both in this world, but not confused together as in the Gospels.

Yours ever affectionately   Robert

I have a feeling that one of the first gospel editors who tampered with the text was a Samaritan who wanted to glorify his own people. I wonder whether he could be identified.

Graves later felt he had identified this Samaritan editor, as he explained in a letter to Podro on 12 September 1949:

Simon Magus appears in Acts 8 and is closely identified with St Paul in the pseudo-Clementine Homilies 18, 19 and Recognitions 10, 61. Eusebius mentions him and his disciple Menander in *Ecc. Hist.* III, 26. He was a liar, a Pauline, a crook, and a Samaritan, like the Gospel editor we have in mind, and worked very early, at the textual sources of both the Synoptics and John. Justin Martyr though a Samaritan can be exculpated – he wasn't proud of being a Samaritan and wrote too late (AD 148).

In 1947 the Dead Sea Scrolls had been discovered, relics of the first-century Qumrân religious centre; Graves later wrote that they add little to our knowledge of the Gospels, apart from the identity of the 'Children of Darkness' and the 'Children of Light' mentioned below, but they do give information on other matters such as the constitution of the early Jewish Church.

17 August 1949   Deyá

Dear Joshua:

Back again, and about to start work. I expect you're very excited about the Scrolls of the Dead Sea. I understand from the *Jewish Chronicle* that 'The Children of Darkness' mentioned by Jesus are now shown to have been Sons of Abraham not bound by the Mosaic Law; while the Children of Light were the returned Judaeans, Benjamites and Levites. By the way, the parable of the Two Sons (Lk. 15, 11), one of whom disobeyed and then repented, the other of whom pretended obedience and did not give it, must surely refer to a) Pharisee descendants of the disgraced priesthood whose place was taken by the Sons of Zadok, and b) to these same sons of Zadok, the Saducees – the Pharisees having made a religious come-back? The Gospel editors have turned it against the Jews as a whole in favour of the Gentiles. What a dirty business it all is!

Our job is to distinguish, particularly, between Jesus's titles. 'Son of Man' can merely mean 'this man', can't it? 'Son of God' was every Jew's title, but Jesus's particular title if he was indeed anointed as King by John the Baptist and saluted with Psalm 2.[78] Hence the distinction between *My Father* and *Our Father* in John.

At the moment I'm merely soaking myself in the subject and getting a clearer picture of the technique of distortion, which is perfected in John.

It is very hot indeed here and Spanish economy is running downhill like the Gadarene swine.

Love to Fanny   Robert

In *King Jesus* Graves described a secret coronation of Jesus very similar to ceremonies and traditions mentioned by Raphael Patai in *Hebrew Installation Rites* (though Graves had not then read that book). After reading Patai's work and corresponding with him, Graves came to the conclusion that the apparent later cold relations between Jesus and John the Baptist would have been traditionally necessary if, as he had originally supposed, it had been John who had installed Jesus as King.

8 September 1949

Dear Joshua:

I quite agree that by the time the 4th Gospel had been edited John the Baptist was made to talk nonsense (in support of a quarrel between Madeans and Christians?) but it is strange that this morning before I got your letter I was working at this very point – the quarrel between Jesus and John – and applying Raphael Patai's findings about the Jewish monarchy to Jesus's case. He proves that by ancient tradition the prophet who crowned the King never saw him again and often behaved like a personal enemy (*Hebrew Installation Rites*, 202–204).

Samuel never saw Saul after the completion of the latter's installation at Gilgal (Sam. 15, 12–34): 'he did no more see Saul until the day of his death.' The same is told of Samuel and David (16, 13). Similarly with Ahijah and Jeroboam (I Kings 11, 29–39). Similarly with the prophet who crowned Jehu (II Kings 9, 3–10). Patai makes an analogy between this relationship and those of African sacred kings and their chief priests. He also stresses the resemblance between Jesus's installation and that of Saul's, though without following up the John the Baptist clue (above) nor two others that I mentioned, independently, in *King Jesus*. So I think you should be cautious about dismissing Jesus's coronation story as a late invention, especially as it occurs not only in Luke but in the very early Gospel According to the Hebrews quoted by Jerome. Pilate at least seems to have taken his claim to the throne seriously.

That the Hasmonean princes were referred to as 'Sons of God' at their coronation is welcome news. It shows the continuance of the Davidic ritual until nearly the time of Jesus. I have always thought that Jesus was Son of God only in the sense of being crowned King.

Do I understand you to suggest that Jesus's remark about the Children of Darkness and the Children of Light is an anti-Pharisaic interpolation? From an article in the *Jewish Chronicle* I understood that the 'Children of Light' were the Jews returned from Captivity and the 'Children of Darkness' the Ammonites and Moabites. *Someone* is wrong.

Yours ever   Robert

Apart from the 4th Gospel I think that the Gospel editors omitted, interpolated and tampered, but otherwise kept to the bones of the story without wanton invention on a large scale.

About Uriel: he was 'set over the world and over Tartarus' (I Enoch 20, 2). Raguel, not Uriel, was in charge of the 'world of luminaries' (5,4). According to another system, with another list of archangels, quoted by Weber, that was Michael's task as archangel of Wednesday, the day on which the luminaries were created. Uriel does not appear at all.

I hope you'll like my broadcast. I should have added that Jerome mentions an alternative version of the *Talents* in the Gospel According to the Hebrews, in which one servant wastes his master's money on harlots and flute-girls and is the one who gets shut up in prison. But this does not help matters much.

Be careful about your quotations: Jesus called him 'a reed shaken by the wind' not a *broken* reed. The first prophesies, though vaguely; the second 'pierces the hand' when you lean on it.

After *The Common Asphodel* was published by Hamish Hamilton in September 1949, Graves wrote again to Alan Hodge – at the bottom of a letter by Beryl congratulating Hodge on the birth of his daughter Jessica and telling him of the break between Graves and Otto Kubler, an Austrian historian who had until then been collaborating with Graves on the novel *The Isles of Unwisdom*. (Graves went on to finish the book alone.)

Beryl doesn't mention she's just had an operation – 'very aesthetically' done by a local surgeon for 5000 pesetas after which she's promised good health in perpetuum. Nothing serious; but bits of interior removed that should have gone in her Woolworth days. Now she's up and about again; but it's been a bit of a bother for all. The doctors would insist on cracking up Oscar Wilde to her. How backward we are here!

I haven't yet had an *Asphodel*, so can't say what Desmond MacCarthy[79] wrote about your blurb which I haven't seen. I forget why he dislikes me; some row years ago – wasn't it about TROYS?[80] I certainly disliked every inch of his seedy Irish person when we met (for the first and last time) in 1927. So glad you liked my Parable. I am very well on into the book in which it will be incorporated: *The Hand of Simon Magus*[81] – S.M. was Samaritan editor of Luke and John who was always boosting

Samaria, and incidentally invented the Christian Trinity theory. His less respectable side appears in Acts 8. Today I've been doing Jesus's remarks on 'Ocular Adultery'. He said that if you saw a pretty girl and got an erection you should pluck out your eye and cut off your virile member. Simon Magus feeling that was going too far in the direction of Cybele-castration changed 'virile member' to 'right hand'. A pity Christians did not take Jesus seriously then the whole religion would have died out.

Love   Robert

To Joshua Podro

23 September 1949

My dear Joshua

I have kept a copy of this introduction with the same page numbers, so that any comment, addition, etc., that you care to send me will be intelligible. I don't know how far you agree with my argument about Jesus's parentage, but I have documented it fully, and if you have anything against it (except that you think it cranky!) you're welcome to make your case.

Now I have started work on the detachable episodes with the idea of getting them, when complete in themselves, into a rough sequence.

This week I did the *Incident of the Greeks* (John 12, 20–43) which I'll send you soon; and the *Incident of the Lepers* (treating the two stories as one). Both leave room for your comment. I chose the *Incident of the Greeks* because it was a very sticky one and had forced itself on my attention – they were of course Greek-speaking Jews, not Gentiles as the editor makes out, and I think Jesus rebuffed them as heretics.

It doesn't really matter what part of the Gospels you work at and what I work at; the work can be harmonized. But I'd like you to comment on the more difficult Jewish problems, such as the Sabbath and ritual cleanliness and divorce, where I'm not so well-educated as you. ·

I find the work intensely interesting and I'm sure you do too. The great thing is to write as dispassionately as possible: our resentment of Paul and Simon Magus will show through our careful sentences, I've no doubt.

Please: *nothing is final* in my contribution. I'm always ready to change my view for one more in keeping with the known facts; and I know you are too; so no disagreement is possible – though here and there we may have to record alternative explanations if the evidence is delicately balanced.

Yours affy.   Robert

My ambition is to stop Jesus from writhing endlessly on that Cross; to give his spirit rest.

4 October 1949

My dear Joshua:

Many thanks for your essay, which I have skimmed and will read properly tomorrow. The material is excellent, though as you realize there's discrepancy between my Crucifixion theory and yours, which will have to be settled.

I am constantly wishing you were here to ask for information on small points, but of course you'll get my work in a form in which I hope you'll be able to supplement easily where I leave lacunae.

For example what quotations (if any) are there in the Lord's Prayer from the synagogue Liturgy?

I feel very pleased with the work I have done in explaining *why* there are four blind men healed in Matt., 2 in Mark, and one in Luke. Once one hits on the principle of distortion it's easy as shelling peas.

About the Common People. Jesus was 'forcing the hour'. Until *all Israel* had a chance to repent, the Kingdom of God couldn't come; so he left the Pharisees to their admirable own teachings and went after the unwashed, while still keeping touch with noblemen Pharisees and others. He didn't love them for being unwashed, as Christians think!

I'll think about the most appropriate way of using the material – don't apologize for your English – it's better than most Oxford historians!

My most important discovery is the principle of 'conflation'. The Gospellers worked on 'Acts and Sayings of Jesus' arranged under headings, not chronologically. Thus the heading 'Rich Young Man' has two entries which get confused. 'Watch' has four which get confused. 'Conflict with Authority' has two, which get confused.

(The corn-plucking as theft; the healing of the withered arm as *Sabbath breach*.) By regrouping the headings, most of the nonsense can be explained.

Love   Robert

I have done so much work lately Karl can't keep up with the typing; but I'll call a halt and get him to retype a copy for you.

No date

My dear Joshua:

About the passion-story. Pilate would have been quite safe to have Jesus crucified, even though a Roman, if he did not plead citizenship, and if his ancestry was known only to a very few and if he could be charged with sedition. Pilate was careful to disclaim responsibility for the crucifixion, by fixing it on Herod Antipas and the High Priestly junta, and could have denied any official knowledge of Jesus's identity if it had been brought up.

The High Priestly party could not afford to be 'unclean until evening' on a day like that. Work on the Passover sacrifice started at 3 o'clock and there must have been a lot of jobs to do. *But please rid yourself of the idea that I consider the Crucifixion to have been a Jewish affair.* The story has obviously been tampered with by the evangelists; but its occurrence in more or less the same form in all of them shows that it is not altogether an invention: that it is Nazarene tradition not just material for a Gentile 'miracle play'. Pilate *did give Jesus an interview*; and that he did so in so petty a case as it was is most peculiar and needs explanation. I find that John though a mass of lies does often point to an older and more reliable account than the synoptics; e.g. the blind man of Bethesda Pool – despite the absurd embroideries on the story. And in the Passion narrative, despite all the obvious lies you point out, there is a good deal, I think, of authentic material buried underneath.

It's a question of *date*; 'Q' was embroidered on, but not invented.

Yes, of course, Antipas wanted to get rid of Jesus, but Pilate and Antipas had had a quarrel, and Pilate would have made him pay for the privilege of having him put away. 'Nothing for nothing, and damned little for a drachma!' was a Roman governor's motto. But *how much* did Antipas want to be rid of him?

What you say about the Jewish authorities wanting to postpone Jesus's case until after the holidays supports your view, and mine,

that the Crucifixion was arranged between Pilate and Antipas –
that though the Levites in the HP's service first arrested Jesus on
a charge of brawling in the Basilica, for which he deserved 39
stripes, Pilate sent for him because of 'information received'. The
question is: *what information?*

About the washing of the hands. Pilate may well have seen the
ceremony and been amused by it, and used it in jest on an
inappropriate occasion.

I'm glad you realize that you have a 'private feud' with Pilate.
It is obvious that he was as corrupt as an 18th Century East India
Company official, and as shrewd. But don't let the feud distract
your attention from historical probability about the date of the
first *undoctored* account of the Passion sequence.

In any case, I propose to leave the question of J.'s identity an
open one.

[Unsigned]

In September, Lynette Roberts, the Welsh poet who had helped
Graves by supplying books and suggestions when he was writing
The White Goddess (see *In Broken Images*, pp. 316 ff.), decided to
move to Deyá with her two young children, on Graves's invitation;
she was in the process of divorcing her husband, Keidrych Rhys,
and was worried over her father's ill health.

Graves, on the other hand, was making preparations for his
marriage to Beryl; he had previously been unable to marry her
because Nancy refused to divorce him on the grounds that it would
mean styling herself Nancy Graves (i.e. *Graves* v. *Graves*) whereas
she had always firmly retained her maiden name of Nicholson.
Finally, however, Nancy was persuaded by Jenny and her husband
and by Graves's mother to accept the compromise of Graves *alias*
Nicholson, and the divorce went ahead.

5 October 1949

Dear Lynette:

We'll keep on writing, to keep you going until you come here.
Solidarity!

How dreadful about your Father! And how absurd about the
assizes! The smell of solicitors' offices is terrible even if one knows
and loves the inmates, as in the case of Beryl's family firm – they're

all in it, Father, two brothers, one sister – and in Wales peculiarly terrible.

Patience, woman!

I'm writing to have you sent my *Utopia* novel just out.

Love to Angharad.[82] I've just had a letter from my only godson, of whom I'd lost sight since the font, son of an elementary schoolmaster. Now ex-Balliol, ex-1st Dragoon Guards Officer, something very important in *Joint Intelligence* whatever that may be – writing to me a learned criticism of my Parables broadcast. How old I must be!

I'm having a wonderful time with a new theory of just how the Gospels got so muddled – your barrister would be thrilled. I've found out from a 2nd century chap called Irenaeus how it was done – by trying to make a chronological sequence of a collection of sayings and acts under *subject* headings, and running them together.

Come here whenever you're ready, let's know the date roughly – somebody *may* be coming out at the same time who could help with the luggage and children if you decided not to fly. But let it be in time for Christmas.

Adultery is not evil, so long as it is not hole-and-corner and serious. Here, where there is no divorce and lots of priests about, it is a sort of escape into the free life – but not serious because it has no future.

Me, I'm technically adulterous still because Nancy has refused to divorce me since I don't know how long; but my sons-in-law have finally insisted, and the papers are going through, so perhaps you'll be a matron of honour at Beryl and my wedding. We wonder, though, whether we *should* marry: an unlegalized compact of love is obviously stronger than a legalized one. There are some advantages of course, such as: *if* we ever wanted to go to the USA together we'd not be allowed to enter, as being of moral turpitude – or is that an advantage? And then of course death-duties, if I die, etc., are less if the family is a legitimized one.

Love from us both

Robert

In May, Podro went to Deyá to work with Graves on the book; as they had now almost finished a first draft they decided to write to T. S. Eliot at Faber offering him the book.

14 May 1950

My dear Eliot:

Since we last met nearly a year ago I have been working nearly eight hours a day in collaboration with my learned Talmudic friend Joshua Podro on the book I promised you – the rescension of the Gospels which we propose to call THE GOSPEL OF THE ZOPHIM. (The Zophim were a Levite sect of apocalyptics with whom Jesus had close relations.) I have been writing at the Graeco-Roman end; he at the Aramaic-Hebraic-Syriac end. Our findings dovetail exactly. It is a very long, very readable, very strange book [*margin note*: I have had to abandon a good deal of what I wrote in *King Jesus*, which was a novel not a historical work[83]] and we claim to have solved on sound historical lines, with every sentence documented, all the outstanding Gospel *cruces*. This, of course, is a very large claim; but we proceed from what is historically certain to what is certainly unhistorical and arrive at the *reasons* for the acknowledged discrepancies in the Gospels and the acknowledged departures from historical fact, and are thus able to restore the original tradition. I mean: it is not (e.g.) enough to say that the two genealogies of Jesus in Matthew and Luke are irreconcileable and that if He was Son of God neither genealogy has any point, even if Mary was Joseph's niece and ward. One must explain *why* both genealogies are preserved and how the tradition that Joseph married his niece arose. One must also explain *why* if Jesus was the son of David, and therefore of the tribe of Judah, he was wearing a Levite vestment at the Crucifixion.

All this we have done in close argument.

Again, it is not enough to say that Paul in Corinthians 15 (the earliest historical document of the Resurrection) is alone in saying that Jesus appeared to 'above 500 brethren at once' when the fact is not mentioned in the Gospels and when according to Acts the brethren only numbered 120 at the time. The number 500 (like the impossible 2000 of the Gadarene swine) has either to be explained away or else to be justified.

And it is not enough to accept the story that Jesus told his disciples: if they had sufficient faith they could uproot a sycamine tree and cast it into the sea. It must either be shown why Jesus used this fantastic figure and what the object would have been of performing so anti-social and ridiculous a feat of magic; or else the various stages of textual corruption which culminate in this text must be traced in a scholarly fashion.

It is not enough to say that Jesus could not have dined with a 'Leper' – who would not have had a house to dine in: one must show how the word *Leper* came to be mistranslated, and from what Aramaic original; and who this Simon was.

It is not enough to say that Jesus saved the woman taken in adultery; one must show why she was in danger of stoning when the capital punishment for adultery had been removed for the last hundred years or so, and what Jesus wrote on the ground, and why her paramour was not also in danger of stoning, and why the story as it stands has been impossibly staged at Jerusalem.

And so on, for 800 pages.

Listen: Joshua Podro is here working with me and is returning to England next week to check meticulous Talmudic points with Dr Epstein, the translator of the Talmud in English; and Dr Patai, the head of the Department of Folklore and Ethnology of the Hebrew University at Jerusalem, now in New York, is checking a few specialist chapters concerned with the Nativity and Baptism. In July, about the 15th, I shall be in London and would like to come to see you with Podro for a session of a couple of hours to discuss whether you really want this book or not; what seems reasonable is for you to catch a bishop, canon, archdeacon or other dignitary who has a sound knowledge of the latest developments of NT criticism, and let him come armed with certain knotty questions about, say, three selected texts. If the solutions to these set questions contained in our book can be shown erroneous, inadequate or historically unsound, then obviously you'll not want to publish; but if they stand up to scrutiny, even though heretical from a Catholic point of view, you'll probably want to publish especially since we not only show the greatest respect for Jesus (and indeed consider him libelled in the Gospels) and even accept as historical the Apostles' Creed as far as: 'on the third day He rose again from the Dead' – though we interpret the articles in a different sense from the Catholic.

If you can't decide in a two hours' test whether or not it is a *Faber* book, then we'll go elsewhere; we want to fix things up before I return early in August to this island. Is this fair?

I'm looking forward to seeing you and Morley Kennedy[84] again.

(Wasn't Thurber[85] good in the *New Yorker* on *The Cocktail Party?*)

Yours ever sincerely   Robert Graves

Eliot replied that he was very interested in seeing the book, though Graves assumed too readily that Faber would definitely publish it, as in this letter to Gordon Wasson (10 June) – one of the many they exchanged about etymologies relevant to Wasson's mycological researches:

My spelling of *Boszegui* is older than yours – see *Oxford English Dictionary* under *Buskin*.

I think this is about all . . .

Why these things plague you – why they plague me – who knows? I don't think profession has anything to do with it. (I make my living by turning my silver *duro* to the new moon every month, and have no investments, and give spare money, when needed, to people I like. It is a primitive economy and, some say, reprehensible. I keep no accounts; which is a job I leave to my agent and income tax adviser.) The Goddess has a sense of humour and to reach down to 23 Wall Street and say: 'You, there, recover my lost mushroom lore, and make Morgan & Co. foot the bill' is just like her.

Regards to your wife.

Yours   Robert Graves

Next month I'm seeing T. S. Eliot again. When I first knew him he was a banker too. He's publishing a heavily documented book, for me and a man called Podro, about Jesus's original sayings. We got the clue to the technique of editorial distortion in the Greek Gospels and between my Greek and his Aramaic, Hebrew and Syriac, we have managed to work out all the *cruces* intelligibly. *The White Goddess* is for poets, this will be for scholars. Very decent of Eliot to publish both these books, because they are heretical in the extreme. I am so glad you like *The White Goddess*. It is slowly sinking in, but the scholars are shy of making any comment on it at all; and have left it alone. The poets get excited about it, and that's nice. I wrote it for them.

That summer in England Graves went to see Eliot; no experts, however, were produced and Eliot 'seemed anxious to turn aside any discussion about [*The Nazarene Gospel Restored*] ... commenting sardonically that he would of course be interested to read it – and that he hoped it might be rather "dry" "if the Faith were to survive" ' (Martin Seymour-Smith, *Robert Graves: His Life and Work*, Hutchinson, 1982, p. 431).

Back in Deyá Graves wrote again to Eliot.

15 August 1950

My dear Tom – I used to call you this once,[86] and propose with
               your consent to revive the custom –
Many thanks for your letter. Of course, I understand the technical problems raised by this book and so long as I know that you and your fellow-directors are genuinely anxious to publish it, that is good enough for Joshua Podro and me. The work won't be finished before December – there are so many cross-references to work out, and texts to check, and then the whole restored version of the Apostolic tradition to type out in sequence (at present the separate passages are considered in scattered sections). And only then will I be able to estimate the length of the book; but I imagine that it will not be much longer or shorter than, say, twice the length of *The White Goddess* – no two volumes necessary.

In any case, I shall get Creative Age Press to do the first printing of it, and if you decide to reprint from the completed book by the same photographic process that you used in the new edition of *The Long Week-End*,[87] that would save a great number of errors and only necessitate a new title page. Also, it would save several months of printing hold-up.

Anyhow, don't let's worry. The book is yours to publish or not, and so long as I know that the only objection that will possibly be raised by your fellow-directors will be one of expense or of printing-difficulties, and not of religious policy, I am (let me repeat) quite happy about it.

All sorts of new points keep cropping up, of course, and have to be settled: for example, the Coptic tradition that makes a sword not a lance used at the Crucifixion and thus gives point to 'a sword shall pierce thy soul *also*' in Luke 2, 35. And a Talmudic text which suggests that Jesus recommended the equal partition of

a paternal inheritance between sons and daughter, in the style of
Job; but why?

Yours   Robert

P.S. I do very much appreciate your attitude that these seemingly
heretical views of Joshua Podro and myself should be given an
airing, so long as they are based on documentary evidence
throughout – as they are.

My admiration for Jesus (though I am not a Christian except by
baptism and confirmation) has been enormously enhanced by our
researches; and my respect for many of the Church Fathers,
especially Paul, correspondingly reduced. As Cardinal Newman
pointed out: 'they thought that, when there was a *justa cause* [*sic*],
an untruth need not be a lie'. I could not disagree with them more!

10 September 1950

My dear Tom (repeat *Tom*; or delete and substitute *Eliot*, see my
                                     last)

Your letter clears things up nicely, but the typescript which I
send you will not have the quotations from the Gospels, apocryphal
works, early Fathers, Talmud printed *in extenso* at the beginning
of each section in which they are referred to; only the references
to them will be listed at the top. This is because I have cut out and
pasted the original printed passages onto separate sheets, to avoid
typing errors, for accurate reprinting in the US edition. But anyone
capable of judging the scholarly value of the work on your behalf
will obviously have access to the originals, so it does not matter.

'Scholarly value' is, of course, a double-edged expression. An
ordinary scholar would perhaps take it ill that Podro and I regard
Eisler as unsound in his interpretation of the Tower of Siloam
incident; or that we take seriously the Ebionite story reported by
Epiphanius that Paul was born of a Greek father and Greek mother
and that his conversion to Christianity was connected with his
disappointment at not being able to marry into the house of
Boethus, or that we respect St Ephraim's interpretation of the
saying about the fish and the tax-half-shekel. But at least no single
sentence is undocumented, and if this is what is meant by
scholarship, then there you are.

We find shocking cases of misquotation and misinformation in

all the leading authorities; most of them due to copying from equally
careless predecessors. Scholarship – alas!

Once you have the corrected page-proofs from Creative Age that
will be that. The only further corrections will be the fault of the
execrably low standard of English printing these days.

Yours ever

Robert Graves

In 1950 James Reeves began a poetry magazine, *Quarto*, part of the
intention of which was to encourage young poets.

~~Sept~~ *October 11 1950 (Posted in pocket – sorry)*

Dearest James:

The problem of encouraging young poets and giving them a
market –

Were you and I encouraged?

I wasn't. I published pamphlets of my own poems, from my
army pay, and sent them round.[88] And a publisher whom I didn't
know did a small volume[89] and sold two editions of it. But I had
nothing printed before that, except a poem I sent to the
Spectator[90] and poems in a magazine[91] I edited at school.

If I were an unknown poet now, I'd select my four best poems,
have them printed on a cricket-fixture card, for a couple of £s,
and send them round to selected addresses; *not* send them to a
poetry magazine. I'd put a note at the top that these were the
first and rarest items of Robert Graves's poetic publications and
advise recipients to keep them in a cellophane envelope in their safes,
after getting them by heart.

But as I'm not an unknown poet . . .

Anyhow, put me down as a £5 guarantor to show that I think
you know what you're doing. As for sending poems, I can't. *New
Yorker* have bought an option on all my poems (universal rights)
and what they refuse goes to Janet Adam Smith of *Spectator* (on
request) and what she refuses goes to *Times Literary Supplement*
(on request) and as I get about £20 to £30 for a short poem from
the *New Yorker* and £7 or £9 from *Spectator*, it isn't economical
to print elsewhere, especially as I don't write many poems. I'll
have a new collection of about 25 out in April but that's four
years' work.

The Gospels continue to engross every spare and unspare minute and I have refused about 20 offers to write on this and that, for this or that, especially poetry, etc.

If I find any unknowns who are up to standard I'll send them to you.

If we hear of anyone who could bring out those records – a pity that there wasn't better liaison between you and Ethel – we'll be delighted.

'I have a little cough, sir',[92] etc. When I once tried to get permission to print a cowboy ballad in that book of mine about ballads I was told that it was copyright because the editor 'had established the text'. The same is true of me and the little cough, sir. If *I* didn't write it, who the hell did, tell me that! You see you can't; and I've put my name to it as the 'Establisher of the Text' – see? I'm protected by the Copyright Act, see? You just try to rob me of my literary property.

Love from us all   Robert

Write me down as a subscriber to *Quarto*.

. . . .

When visiting his daughter Jenny at Porto Fino in June, Graves met the thriller writer Selwyn Jepson, a friend of Jenny. At that time he was using her toolshed to write in. Jepson's wife Tania was a bookseller and dealer in rare books, and Jepson had been for some time a collector of first editions of Graves's works.

Graves has always enjoyed reading thrillers and admires Jepson's more than most; in an article on 'Crime and Detection in English Literature' he said he found, on the whole, British crime writers distressingly flat-footed: ' . . . A refreshing exception is Selwyn Jepson, who dispenses with a detective stooge and provides intense excitement by keeping his hero (or, more usually, his heroine) on the run from constantly threatened crime: thus using detection not as an amateur foray into situations which should properly be handled by the police, but in desperate self-defence . . .'

During the early fifties Graves became very close to Jepson, who was later to be of great service to him as his business adviser.

No date

My dear Selwyn:

Got the Volturius from Mr *Sivad* and what a Volturius it is!
Why didn't we know before about your books? Is it because your
publisher puts such awful covers on your books you have to remove
them before you send them to us; or because no decent
Englishman would ever waste time on the *Saturday Evening Post*?

Anyhow, we have had more pleasure from these two books read
aloud than from any others in a long reading-partnership and are
exceedingly grateful. It was so nice too that we know Lowestoft
and Saxmundham and the very beach from which the *Nancy Jane*
sailed. The only unfair thing in the books is that it's always summer
at Marsh House; but then of course it's always winter in Simenon's[93]
books, or at least raining.

Ever so many thanks. The Gospels are coming along fine. I'm at
the Judas business in the third go over, and all the Gospels contradict
one another as usual, and though I had got the main points decided
I had missed Jesus's 'Thou sayest' to Judas when he asks 'is it I?'
This is ATTA AMARTA in Aramaic, and means not 'Yes it is' but
'You may so say if you like'. In other words, though he had been
looking for someone to 'smite the (<u>worthless</u>) shepherd' (whom he
was then impersonating by preaching false doctrine in order to
fulfil a prophecy of Zechariah which would bring the world to an
end) [*margin note*: Crazy; but inescapably the only explanation
of his final performances] he couldn't tell Judas outright: 'Take the
bag, buy a sword, and be prepared to kill me as a sacrifice for the
people's sins' – that would be forcing things – so he says: 'That's
up to you; but get on with it, if you feel that way.' But Judas
funks the assignment and gets him put into protective custody
(after accepting the paltry sum of 30 shekels, at which the
'worthless shepherd' was valued in Zechariah) but doesn't realize
that the High Priests will hand him over to the Romans for
crucifixion. So he hangs himself, because that was in the book-of-
words which Jesus and the disciples always followed: Achitophel
did so when he had made a mess of betraying David. Poor Judas:
the universal weakness of Jews and almost their only one:
'knowing better than the boss'.

Nice letter from Jenny. Love to Tania.

Best love from us both

Robert

I say! I see in the *New Yorker* that there's a new book in which Eve figures again with Ordinary Smith. Shall send for it.[94]

My next book is called *Occupation: Writer*, a collection of assorted nonsense about all sorts of things. I'll send you a copy when it arrives at Christmas.

No date

My dear Selwyn

The Spider's Web[95] [sic] (not to coin a new phrase) does the hat-trick; we both love it.

It was a splendid knock-down ending, and I'm glad that Eve's not going to marry Ordinary Smith, because everyone (including most of your male readers) will be so jealous of him. Also I'm glad that Mulligan is still about.

In part payment I'm sending an *Occupation: Writer*;[96] I had just inscribed it to you when the English proofs came and had left out six pages! so I had to send Cassells your copy (because I had not the original) and ask them to print from it and then send on to you.

No news from anyone you know, recently.

The Gospels still engross me, and even the third time over I find obvious things which eluded me (and everyone else) before; such as yesterday: 'Ask and ye shall be given (what?) seek and ye shall find (what?) knock and it (what?) shall be opened to you.' As usual the evangelists have cut out Jesus's Biblical references, so one has to find out. The answer is (Psalms, Proverbs, Esther, etc.): Ask for *Peace*; seek *Wisdom*; knock at the gate of *Mercy*.

This is not very exciting until you realize that *Peace*, the *Spirit of Wisdom*, and *Mercy* were *Son*, *Mother* and *Father*, the 1st, 2nd and 3rd persons in the Pharisee pre-Christian Trinity; which got turned into Father, Son and a *masculine* Holy Spirit by the Catholics; and that Jesus elsewhere (Gospel According to the Hebrews) said 'My (it should be 'Our') Mother the Holy Spirit (of Wisdom) seized me by the hair of my head and carried me (in a vision) to Mount Tabor.' In other words the Catholic Trinity doctrine is Jewish pre-Christian in origin, and Jesus was not *Peace*, the Second Person (though he was later called 'the Prince of Peace') and had no part in it.

This is just to show you the nature of my daily problems. In the afternoon I bathe still; the water is still as warm as it ever gets in the Channel even at the end of August.

A queer bloke called Ronald Duncan came to see us with his wife; claimed to know you. Couldn't quite make him out until his passport fell open at the appropriate page and I saw that he was a disguised Rhodesian; why are they all so ashamed of being colonial, eh? Liked him a lot, though.

Love to Tania and ever so many thanks.

·Robert·

In 1950 the first of Graves's four 'Muses' entered his life. His central argument in *The White Goddess* is the persistent survival of faith in the Muse among 'what are loosely called "Romantic" poets who derive their imagery, either consciously or unconsciously, from the cult of the White Goddess'; he suggests that the 'magic' their poems exert depends on their closeness to describing the Goddess or her presence. Now that the ancient Goddess religion has long been dead, however, 'She' has become a personal rather than a national or public deity and to experience the Muse fully Graves came to believe that the dedicated poet, one who writes private as opposed to public poems, must fall in love with a 'Muse-possessed' woman and suffer at her hands as the ancient myth is acted out, the White Goddess myth which he claims is the archetype of which all true love poems are either fragments or variations.

When interviewed in the *Paris Review* (no. 47, summer 1969) on the role of the 'Personal Muse' Graves replied: 'She serves as a focus and a challenge. She gives happiness. Here I use the English language precisely – hap: happening: happiness. Tranquillity is of no poetical use. The first to use the Muse in the sense of the White Goddess was Ben Jonson – then it dropped down into weakly meaning self-inspiration of young men.'

This first 'incarnation' was a seventeen-year-old girl (Graves was told she was twenty-three – see page 260) called Judith. As Graves wrote in the following letter to James Reeves, nothing 'historical' happened and he interpreted the experience in almost wholly mythological terms. His first poems to her were published in *Poems and Satires* (1951) and included 'Darien', 'The Portrait' and 'Prometheus', and from this time on his poems about the White Goddess are less poems about a mythological or 'metaphorical' phenomenon

82

and more a charting of his own personal (later horrendous) experience of her.

Judith, like her 'successors', was Graves's Muse, not mistress, and like the others, except Cindy (see pages 233 ff.), was immediately incorporated as a close friend of Beryl and the rest of the family.

14 December 1950

Dearest James:

Rummaging idly in the attic I came across unpublished enclosed, of 1923–24 vintage, and wondered if they would suit your Heinemann anthology, either one, more, or all. They are a bit mannered but have a certain wild charm in spots; you may have them cheap.

The Goddess has been plaguing me lately, very cruelly, and I have managed to satisfy her by two or three poems written in red arterial blood; she appeared in person in Deyá during the last full moon, swinging a Cretan axe, but is now away again. Put into historical terms the story isn't really interesting; no liaison dangerous or alteration of the local ebbs and flows. But there are the poems; their publication in my new collection is the only impingement of poetic on historical truth; I'll send you a copy when it comes out in the Spring.

The cheque is for the children in whatever proportions you please to decide.

About the record – I quite agree about the bore – : a girl called Eileen Hawking, Oxford pal of Beryl's, is coming out next month we think; give it to her when we know for sure.

Beryl and the children are fine.

Love to Mary and all –   Robert

Although Judith caused Graves considerable anxiety and concern (in particular he was 'much exercised' by the suitability, or unsuitability, of her boyfriends – see Martin Seymour-Smith, *Robert Graves*, pp. 442–5) he was not so single-mindedly involved with the 'theme' as he was to be in his later dealings with the Goddess. Nor did he have a confidant in the affair, as he was later to have in Idries Shah, and in fact hardly mentions her in his letters.

To Derek Savage, who had written to Graves about a dream he'd had of an encounter between Jesus and an 'extortioner'.

3 January 1951

My dear Savage

If I were the Pilgrim Trust or Signor Guggenheim or Carnegie's Executors, I would confer an *OED* on every writer, real writer, in England. [*margin note*: It would not involve great expense – half-a-dozen copies would be too many!] I have advised many rich and incorrect writers to sell their astrakhan collared coats and frigidaires and Baxter prints to the same end. It is not a faultless work, of course – I am often catching it out – but necessary ... I starved, like you, for years and my critical work suffered in consequence: good dictionaries and plain texts were what I lacked most; and I never could find time to work in a library.

About Jesus: yours is a nice story, but since he was a Pharisee, and therefore bound to consider even Roman swine and Phoenician dogs as God's creatures, he would not have approved of the usurer (the text about 'spoiling the Egyptians' was out of fashion in the 1st century) and would not (even ironically) have wished that the usurer would transfer his extortions to the Children of Promise. He made a nice crack about the High Priest's privy (quoted in the Talmud) which the HP used during the Feast of Atonement; and he made ironical remarks about the Lord (of the Unjust Steward)'s pleasure at being defrauded, and about the Sadducees' reserving seats in Heaven. But there I think he would merely have reproved the usurer for his unfair dealings and told him to restore the stolen money fourfold according to the Law.

Yes, isn't a conscience a damned nuisance? Here I am spending 18 or 20 months on a book that will bring me in 4 months' living expenses. But it has to be done. However, now that I have got to 55 and have a lot of work behind me, sudden gifts drop from Heaven like unexpected sales in Germany or Hungary of books I wrote 15 or 20 years ago. And I've never been forced to abandon my independence which I swore to keep when I left the army in 1919. Read a poem of yours about the water and potatoes in Oscar Williams's[97] swollen *Treasury* – it touched me, remembering my own stolchy allotment and how I fed four children on spuds, milk and a weekly tin of bully – Army surplus. But I still refuse to invest money and cannot look more than a year or two ahead.

I have been spending Xmas solving the problem of the first four chapters of Genesis which, mythologically speaking, stink to

Heaven yet muddlingly incorporate most of the usual Eastern
Mediterranean creation-myth elements. I have got the answer at
last and checked it from the textual commentaries and now I'm
happy.[98] You'll understand me when I say that I feel very pleased
to think that you are keeping on, in spite and still; out of every
ten writers, eleven [*sic*] sell the pass to the Persians.

Yours v.s.,   Robert Graves

Have you a subscription to the St James's Library?[99] If not,
please let me know what it is now and I'll be very pleased to send
it you as a new year gift. Apart from theology and ballet (blitzed
during the War) it is extremely good. I used it throughout the War.

On 16 January Graves wrote to Gordon Wasson to 'consult' him
about the case of Agnes Beaumont, a seventeenth-century East
Anglian girl who was accused of poisoning her father. An American
friend of Graves in Deyá was investigating the story and both he
and Graves came to the conclusion that Beaumont, although
acquitted, really had murdered her father. Graves suspected mushroom poisoning, so sent Wasson an account of the father's symptoms
and death and asked his opinion; at the end of the letter he wrote,
'I miss our queer exchange of letters, but until today have had no
occasion to consult you.' Wasson suggested, in reply, what mushrooms might possibly have been used, and announced he would be
visiting Europe in the spring and hoped to meet Graves.

1 February 1951

My dear Wasson:

Very many thanks for your prompt answer about Agnes
Beaumont and her Venomy.

Witchcraft was very strong in the Eastern counties in the 17th
century and it is a subject which has always interested me.
Especially 'flying ointments' which are a nice mixture of active
drugs such as foxglove, aconite, and water-parsley with ritual
ingredients such as soot, baby's blood and various five-leaved herbs
in honour of the five-fold Goddess who originally sponsored the
flight.

I have never been envenomed by a toad but I had a most
interesting clinical experience in 1946 when I was bitten in the
heel by a Pyrenean adder which are statistically eight times more

mortiferous than the English variety. The poison worked on my retina by forming a sort of silver patch with jagged edges; this gradually spread across my entire vision until I could not see. As a result I solved an outstanding problem about 'Silver Island' or 'Leuce' where heroes went when they died after their ritual death by a snake-bite in the heel – Mopsus is the Classical instance. The venom was sometimes conveyed with an arrow point as in the cases of Achilles, Cheiron, etc., sometimes with the bristle of a boar in Irish myth; and sometimes it was a scorpion, as in the case of Harpocrates.

I'm afraid I can't tell you about Guillermo Mesquida[100] off-hand but will inquire.

Thanks for putting me wise about sanguifluus, and for the trouble you have taken about toads.

I am so glad that your book on mushrooms is going well – so is mine on the even more complex subject of the technique of editorial distortion by Greek editors of the Aramaic *Sayings of Jesus*. What always amazes me in this world (and I am sure it has amazed your wife and yourself) is the crippling lack of liaison between specialists in particular departments of knowledge. For example, no expert on mythology has or wants to have any knowledge of astronomy, botany or sexual pathology. No mycologist (except yourself) troubles to use a Dutch or Breton dictionary or sends for an oil-lamp wick.[101] No New Testament critic studies the procedure in Jewish native courts of the 1st century. No expert on Roman history could tell you exactly how oil was extracted from olives,[102] or what the range of the Balearics' sling-shots were, or how one cooked mallows and lupins.

The Lascaux caves? Are those the Dordogne ones that my friend Miss Garrod discovered? She is a very proper girl as well as a brilliant archaeologist and has been much disturbed by the very frank pictures of ritual bestiality unparalleled elsewhere, on which she has to read a paper to some learned society. (That's another subject which, I guess, nobody has tackled. There must have been a good deal of it in Palestine in the 6th century BC for the author of Deuteronomy to have included it in his bans on ritual prostitution and sodomy, eating of the Zagreus kid, shaving the head in honour of the God Ker, and the like.) It will be a great

pleasure to meet you this Spring; we are only sorry your wife won't
be coming too.

Yours v. sincerely   Robert Graves

The following letter to Lynette Roberts (who had changed her mind
about moving to Deyá and decided instead to remain in Wales) is
incomplete.

No date

Dearest Lynette:

So glad to hear from you and to know that you are still at peace
with the world and us. More and more we congratulate you on
getting clear of that self-tormented monster K.

About Jesus: you see, you're a woman and your problems are
different anyway because of your different sorts of blood. I have
a lot of Scottish and German intellectual in me, combined with a
queer streak of cypher-guessing intuition, and that has to be
harnessed and kept apart from the purely poetic part of me. So
what happens is that I don't feel obliged to write poems if none
are about, and if any are, as recently – owing to the appearance
of a living muse in Deyá – then what a relief to get away from
the damned Pharisees and apocalyptics and be my madder and
essential self.

You see: there's this job to be done in aid of the poetic theme,
to say 'OK this is the damned, illogical, faked, fifth-rate pseudo-
mystery that you have made of religion; the *real* truth is in poetry,
not Church dogma, and if you think that a poet can't think as
accurately and historically as the best of your so-called theologians
take this in your faces – slosh!' So really you see the intellectual part
is allied with, though separate from, the other.

About the ring: doesn't sound right. V. ought to wear that on
his thumb if he wants what it portends; little finger is for poetic
inspiration, anyway, and should have an oracular design – raven,
sow or serpent.* If you want the complementary thing to the
phallic emblem, there's no need to have any design cut: a $\bigtriangledown$ in
malachite is what Merlin ap Merddin Robert recommends –
malachite is found in copper which is the Cyprian metal, and $\bigtriangledown$
is the symbol of woman. O – you could put a buskin on it –
can't draw buskins but it was what the priests used as

87

a yonic symbol in the mysteries. That would make you into the
Eskimo Nell of all Soho – what am I saying? this is very rude.

* I have two rings: one with Sow; one with the doomed stag –
you saw that one I think.

To James Reeves

26 February 1951

Dearest James:

I read *Mulcaster Market*[103] in a favourable moment, convalescent
from flu, still in a warm bed with plenty of orange juice around.
It's hard to criticize because I don't know the problems of school
plays, and because I knew the originals both of the Bacon play
and of the Man on London Bridge; also because in restoring the
original text of *The Nazarene Gospel* I have to be frightfully
careful to keep to pure Elizabethan English and your, perhaps
necessary, compromise between Tudor and neo-Tudor often jerks
at my conscience. But they seem to be actable and certainly are
pleasant and thank you very much.

We have all had flu now and feel awful, and though the sun is
hot the wind is cold and treacherous.

I have got off the page proofs of my *Poems and Satires* but
they'll not be out for another couple of months I think; so if you
like to use the poem that naughty Martin has been sitting on so
long, the one about the New Queen,[104] do. I forget (I forget
everything) if I told you that I thought *Quarto* was up to
expectations; a very much higher technical standard these days
than when we were young – especially than when I was young.

So glad you appreciate my remarks on Keats. As for yours – I
think one gets cross with Keats because he might have been so
much better, with a little less Gothic vulgarity and Cockney
ambition and Della Cruscan flabbiness. But he was so much better
than any of his contemporaries except Coleridge, and I don't think
you're fair about the 'unravished bride of quietness' – though it's
not a very good phrase I admit – he means that the urn was put
under the earth to be the bride of quietness, and even the mattocks
of the peasants who discovered it haven't broken the damned thing,
and it has actually survived the voyage and the customs. 'Two

faousand years old, coo!' Cockney Keats breathed reverently. 'Bride of quietness, eh? Werry good phrase, Severn, old cock!'[105]

Love from all   Robert

To Derek Savage

23 March 1951

My dear Savage:

It seems waste of a two-penny stamp to tear up that cheque, and my economic soul revolts against such a deed; but it's made out to you so I think you had better use it on reference books, which was the original idea, and if I thought that you were sending it back for any but technical reasons, I should be vexed. I mean reference books to buy and keep: such as dictionaries and biographical dictionaries and the like of which I have slowly amassed a necessary bookcaseful and can't imagine how I managed without them.

But about the London Library; I found that they were very helpful and sent me a typed list for example, when I was writing *Wife to Mr Milton* of all the *Lives of* they possessed; and then when I had a good one I found a bibliography at the end and asked for what I needed. I have not used them for my present *Nazarene Gospel* because mails aren't safe and their theology department got blitzed. However: that's up to you.

The plan at the back of my mind was roughly this. We have three children, boy 10, girl 7, boy 6, and education here is pre-Reformation – post-Fascist. We don't want to live in England, for all sorts of reasons, mainly climatic, and we don't want, and can't afford, to send the children away to school there until they are 14 or so, if then. At the moment I have a tutor here, a Princeton graduate,[106] for the elder boy; but he's not a great success and the money seems wasted. . . . I gave him a furnished house and access to my library. After June, he'll have to go. Anyhow Beryl (my wife) and I have to teach him arithmetic and Latin at home.

I thought, vaguely, that you might all like to come out here and make some sort of common educational front with us, if you have children of the right sort of age and find Cornwall too wearing: the question of money needn't worry you and the amount of teaching wouldn't be enough to interfere with your work, especially if your wife could cooperate. It's only a vague idea, because we don't know each other, and you might hate to tear up your roots. The advantage would (1) be that your children would have (to coin a phrase) their horizons enlarged and that you would find plenty of time for your work and none of the worries that beset – in my own experience – life in the West Country. In the last 20 months I have finished a job that in England would have taken at least five years and been scrappily done too. (2) The advantage of this island is that the children learn independence and languages; bi-linguality has a great effect on the intelligence. As for education, all I really care about is that they should learn to write English well, which means an exercise of judgement not (as in the case of the Latin language) of memory and rule.

And how few can teach that!

Yours ever   Robert Graves

To Joshua Podro

25 March 1951

My dear Joshua

You'll be glad to hear that the job is now complete apart from incorporating stray texts, revising, and deciding on the sequence of the events of the ministry; and rewriting our prefaces in the light of our discoveries.

Three Oxford-American DPhil students visited me here the other night. They are in the forefront of modern theological fashion and it was a very interesting talk we had; they had no criticism at all to offer of our theories except that *every* theory can be rebutted by challenging the validity of the source on which it is based. But apparently the general trend is in the direction of our own conclusions though a long way behind. I got from one of them a useful OT parallel to the storm which Jesus stilled which incidentally explained the pillow on which he lay [*margin note*: The reference is to Jonah's sleeping in the ship; *the* pillow seems to be derived from a synagogue picture of Jonah mistaken for Jesus]; and also a reference to Schmeidel[107] [*sic*] (if that was the name) who bases his reconstruction as we do on certain obviously Pharisaic sayings of Jesus which have escaped alteration by the Gentiles.

You are obviously entangled again in family or business worries, because a great many answers to my letters are outstanding. But we do hope you and Fanny are really coming; Deyá is enchanting now that summer is starting and will be at its best between now and the end of May. Tell her you'll not be called on to do more than a little work; the rest you can take home with you to England.

The *Leader* were very much impressed by the trial article, thank you again so much for your part in it.

If you can send me the remark that Gamaliel I (or was it another Pharisee?) made about getting into trouble because James told him of Jesus's witty answer about the High Priest's lavatory, that will be a great help in getting the sequence of incidents straight. With that, there will be 120 in all (some only three pages, some fifteen or twenty) for rearrangement. The book will be large crown octavo of some 800 pages!

The odd thing is that so far, and there's almost nothing left, not a single text that has anything of a genuine ring has failed to explain and document itself.

The Wandering Jew himself,[108] I think, has worked it all out for us; he wants to have his effigy removed from about 100,000,000 crucifixes.

Love

Robert

What's the address of your private bank?

Your quotation from Jerome 22, 10 is magnificently apt. But it must have been spoken to Mary *after* the Crucifixion, when he had decided to be the Wandering Jew.

The blood of the *New* Covenant or *Sacrament* is a frightful sin; annulling Ex. 24, 8–10.[109] How Paul seized on it!

Paul was, with Hitler, one of the two nastiest characters in history; but Paul was a triple or quadruple renegade, Hitler only a simple one.

I bless you every time I find a neat Talmudic comment in your handwriting; which fits with a sigh of satisfaction into the argument I deduce from the Greek.

To Derek Savage

11 April 1951

My dear Savage or shall we say Derek:

Beryl and I were charmed by your letter and the photographs, and have been thinking a lot about the problems involved.

To begin with: we think that your attitude to education couldn't be improved on, and who hasn't got dismal gaps in his schooling? I certainly have. All that matters is to encourage in the children close attention to what they're doing and a continuously critical mood and the sense that what they're doing is both necessary and amusing. And I don't think that can be done in a large class however gifted the teacher.

The size of your family is the only unexpected feature; four children need a lot of keeping in any country, but here one can live cheaper than in most parts of Europe if one keeps to native tastes in food and clothes. The working-man's average real salary, after deductions, is about £1 a week and he manages to put in a good day's work.

We had hoped that you could manage French but it doesn't really matter; we can always arrange French lessons with a local teacher, or I could give them myself.

About your book. I sympathize, being just at the end of a book which I feel is of extreme importance – two years' solid work on it, a detailed recovery of the original Aramaic Gospel of which the Canonical ones are caricatures – but don't feel at all that it doesn't matter whether I continue to write afterwards or not. In fact, I have other important jobs waiting. But the autumn term here doesn't begin until October, so the time factor needn't worry you.

We will be coming to England in July and will return here some time in August, so then will be able to meet and talk things over more definitely if necessary.

Your family are damned good-looking.

My view is that to be bi-lingual is of great importance in learning the comparison of idiom and syntax. Your boys and girl would certainly benefit greatly from Spanish, though thirteen is a bit late to pick it up naturally as ours have. The trouble here is that two languages are spoken here: Mallorquín (a sort of Provençal) in the playground, and Spanish is the school-language and the official language – rather like English in North Wales before Welsh became compulsory in schools. You'd pick up Spanish in six months without particular trouble. The climate is very healthy and there are no diseases like malaria to fear.

Deyá is a village in the hills five miles from the nearest town of any size and 17 from Palma the capital. Its isolation and nearness to the sea and its height above sea-level makes it the best all-the-year-round place; but we think that for the winter we ought to take a flat in Palma where there is more going on and where the sun strikes more genially, which would mean getting one for you too. We are not quite sure yet of the economics of this plan, but it has obvious advantages and would, for example, be a good deal cheaper than sending even one of the children to school in England!

I think this is all that need be said at the moment except that the advantages of the idea seem greatly to outweigh the disadvantages. All that we want for our children is for them to have a good knowledge of ordinary school subjects, while keeping their independence; we could not, for instance, bear our Lucia to turn into a horrid little English school-girl, and with Romer she would feel happy. I am so glad you liked 'Loving Mad Tom'.[110]

Yours ever

Robert –

Graves and Beryl reluctantly decided, however, that the problems, particularly the size of Savage's family and his inability to teach French, were too great and Graves wrote to tell him. A new tutor for William was still needed, however, and that summer when in England Robert and Beryl arranged for Martin Seymour-Smith to come back with them as tutor, and for his wife Janet to assist Graves with his next work, *The Greek Myths*.

To Gordon Wasson

6 May 1951

My dear Gordon Wasson:

Your *Russian Policy* speech is the most temperate and sensible thing that I have seen written by an American – or for that matter by any English-speaking person – on the subject for a great many years, and it is most cheering to know that you were not howled down.

(Beryl and I looked naughtily at each other and said: 'But perhaps if the Russians had been mycophobes . . . ?')

You gave us a half-promise that you'd visit us this Spring. Let us know in good time, lest your visit should happen to coincide with a few days we want to spend in Madrid – to celebrate the end of two years' work on the (politically) most important book I have written: the dry, careful and well-documented anatomy of the Greek Gospels, showing the deliberate technique of anti-Pharisaic distortion to which Jesus's simple orthodox eschatalogical message was en-subjected. It comes well from me as a Bishop's grandson, though I have had the close collaboration of a learned Talmudist – not a rabbi, of course, the rabbis are as narrow or dishonest as any Catholic priest – but a simple business man with no Chair or position to lose. Farrar and Strauss [*sic*] will be publishing it in the autumn. There's not a mushroom in it, I fear. The Jews seem to have been mycophobes – unless manna counts (it was a sort of edible lichen, I gather).

Really, I was very pleased indeed by your speech.

You seem to be a lawyer; I have come to appreciate lawyers, Beryl's father being an ex-President of the Law Society, and her two brothers, a sister and a brother-in-law also being branded as the 'Devil's Own'. A great deal of the argument in this book depends on a close and accurate knowledge of Roman provincial Law; procedure in Jewish native courts; and procedure in the collaborationist courts which dealt with political or semi-political cases on behalf of the Procurator.

Jesus was admirable. But there is a regrettably close similarity between the Stalinist technique of documentary perversion of history (e.g. in the treatment of Trotsky's part in the war) and that of the Evangelists.

Yours v.s.   Robert Graves

In May Graves finally finished *The Nazarene Gospel Restored* and sent a copy to Eliot at Faber, with the following letter.

23 May 1951

Dear Tom:

I have sent off the top copy of this book to Farrar, Straus & Co., who have swallowed up my former publishers Creative Age

Press, and have a lot of money behind them for launching it
properly. They will print it as soon as possible.

The only difference between their copy and this is that theirs has
the relevant Gospel texts pasted on sheets at the beginning of
each chapter, whereas this merely has the reference given, so that
you will need a New Testament handy for reading it, and a copy
of the Apocryphal Gospels. But the more abstruse source-texts
from Clement of Alexandria, the Agrapha, Origen, Jerome and
the Talmud I have appended with the relevant chapter-references.

As you see, it is a long and condensed argument; but Podro and
I have been at pains to assume that our public come fresh to the
subject, and to write as simply as we know how.

If you decide that the book is as scholarly and temperate as the
subject requires, then you'll have no difficulty in coming to terms
with Watt on my behalf. (The contract will be with me, and Podro
will have 1/5th share.)[111] But it will save a great deal of trouble
if you print from the corrected US proofs rather than from the
typescript.

The argument has been greatly refined and strengthened since
Podro and I saw you last August; I have been working 8 hours a
day on it ever since, in constant touch with him. If your publishers'
readers think that they can lay a finger on any major flaw in the
argument, let them quote the appropriate historical document and
refer it to Podro, if it is an Aramaic, Hebrew or Syriac one; and
to me if it is Greek or Latin. It may sound boastful, but I really
think that we have solved the main historical cruces and that our
point of view will hold the field within a few years; though of
course slight revisions are bound to be made. And we are grateful
to you for your willingness to publish if the view has *prima facie*
plausibility at least; knowing that your motive is one of conscience
and not of commerce.

You will find the restored Nazarene Gospel printed in sequence
in Part III. I have an idea that this, with a few additions and revisions,
will one day be printed by itself[112] in a popular edition, and
translated into one hundred-and-fifty-three languages.

I missed you in Madrid the other day, but you were still in the
south; one of my spies had seen you in El Greco's house[113] a few
days before.

Yours ever   Robert
P.S. I'll be in London on July 4th for three weeks.

Between Moon and Moon

To James Reeves

7 June 1951 'San Roberto'

Dearest James:

Beryl insisted that I hadn't answered your letter, I insisted that I had. As usual she was right.

So I must have written and posted it in my head on the way down to bathe.

We are coming to London on July 4th and will be at 9 Gardiner Mansions, Church Row, near Hampstead Tube Station for about three weeks, up 85 steps; and are very sad and vexed about your postponed operation. It isn't fair.

Thank you for the Clare extract; most apt.

Some enemy, anonymous, wrote in the last *Times Literary Supplement* that it constituted a minor blemish on someone's 'Dictionary of Myth' that *The White Goddess* was frequently cited, since I was not an authority. I have asked the editor mildly to correct this statement, which is technically libellous and also uncalled for.

Spender goes on making money from articles on poetry not paying; perhaps this is because (as his brother Humphrey told us last week) he finds he can't write poetry now. Query: why the qualifying 'now'?

Man Friday[114] is very good and very useful to Wm; and thank you. Just the ticket. I go on writing more poems than is decent, and have already added twelve to the new collection that will be published I suppose four years hence; if they wear well enough. Will show when we meet.

So glad you like the *Common Asphodel* Things. I had quite forgotten the book, immersed in *The Nazarene Gospel* which has just gone off, and in the translation of the Spanish novel *Enriquillo*[115] for Unesco which Beryl and I have been doing and should be ready before we leave. We are visiting Italy for a week, at Jenny's command, next week.

There is a new woman poet in Canada called Jay Macdonald or Macgregor[116] – I forget the clan. Aged 21 and spends her holidays with a friend of ours called Greta (who's an Esthonian of English descent, married to a Swiss who grows Asparagus in the wilds of Two Mountains). I tried to find something wrong with her poems but could not; you know how grudging I am of praise, but these were the real thing, though from Canada. Greta says that she's brilliant at Classics, hates Canada, is utterly lonely and also beautiful: what troubles lie ahead for that girl! I think of Laura.

A fiendish sirocco is blowing the algarrobas from the trees and banging the doors. Love to Mary and you all.

Robert

T. S. Eliot wrote to Graves acknowledging receipt of the manuscript of *The Nazarene Gospel Restored* and at the same time warning him that it was a book he and his colleagues at Faber would have to 'think twice about' before publishing. Graves replied from Deyá.

26 June 1951   As from 9 Gardiner Mansions
Church Row
NW3

Dear Tom:

I agree that *The Nazarene Gospel* is a book to think twice about before publishing; but only for reasons of private or public policy which can be decided only at a F&F board meeting. The argument is documented throughout and where it cannot be checked merely by flipping over the pages of the Old and New Testaments, demands the services of a Talmudic scholar. Since the Talmud and the Mishnah are unindexed and run to millions of words, I suggest that whatever expert you send the book to for reading should be put in touch with Joshua Podro (19 Raleigh Close, London, NW4), who has the largest private library of Hebraica in England and would be pleased to take down the relevant tomes from the highest shelves and put his finger on the justifying quotations.

I shall be in London at 9 Gardiner Mansions on July 4th for a month, and if you can give me a decision by July 24th – exactly a year after our last meeting, at which your experts failed to materialize – it would give me a week to find another publisher before I return here. 'A few weeks' is an uncomfortably elastic term. As for private or public policy: yes, I foresee great searchings of heart as in Judges 5, 16 and hope that F&F will escape the curse of Meroz.

Yours ever   Robert

In London Eliot informed Graves of the board's decision not to publish the book, as Graves told Wasson (10 March 1952):

The Nazarene Gospel: that got finished last June. It is about 230,000 words, very concentrated, objective, documented, but has an inner excitement which led T. S. Eliot (impelled perhaps by his crippled *malus angelus* John Hayward[117]) to write me a strange letter turning it down: 'if it had been duller and dryer, I should have published it'. Poor Eliot: he made a brave effort to do right, but could not. However, a quarter of an hour after getting his letter I was able to ring him up (this was in England) and tell him that Cassells would be delighted to publish it. Now Cassells and Farrar Straus in New York are arguing as to who is to bear the cost of printing, and in what proportion, but it should be out by this fall.

In the end Farrar Straus also decided not to publish, and the book was offered to Doubleday, who published it in July 1954 in an edition of 5000. Although one of Graves's best books, it has never been reprinted either in the USA or in Britain. It was almost universally attacked when published (see page 134), though many of the ideas in the book have since gained currency, even in established theological circles. Although some of Graves's and Podro's postulations may be disagreed with, the book remains an intensely interesting and unbiased historical analysis of the Jesus story and is one of the best examples of Graves's power of historical detection and imaginative scholarship.

PART TWO

1951–1957

In September 1951, the Graves family moved to Palma for the children's schools; they rented two flats, one above the other, in the new, northern outskirts of the town. The family lived in the lower flat and Martin and Janet Seymour-Smith lived in the upper one, where Graves also had his workroom and where William received his lessons from Seymour-Smith. The family enjoyed life in Palma, but on weekends and school holidays they always moved back to Deyá.

Graves was now employed on another vast work, *The Greek Myths*, commissioned by Penguin Books as a companion to their Classics series.

To Selwyn Jepson

29 October 1951   Calle Guillermo Massot 69; Pral 2
                                                                      Palma
                                                                      Mallorca
                                                                      Spain

Dearest Selwyn and Tania –

I haven't heard your news for some time. Here we are pretty good. There was an early winter, which may now be past until Christmas, because it has been hot again and I've bathed three days running, and of course the leaves are still on the trees; but it was cold enough for fires. We have a flat in Palma with a terrace. A new block of flats, rather good for flats, at £4.15 a month, and we have furnished ours, also one above where Martin Seymour-Smith (Wm's tutor) and his girlfriend Janet de Glanville (who works with me, she's a Greek and Latin scholar) live. We have a dog-track two minutes off, no entrance fee and sixpenny bets, and brandy at 3d. and no big money or rich swindlers, and the

101

dogs are faster (Martin says) than any outside the White City. We return to Deyá at week-ends and on fiestas which are many. I like a bit of urban life, as we're in the unfashionable part and have no visitors. Work: I have written three or four poems, and two or three articles[1] (for US but one in next issue of *History Today*) and got two-thirds of the way in the draft version of a book on Greek Myths for Penguin Classics. It will run to 80,000 words and there will be a companion volume on the heroic tales, of about the same length. I have been learning a lot in the process. Also working with Jan on a translation of Lucan's *Civil War* for Penguin. And Beryl is translating Alarcón's[2] *Niño de la Bola*, an 1800ish Spanish novel; and I'm in on that a bit. And Martin is writing a novel about Zuleika Dobson in modern Oxford, and doing an edition, definitive, of all the Robin Hood ballads, because he's found some good obscene unpublished ones – a hive of industry. By the way, my poems will be broadcast on (I think) Nov 12th in the Third Programme; I recorded an introduction.

In return – how are the Gills of East Anglia getting along? We enjoyed a brief mention of the Commodore in your last book, which we *did* enjoy. But Eve?

What I'd like to know is how and where is Jenny? I heard bitterly from her over three weeks ago about Alex's illness – she was standing by in Porto Fino to join him in USA; and I wrote at once. But no answer. And now I hear that Diana[3] has seen Alex and says he looks bad and doesn't seem to care whether he lives or not;[4] but Dick, who told me this, didn't mention Jenny. Please let us have all the news we can. Obviously, by now Jenny's back at the Albany – but what's happening?

Beryl may be flying briefly to England next week because her mother has had a second operation for cancer, and it isn't certain whether she'll have force for a come-back, as she did after the first one.

Judith is living a sort of Trilby life in Paris with a young man whom we have no particular use for – but it is hoped that this is a sort of convalescence after the last one, who was a monster. This one is a gentle spiv with eyes rather too close together, but affectionate and a bad writer. She writes regularly, at least.

I shall send you my new poems[5] when they arrive, as they should any moment; unfortunately some of the better ones of the series were too late for inclusion.

The Gospel Book is having its layout studied by Farrar and Straus but won't be out I suppose before March or so at least.

It would be lovely if you could both come here this winter. It hasn't the beauty of Italy, but is far better for work.

Much love from us both   Robert

The children's schools at Palma are a success, so far.
A warm embrace to Wendy.[6]

To James Reeves

15 December 1951   Deyá

Dearest James

The Speaking Oak[7] arrived by the same post as your letter. Thanks very much. Martin will use it on Wm. It looks very good.

I'm glad you still like 'The Portrait' and that you still like 'Darien'. Why 'Darien'? Because that was his name. Judith (the subject of 'The Portrait') had named him so prophetically even before I met her; and that incident in my spiritual autobiography was recorded a year ago at Deyá. Spiritual as opposed to physical autobiography; my physical head is still firmly fixed between my shoulder-blades and 'the damage is irreparable because there is none' (quotation from Laura). The word spiritual has been abused by Xtians but has no synonym. Martin says that you should not have applied 'philosophical' to Blake's *Auguries of Innocence* unless you meant to deny that it was a poem.

Anonymous thoughts about your poems are hard to supply unless I can see them set out in sequence.

The *Times Literary Supplement* have given me the leading article on my poems – very kind gentlemen who quote mainly from my suppressed poems – and I am haunted, and in perpetual retreat they say. God bless my soul!

Much Love –   – Robert –

To Derek Savage

21 January 1952   Deyá

My dear Derek:

Thank you very much for your letter – I'm glad you are still afloat. It must be horrible in Cornwall now; there is snow on the hills here and a wind from the Pyrenees, but Spring began some weeks ago with the almond blossom & narcissus, so we call it a Buchan spell.

I agree about the insanity of the Baconians – my former headmaster was an Earl-of-Oxford-ite which is almost as bad; but there's a frightening Baconian way of proving that Shakespear wrote the psalms – four vowels in his name, six consonants = 46. Take Psalm 46 in the King James Bible (or is it the Psalter version which is different? – I forget): count 46 words from the beginning and you get *Shake*, and 46 from the end and you get *spear*. That's an object lesson against being misled by theory and circumstantial support of coincidence: humiliating, I call it.

Thank you very much for your review of *Occupation: Writer*; but if ever I find you castigating my work, I shall know that it is deserved. Am nearly half-way through a carefully documented and argued dictionary of Greek myth for Penguin Classics. The important thing is to separate myth from allegory, fable, decorated history, streetcorner anecdote and novelette: the whole corpus of myth is in a dreadful mess. But it is very easy to be deceived into taking, say, the myth of Arachne and the spider to be a simple moral fable in the Hiawatha style: when you learn who Arachne was and who turned her into a spider, it becomes a story of Athenian trade rivalry with Miletus, the biggest textile exporters of the day whose trade mark, inherited with Cretan Miletus, the parent city, was a spider.

My enormous *Nazarene Gospel Restored* is being hung up while Cassell argue transatlantically with Farrar Straus about the printing expenses. It must be 250,000 words, and compressed at that. The present job is a mere 200,000. I wish I did not have to take each page into five drafts; but I still do, after thirty-five years.

Good luck to you all. Hope to see you in England this summer if I can afford to make it; it was silly of me (to speak in a worldly way) to spend two solid years on the Gospels without hope of any return for at least another two years. But the mythology is doubly commissioned, and I'm also writing a modern sex-novel on the side,[8] so all will be well I trust.

Yours ever   Robert

To James Reeves

No date

Dear James,

   . . . . [9]

Thanks so much for the poems, and for the children's *Wandering Moon*;[10] for the unpublished nursery rhymes which you are kind enough to want for the Heinemann anthology please decide what you want to pay and have the cheque sent to Watt with a statement: 'by private agreement with Mr Graves.' If it doesn't go through Watt, I have trouble with the income-tax accountants; and anthology rights are (for some unexplained reason) free of tax whereas book-royalties and poems read over the radio are taxed at 9/- in the £!

Nice that you and I will both have poems out this year; at the last moment I wrote four very romantic ones which set off the rather acrid satire of the greater part. As a reaction from their youthful élan I'm now crippled with rheumatism and a back ricked from too profound a cough.

We like the poems; though we don't think that the last verse of the 'crabbed old man' [*sic*] says anything that hasn't been contained in the first four: but that could be got over by putting it in italics as a formal moral. And in the voyage, there seems a sort of half-contradiction between the moon in the first stanza and the moon in the last. For 'moonlight' read 'starlight'?[11]

For a holiday task I'm solving the secret of the first four chapters of Genesis which, as primitive myth, stink to High Heaven yet contain all the ingredients of the corresponding 'Orphic', i.e. Libyo-Thracian, creation story and sequel. Shall make a little book of the real story with pictures,[12] beginning with 'Eve's' sexual dance with the North Wind (which resulted in the Cosmic Egg) and ending with 'Lamech's' killing of his brother 'Cain' in revenge for 'Cain's' killing of his uncle 'Abel' who had killed Cain's father Ephron, the oracular hero of the Hebron Garden of Eden. Love from all to all especially Mary and my dear Stella.

                                        – Robert –

Between Moon and Moon

To Joshua Podro

March 1952

Dearest Joshua:

Yes, I should have written but it has been the season of colds and electricity cuts and the Myth book is getting a bit out of hand – twice as long as I expected and now I am stuck with the proofs of the amended *White Goddess*.

There has been 'some little stir' caused among Gentile readers of *History Today*; Alan sent me three letters to answer. But they would have taken too long to answer in detail, and the most sensible of them turned on the question of our textual assumptions. So I have sent Alan a modified form of the general foreword to the book, called 'How the Gospels were Written', to explain how useless it is to find the *written* original of what was orally handed down and how the only hope of restoring the original is by internal discrepancies, quotations from lost or heretical Gospels, and by comparison with the Talmud. He may print it; he may not.

No pills have yet arrived; but they will in time – have just had a Christmas parcel posted in October – thanks awfully.

As to the general reception of the book – which is on the point of going into production – it will 'rend the veil' of the Protestant temple from top to bottom. The Catholics will say as little as possible. The Jews who can afford to do so (but that is a limited category) will be delighted. The ordinary agnostic will accept it as the solution he has so long been waiting for, heave a sigh of relief, and support us staunchly: glad to know that the story is a real one, that Jesus was not a charlatan, and that the ecclesiastics have been dishonest. The only recent additions I have made to the argument concern Claudius's edict against Jewish grave-robbing which has been misunderstood; it seems prompted by a report from Jerusalem that many tombs have been secretly opened and the dead bodies removed by unscrupulous fanatics who wished to strengthen the belief that the Resurrection of the Just had already begun (Matt. 27, 52). The other concerns Origen's report in passages about Jesus no longer found in Josephus; and the Jesus passages in the Slavonic *Wars of the Jews*. I don't think that we'll

106

have to amend our text much in further editions; it is a pretty complete treatment.

Love to you both   Robert

In their mycological studies the Wassons had turned to the problem of mushrooms in ancient religion. Again Graves became interested in the subject and although he had no time to devote to it himself, he sent the Wassons a great deal of information he came across in his readings, and his opinion on several etymological questions. He also had a number of inspired or 'serendipitous' ideas and came across several 'clues', which he duly forwarded; these included a myth of the Corinthians' origin from mushrooms, a myth about Perseus's discovery of a mushroom on the site of Mycenae which he then made his capital, and the following drawing of a mushroom in the corner of an Etruscan mirror.

No date [received by Wasson on 8 April 1952]

My dear Wasson:

Many thanks for the copy of your letter to John Farrar; which incidentally gave me news that pleased me: Farrar Straus have a translation series with Galdós[13] in it. My wife and I are nearly finished with a translation of Alarcón's *Niño de la Bola*, and Alarcón is one of the few really good novelists of Spain and outshines Galdós – so I have written to tell Farrar Straus to keep a space open.

But the immediacy of this letter is an illustration on page 204 of A. B. Cook's *Zeus* (Putnam's, New York) from an Etruscan mirror 'in the British Museum, case C of the Bronze Room' where there is a mushroom shown on which he makes no sensible comment. Its importance has escaped his usually shrewd eye: the icon is of Ixion on his seven-spoked wheel, which Cook rightly connects with the firewheel, used in kindling the sacred fire. Now surely the mushroom is there because of the tinder it supplies to the fire-wheel? You know all about this – to me it is only a vague fact in a mental pigeon-hole that one of the most serviceable tinder sources was dried mushroom.

Cook says 'the flower introduced between adjacent spokes serves as a stop-gap and has no special significance'. He should know that *no* detail in a Bronze Age icon is irrelevant, and he should be

able to distinguish a mushroom from a flower.
  – this is how it is
    engraved

This seems to be of prime importance for your work. The Etruscans were of course kin to the Lapiths and Satyrs and Centaurs, whom Ixion fathered on Pelion. I know of no other mushroom in Greek art; but perhaps you do.

Yours ever   Robert Graves

This discovery reached the Wassons just as they were finishing their book, *Mushrooms, Russia and History*, and fitted in with their discussion of the relation between tinder and mushrooms, especially as the mushroom represented resembled the agaric mushroom *Polyporus officinalis*, known in the old pharmacopoeias as the 'female agarick' and used as a cathartic and as tinder. This was linked, Wasson explained to Graves, with the double meaning of 'punk' in English, 'tinder' and 'strumpet', and of 'spunk', 'tinder' and a fungi of the *Polyporus* species; both 'punk' and 'spunk' are words of unknown origin but Wasson suggested they derived from the Greek σπογγος, sponge. He was, however, 'baffled' by the fact that other fungi used for tinder used to be called 'male agarick', though he was unaware of the bawdy meaning of 'spunk' which Graves explained in the following letter.

Graves's letter about the mirror came 'in the nick of time', Wasson wrote:

We are most appreciative of it, and at the same time a little frightened. Your capacity for detecting inner meanings is so extraordinary that we wish you had been writing our ms. It would be much better than it is.

15 April 1952   Deyá

My dear Wasson:

  I am delighted that you got my letter in time to take stock of that Etruscan mirror, and that you agree with me about the mushroom; as I also agree with you about *punk* and *spunk* – and would tentatively add *sponge*, English dialect word for 'leaven', reported from Yorkshire and the Eastern counties. *Spunk* is *Sponk* in Scottish: even nearer to σπογγος. About the male and female agarick: the point seems to me to be whether you regard the *spunk* as a) the female receptacle in which the male fire-stick is amatorily twirled, or as b) the *spunk* (which is used in English dialect and university-bawdy to mean *semen virile* – the *locus classicus* is a dirty limerick written by Tennyson in his nasty old age beginning: 'There once was a Chinaman drunk') which procreates the desired flame. If *a*, then the agaric is female; if *b* then it is male. QED.

In reply to your letter of a few days ago: we shall be in Mallorca until July 14th when we are taking a flat (no. 8 Gardiner Mansions, Church Row, Hampstead, London, NW3) for three weeks. We pass through Paris, but will have our three jaded and boisterous children in tow, and so hope rather to see you in London – or, even better, here. It is about time we met.

Very busy settling the historical basis of early Greek mythology: a task shirked by all but a very few independent-minded scholars; and they all fall short at the real problem, which is the relation of the myths to the ritual theory of royal succession varyingly held in different parts of the Greek world at different times. *How* the sacred king dies: whether netted in a bath, pushed over a cliff, eaten in a stew, killed in a staged chariot crash, bitten in the heel by a viper κτλ, κτλ.; *when* he dies, whether in June, October or New Year; and *after what length of reign* – these are the relevant details. The rest is mainly local anecdote or cathartic drama. The clue to a great deal of the corpus is found in Irish, Welsh and Latin myth; and occasionally in the Pentateuch – there are a great many points of contact between Corinthian and Palestinian mythology.

I am anxious to rescue myth from the ignorant Jungian psychologists ... I learned today Theophilus the 11th century writer on the metallurgical crafts of his day explained the meaning of such alchemical fantasies (exploited by Jung in a nonsensical treatise) as 'marry two *red cocks* and set a *toad* to hatch their *eggs*', by pointing out that these are code words for chemical substances used for the sake of secrecy by Spanish alchemists. The 'precious jewel in the toad's head' which has always puzzled me (and probably you) makes perfect sense as the by-product of a chemical process – the extraction of silver from lead ore by the addition of sulphur, I think it will have been.

But this piece of paper is coming to an end; and I must get back

to Orestes and the tell-tale robe embroidered with wild beasts
which he wore.

Kindest regards to your wife.

Yours v. sincerely   Robert Graves

What astonishes *me* is how you manage to think so clearly
about these problems in the Banking district of New York.

Although some of Graves's own theories (particularly in *The White
Goddess*) are described as 'Jungian', Graves despised the Jungian
response to mythology, attacking it in an article in the *Hudson
Review* (no. 5, summer 1952, pp. 245–57) and in the introduction
to *The Greek Myths*, where he wrote:

A true science of myth should begin with a study of archaeology, history
and comparative religion, not in the psycho-therapist's consulting-room.
Though the Jungians hold that 'myths are original revelations of the
preconscious psyche, involuntary statements about unconscious psychic
happenings,' Greek mythology was no more mysterious in content than are
modern election cartoons . . .

He went on to describe his own method of assembling all the
scattered elements of each myth,

supported by little-known variants which may help to determine the
meaning, and to answer all questions that arise, as best I can, in anthropological or historical terms. This is, I am well aware, much too ambitious a
task for any single mythologist to undertake, however long or hard he
works. Not for the first time, I will find the scholarly specialists combining
to criticize me on points of detail which they have made their own, though
not combining to suggest an alternative general hypothesis, and each disclai-
ming acquaintance with the other's small department of knowledge, even
where it is necessary for a better understanding of his own. What seems to
be lacking today is centripetal, rather than centrifugal, scholarship.

In August Graves heard from Derek Savage, who was having trouble
with his publisher, Frank Morley of Faber.

11 August 1952   Deyá

Dear Derek:

Frank Morley had no right to accuse you of irresponsibility
towards your family; that was clumsy: and really a reflection on
your relations with your wife; on the other hand as your publisher

he could not offer to subsidize you – the firm is largely the financial concern of Brendan Bracken[14] – or pay you royalties incommensurate with the probable sales of your books. Nor would you expect it. As for that: three years', no 3½ years', solid work on two books – one of 1251 pp the other probably 1000 pp crown octavo – will have earned me in royalties £300 in England, less agent's fee and tax = £150; and 1500 dollars less agent's fee and US tax = about 900 dollars. Research and secretarial expenses: £1000; and what about the cost of my living for 3½ years? It doesn't add up; but I have survived on previous earnings, and new editions of old books, and poems, and both books *had* to be written. [*margin note*: Yes wouldn't it be lovely to pay £1000 income tax like Herbert Read (after all ingenious deductions have been made by a clever income tax consultant)?]

Frank also had no excuse not to read your book so far; but he has you very much on his conscience. He really admires you, he has an odd passionate belief in you (he has told me personally) and would work very hard and long to get you safely established in some University or other job . . . In 1925 T. E. Lawrence felt for me like that – four children, poet–critic, no prospects – and got me my Cairo professorship-job. I was to be my own master there, so accepted; and it gave me the break I needed. I have been solvent ever since, though I resigned after six months.

The question is when is breaking-point reached? I reached it in 1925. If you can tide over the present crisis, good. If not, Morley is genuinely concerned to help you and that is to his credit, and if he can do anything for you which it is within your realm of principles to accept, don't kick him in the face. But I know you won't. He's a good chap.

Meanwhile: if a loan of £100 is any good, repayable when God blesses you, let me know where my bank is to send it to your bank.

All well here: but devilishly busy

Love from us all   Robert

Briefly: you are the only honest and discerning critic about and you have very properly refused to play ball with the boys of the journalistic world. But you can still publish books, that is what you somehow *must go on doing*. For all our sakes.

111

That autumn James Reeves's *The Password and Other Poems* was published.

11 December 1952   as from – Deyá

Dearest James:

I have been waiting for the right moment to sit down and read your poems and now it has happened and thank you very much. I like them together a great deal more than separately which is as it should be – the personal smell and flavour comes out more strongly. There are a few which will necessarily be omitted from your *Collected Poems*, and which seem to be there because you worked so hard on them that you feel they must be all right; and occasionally I feel that your ear has cheated your eye – the eye is much the cannier organ – but on the whole it's admirable Reeves especially when you are at your nastiest – in 'The Stone Gentleman', 'The Infernal Machine', 'Novels I Have Never Written', 'The Little Brother', etc. – or your most detached, as in 'The Newcomer'.

I have just sent off a slim volume to Cassells, only half the size of yours, and also dripping with heather honey and black gall; to mark the close of an epoch.[15]

We have sent you Christmas card and Christmas fare (to No. 47 by mistake) and Jan tells us your house is very much like home; that is good.

Beryl has lost three teeth to the coming brat, but is being very gallant, and has to pass the water-jump of Christmas and the hurdle of holidays before it gets born. . . . Jan and Martin are fine. The book (see overleaf[16]) should be ready by March. On Dec. 23 at 7.15 (Third Programme) you will (or will not) hear me in a *Personal Anthology*. The children are in good health and we love you and Mary right well.

Robert

The line I like best is:

The gaoler's daughter with the purloined key –

can't say why, but it gets home like a knife.

112

In reviewing Reeves's poems, critics again emphasized the influence of Graves. Both Reeves and Graves, however, thought the question of influence overstated.

In January, Beryl had their fourth child, Tomás, who was born in the flat in Palma.

13 January 1953   Palma

Dearest James:

We are daily expecting the new baby, who is intended to be born in the flat above us, which Jan and Martin vacated but where I have a workroom and Wm a schoolroom. It's rather like going back in history this business of cots and baby-clothes and napkins but as my sister Clarissa solemnly says: 'Every baby finds its welcome' and this one brutally insisted on being born, so good luck to it!

What a terrible Christmas dinner. (We sat down 13 but the baby was what is legally called 'viable' so that made 14.) How is Mary's father now? (I remember only her dainty mother that day at Bognor Regis.)

Have duly subscribed to *Quarto*.

'What is a *chock*?' I'm in bed with a cough and the dictionary is upstairs, but I know that a chock is a stone you put under a wheel, or to fill a crevice, so perhaps that's it.

Yes, of course; those artful critics. It would never occur to them to say that W. H. Auden[17] has lifted from me. Whereas you who have never taken anything from me but merely shared the same poetic climate, with rhythms all your own too – it's just silly, isn't it?

Martin and Jan seem to be running a concern called the Roebuck Press decoyed by the cheapness of printing here; it keeps them busy. I forget if I told you that I have sent some new poems to Cassells for publication – twenty-seven of them – and that on January 19th and 22nd I am recorded in 3rd Prog. reading my poems with a dry mouth and pounding heart.

Love to you all   Robert

[Postmarked 24 March 1953]   Palma

Dearest James:

Have been struggling with a cold and with proofs of *The Nazarene Gospel* and with *Greek Myths and Pseudo-Myths* and with the weather; should have answered before.

About speaking and reading poetry. No anecdotes handy but personally I never trust my outer ear as a judge of poetry; but only my inner ear, informed by my outer eye. This protects me against such frauds as Bridges which an elocutionist can do wonders with, but looks wretched on paper. Spoken poetry has a much coarser mesh than written. And that the test of the written is much more severe than the spoken is shown by the question: 'Do you *write* poetry?' rather than 'Do you *compose* poems?' I have only known one modern composer of poems, and that was Vachel Lindsay.[18]

His 'Congo' and 'Bryan, Bryan' and 'Rachael Jane' and 'The Golden Whales of California' are magnificent as spoken performances but lie as dead on the page as do, say, successful modern stage comedies. Have you ever tried *reading* Noel Coward's *Private Lives*?

Tomás's arrival hasn't made any fundamental change in our life yet, but he does take a lot of Beryl's time ...

    . . . .
Much love   Robert

In April Norman Cameron, the poet and translator of Rimbaud, died. He had been a close friend of both Graves and Reeves.

14 May 1953   Palma

Dearest James and Mary:

Thanks for letter about Tomás; and book about Hopkins.[19] The book is extremely useful and well done.

Poor Gerard. 'Carrion Comfort' is as positively revealing as the 'Drummer's Communion' is negatively; and even in 'Carrion Comfort' technique interposes 'oddity' between what he means and what he says. I got a sudden revelation when I looked at the *facsimile* poem in Desmond Flower's[20] *English Poetic Autographs*: I exclaimed, aghast at the hand writing, 'That man bites his nails.'

'Yes,' said Grete (our tame-but-wild graphologist) 'and has other comfort habits!'

Alas: dear Norman! I wrote the *Times* an appreciation, but they did not print it. Tom Matthews suggests a single-volume collection of his poems;[21] but there are probably copyright difficulties – he was even more careless than I am about business: at least I keep an agent . . .

Just about to send off my *Greek Myths and Super-Myths*; page proofs of *Nazarene Gospel* on the way; am writing a piece about Saints for *Botteghe Oscure* called 'I Prefer Some Saints to Others'; and have written a Coronation poem[22] – not exactly for a bet with myself, but because it happened to come into my mind. Unless you have also coincidentally written another, it is likely to be the only one that means what it says. I have asked Watt if he can market it at 6^d to the crowds! But the time is limited.

All well, and much love   – Robert –

While Graves was living in Palma, Karl Gay remained at Ca'n Torrent in Deyá, with his wife Rene and their young daughter. He did all the typing and other secretarial work there, and first thing every morning he would put completed work, along with any mail that had arrived, on Gelat's bus which stopped not far from Graves's flat in Palma. The bag containing work was collected and new work put in its place before the bus returned to Deyá at 2.30 p.m.

Gay was an excellent secretary, industrious and meticulous, whose nature and training (by Graves, who also taught him English) demanded perfection, and without him Graves could hardly have produced the amount of work he did during these years. He learned, and maintained, Graves's own very high standard of workmanship – rather like 'a pistol aimed at their originator's head' as Seymour-Smith observed. Before typing, he would read Graves's manuscript very carefully, annotating it for mistakes or shortcomings of style, and then often would 'demand' that whole passages be rewritten – which, often after a heated argument, they usually were.

Since they both had passionate and perfectionist natures, it is not surprising that such a close personal and working relationship sometimes became strained. Graves wrote a brief letter to Gay from Palma every working day, and read all together these letters give considerable insight into how Graves worked and into the ambience of his household. Because of lack of space, however, I give only a few here. The following short sequence (the first letter in reply to Gay's insistence that Graves's article, 'I Prefer Some Saints to Others', was really not up to standard) illustrates the intensity of their relationship and the somewhat ferocious perfectionism of Gay, which here leads to one of the worst of their arguments.

9 June 1953   Palma

Dearest Karl:

Thanks so much for seeing about the key problem.

The dung was burned by Juan in a 'forest fire' . . . I thought I'd stamped it out.

About the Saints. No: the *slant* is right, but it needs a lot of jacking up still. (*Avant garde* my foot! The Avantgarde nowadays is a rear-guard trailing behind Joyce – Scott Fitzgerald – Hemingway – Auden – Wm James. And *Botteghe Oscure* isn't erudite, just Roman, and the Countess or Princess Cayetani is a famous anti-clerical.)

Sudden heat.

Sorry no *Times* today.

Love   Robert

16 June 1953

Dearest Karl:

I thought I made it clear that I shall send 'Saints', first, to Patrick Crosse in Italy as a Roman intellectual, a cradle Catholic and a responsible journalist; I have cleared up the only points which I consider doubtful and have no local expert handy whose advice I would accept on the advisability of printing the article as amended.

Your 'I always wonder why I bother when you don't' is a bit overstated, surely? You know how grateful I am to you for your tirelessness in working for me, and your keen sense of when a chapter hasn't yet jelled, and your anxiety that I shouldn't write anything slipshod when I am, for some reason or other, off my balance. And you know that I have come to rely on your judgement in the wide critical area which you have made your own. But your moral judgements, even when prompted by generous impulses, are sometimes based on factual misconceptions

116

and become obsessions, and you try to force them on me, so much so that I sometimes have to struggle hard with myself not to say something irreparable. E.G. If you thought that Vladi had overcharged you for the battery why didn't you suggest that he had made a mistake and ask to see the account? Instead of brooding, and then bursting out about the Sullys a few months ago: 'If they are friends of Vladi and Helen they can fuck themselves'; and the day before yesterday refusing my offer of a lunch at the Cala with a graceless: 'Certainly not; you have your company.' I mention this because it seemed to get mixed up with the 'Saints' problem, with which it had of course nothing to do; and it is only fair to bring the problem into the open instead of letting it get worse by shutting it up in a damp cupboard. There are all the years ahead. And please don't take this amiss.

Love   Robert

Gay did not, of course, take it amiss, but nevertheless stuck to his guns about the article.

Graves's next letter began:

17 June 1953

Dearest Karl:

Thanks very much indeed for the tone of your letter.

I shall take another good look at 'Saints' and see whether by cutting it down to five pages I can keep what I know is good in it. Beryl agrees with you that it isn't up to standard, though doesn't think that there is any danger of publishing it.

If I can't get it right I shall send the Countess or Princess or whatever she likes to be called, other than Biddle, the 'Penthesilea' poem.

In the end Gay had his way and the article was not published (though the poem was).

In June Reeves sent Graves some poems, including a long five-part poem called 'The Savage Moon', a meditation on the life of the Northamptonshire poet John Clare. Graves was now thinking about writing another historical novel, and considered several subjects.

117

15 June 1953   As from Deyá

Dearest James and Mary:

Beryl and I will be in London for only a few days arriving July 3: at Sally's house. 108 Clifton Hill, NW8.

I don't think I wrote to admire 'Daffodil Water'; in your true vein. The long poem is episodic: very beautiful lines, some, particularly the last lines of *IV* and *V*, but the whole is loosely coordinated and too sorry for itself to hold up its head. *IV* begins with a reminiscence of:

> Adam, a lean old vulture in the rain,
> Huddled beneath his wind-swept olive trees . . .

which S. Sassoon wrote in Sinai in 1918 while he was still alive.[23]

My Coronation poem couldn't get onto the streets in time; so got a neat carton to itself in *Time and Tide* and gawped out complacently.

No: Saul's period is a good one, but the whole of Kings is so dishonestly written that it would be a very difficult novel to write. My next novel is about Queen Salote of Tonga's Great-grandfather (from 1787–1893); and then I go to Sicily in 900 BC about.

Love   Robert

You sound fine.

In fact Graves did not write the Tonga novel, though he did assemble much of the material for it. Instead he went directly to Sicily.

When translating the *Odyssey* in 1891 Samuel Butler made the discovery that the geographical setting of the poem was Sicily and that the poet must have lived at or near Trapani; he also became convinced that it was written by a woman, in fact the girl 'self-portrayed' as Nausicaa, whom Butler considered to be 'a sort of ancient Jane Austen'. Butler's theory of female authorship was not taken seriously, but when Graves was working on *The Greek Myths* he found both Butler's arguments irrefutable, and set himself to write a novel recreating from textual and historical evidence the circumstances surrounding the writing of the *Odyssey* (using Henry Festing-Jones's *Diversions in Sicily* for local colour).

Selwyn Jepson was now advising Graves on his financial affairs and offered to act on Graves's behalf in dealing with the large New York publishing firm of Doubleday and in getting the new novel (to be called *Homer's Daughter*) serialized for a large fee in the USA.

Dearest Selwyn:

Isn't it hell getting into a new house, unless it happens to be one which you have built yourself with exact foreknowledge of your requirements?

Thanks awfully for your letter, and in principal [*sic*] I agree. The point which the Watts always make, and which I cannot lightly disregard, is the question of copyright; but I cannot believe that unless a book is a humdinger or crackerjack there can be any great danger of piracy. The Trianon Press, Paris, distributed by Faber and Faber, are doing the *Infant with the Globe* translation (with introduction and a cutting of Victorian excrescences) and my short book on *The Creation Story in Genesis* solving the mythological *cruces* that it contains. I can hardly think anyone would pirate either of these in US. The *Poems* are different, and will ultimately be a valuable property.

I should like you to write to Ken McCormick[24] and tell him as follows: The *Odyssey* originally consisted of a straightforward early Homeric saga about the return of Odysseus from Troy, only to find that his wife had been unfaithful – to which (after the first eighty lines) has been added a fairy-tale, unconnected with it, about a hero called Ulysses who escaped various kinds of ritual death. But when these two separate elements have been removed, there remains, as Samuel Butler first pointed out, a substantial mass of realistic modern novel-writing which reflects a domestic and political crisis in a Sicilian court about the year 730 BC. I have worked this background story out and it makes a very exciting drama full of suspense: centred around the Princess Nausicaa (a sort of Ionian Eve Gill) of whom such a charming portrait is given in Book VI of the *Odyssey*. It will be about 70,000 or 80,000 words, and I have already written about a quarter of it. That will be my next book, on which they have an option. If, without prejudice, they care to publish my *Collected Poems* (last edition in US was 1938 and copyrights are freed now) I should be glad to let them do so. Most of the newer poems have appeared in the *New Yorker*, *Atlantic Monthly*, *Poetry*, *Hudson Review*, etc., and no anthology which includes poems by English authors ventures to omit me now. But I should not like to force the book on them, unless they realize that it is a solid literary property which should be greeted with a grin, not a sigh.

Love to you both   Robert

P.S. A title has just been put into my mind doubtless by the Goddess [   ] BLIND HOMER'S DAUGHTER. All right.

4 November 1953   Palma

Dearest Selwyn:

You are a good friend and I hope you find me the same. I agree with all you say. The trouble has been hitherto that I have been too busy writing to think about marketing: in fact the case of Hokusai comes to mind. He used to live in a bamboo house and when people came to buy his pictures he used to tell them: 'take what you want' and when they asked 'how much?' he answered 'what you like!' Still painting vigorously he reached out his left hand for the money and put it on a shelf above his head. Then came the man with rice and sesame and cucumbers. He simply reached up to the shelf with his left hand, paid the money, said: 'Leave what you like!' and went on painting. It might have been 100 yen or 20 yen, *he* didn't care . . . But I got a scare last July to find only about £400 on the shelf and decided to be more practical. *The Naz. Gospel* and *The Greek Myths* really absorbed all my faculties but now they are done, I can relax. *Homer's Daughter* – I think *Blind* is unnecessary – causes me no trouble. I shall have finished the first draft in about a fortnight and can then concentrate on embellishments. Never have I found a book so easy to write, and the suspense is kept up, and there is a strong love-interest and lots of murders.

Poems keep on happening: including one or two crucial ones. And two odd things: Trinity Coll. Cambridge have asked me to be Clarke [*sic*] Lecturer next year on Literature, and since the six lectures can be done in three weeks and I should like to be in England while Wm is starting at Oundle, I have accepted. Shall probably talk about 'Professional Standards in English Poetry'; this year's lecturer Dr G. Trevelyan[25] chose 'A Layman's Love of Letters'. The other odd thing is that Warner Bros. want me to do a script job this winter on a subject and with a distinguished collaborator of which both names are withheld. Bill Watt is asking for details. If I think the game is worth the candle, I shall ask you to advise me *yes* or *no*.[26]

Thanks ever so much for the Ken McCormick softening. In a letter to me he mentioned the novel, but not the Poems. *Poems 1953* are having a fantastically 'good' press: meaning that people have decided that it is time I was recognized. 'Father says turn, and we all turn . . .' No review yet of *Naz. Gospel.* Theologians are stunned and wildly thumbing their exegitical cribs. It is all very amusing.

Gordon Wasson of the Savile, Brook St, and Morgan and Co., Wall St, has been here to study Mallorquín mushroom lore and consult with me. He is the most civilized American I have ever met: and is frightfully pleased because I put him in the way of solving three outstanding mycological problems: the sacral use of the shelf mushroom in ancient Corinth; the exact circumstances of Claudius's death; and, the most exciting of all, the sacred narcotic mushroom cult of the Aztecs.[27] He is just back from Mexico where he took part in a divinatory mushroom session in a backward Indian tribe and got a very excellent divinatory message, and brought back the mushrooms in formaldehyde for identification by Paris savants. His bank has just condescended to recognize Franco Spain; so he has been busy in Madrid, too.

Now, about policy. You have to realize that I find it impossible not to work all the time at something. Occupational neurosis. But there are a great many things I can work at which don't interfere with the money-making ones. E.g. the back of this concerns a book about the Genesis creation story, of about 30 pp of text and 40 of pictures which solves the problem of the historical origin of Adam's rib which, mythologically speaking, stinks and is only 6th century BC it seems; and of why God made grass before he made stars. And poems don't interfere. Nor does my coming translation for Penguin Classics of Lucan's *Pharsalia*. Nor does the now revised and brushed-up translation of Alarcón's *Infant with the Globe*. Nor do incidental anthropological articles and so on. These things are by another man of the same name: like Lewis Carroll's mathematical and logical treatises. (By the way: Gordon Wasson finds that Alice's mushroom was a real one whose illusionary properties were described in a book published just before *Alice in Wonderland*.) But I agree about not overproducing books capable of a large sale; and, between you and me, Bill

Watt is not capable of managing anything of the size you mention
in the fiction-serial line, but I love him well and don't like to
pension him off because he manages the lesser things well enough
and is smart at contracts and I have had dealings with him since
1922! So what I shall do is: not send B. Watt *Homer's Daughter*
when completed around Christmas, but send it to you for advice.
There is no reason why the serial version should correspond exactly
with the hardcover version, and adjustments may be necessary.
Then, if you think it feasible, please, please, approach the New
York people you mention and let us present Bill with a *fait
accompli* before he realizes that the book is written. It is to his
advantage and his son and heir-apparent Peter Watt, who manages
the foreign language business, is a smart chap, and when Bill retires
will be capable of modernizing methods. Thanks 1000 times and
love to you both.

Robert

Correction: when I write a book there are three priorities:
Beryl, the children and poems; mustn't forget the poems.

After his controversial biography of D. H. Lawrence, *Portrait of a
Genius, But . . .* , Richard Aldington (the author of *Death of a Hero*)
set out to 'debunk' the other legendary Lawrence, and in 1955
Lawrence of Arabia: A Biographical Inquiry was published.
Aldington attacked Lawrence (who had died in 1935) as an
'imposter, a congenital liar, insanely ambitious, a homosexual and
a hater of women'. Even before it was published the book aroused
intense indignation among Lawrence's friends and trustees who at
first determined either to prevent publication or to bring a legal
action against Aldington after publication (but did neither).
Following an *Evening Standard* article on 19 January 1954 about
the book, Basil Liddell Hart wrote to Graves asking him if he had
been consulted by Aldington. Liddell Hart and Graves had both
been close friends of Lawrence and had written biographies of him
in his lifetime. They had also collaborated on *T. E. Lawrence to his
Biographers* (1936).

My dear Basil:

How nice to hear from you again.

This is the first I have heard of Aldington's interest in T.E. He never wrote to me, or to my agents asking permission to quote from either of my books, both of which are copyrighted in USA and Great Britain.

One can't libel the dead. The only punitive action one can take, apart from action in defence of copyright, is to publicly strike Aldington and plead the book as provocation. This I should be glad to do myself were I in New York, or Paris, or wherever Aldington hangs out.

Whatever I checked in T.E.'s stories always proved true or even understated; I went to see Allenby, my brother Philip of the Arab Bureau, which handled the Arab campaign officially at Cairo and has checkable files as you know, Buxton, Hogarth, Richards, his brother Arnold, his mother, George Lloyd, Sergeant Pugh[28] and a dozen more, and when I wrote to Buckingham Palace to get the truth of T.E.'s famous interview with George V[29] the letter I got back from George *via* Stamfordham improved on the story T.E. had told me. Also, I knew T.E. for fourteen years intimately, and never caught him out in an untruth, though he often foxed, e.g. at his enlistment.

The suggestion that he was a homosexual is absurd and indecent; the truth seems to be that he was flogged into impotence at Deraa and thus unable to consummate his heterosexual love for S. A.[30] A letter from her to him came unexpectedly into my hands in 1927; I read only two or three lines and the signature, realized it was not for me and forwarded it to him in India. (He had asked me to read and destroy any fan mail sent to him *via* me as a result of the publication of *Lawrence and the Arabs*.)

The odd stories in Lowell Thomas's book[31] were Arnie Lawrence's 'stuffing' of Thomas when he came calling for information at Polstead Road in 1923 (or whenever the date was).

Well: I think that the first action to take against Aldington is to get him on copyright. The Lawrence Trustees, my agent (Bill Watt) and your agent should between them smother him with prohibitions – will you please ring up Bill (W.P.) Watt who also acted as T.E.'s agent before Savage[32] . . . and briefly explain the situation and ask him to protect my copyright in *Lawrence and the Arabs* and in *T.E. to his Biographer R.G.* (He will be enraged against Aldington.) Then turn the heat on Collins.

If Collins continues to handle the book in spite of all these demarches, we can think again about punitive action. But is Collins aware that Mrs Lawrence is still very much alive and that any reflection on T.E.'s birth[33] and that of his two brothers killed in World War I and of his missionary brother, and of Arnie who holds an important museum position in W. Africa (he has just been trying to identify a unique Akan gold-weight for me) would be outrageous?

It will be impossible to stop publication in USA, I fear; but we could 'lay on' reviews and *dementis* in good time.

Ourselves fine: Wm is just about to sit (in the British Consulate) for an Oundle scholarship exam (preliminary); Lucia is learning ballet; Juan is wild; Tomás is one year old.

Myself: have been running into trouble with the Academic Protestants over *Naz. Gosp. Restored* (self and Joshua Podro) which seems to be historically unanswerable and has the approval of the Prof. of Rabbinics at Oxford and the Lecturer of same at Cambridge; the *Manchester Guardian* printed such a scurrilous review of the book that we got a public apology and lawyer's costs. *The Times, Telegraph, News, Sunday Times*, etc., have funked any notice at all. It is all very interesting.

Have just sent off a novel about Sicily in BC 750 to Doubledays and Cassells which may keep me in money for a year or two and have three other books scheduled for this year.* In October I am lecturing at Trinity Coll. Camb. on English Lit. (the Clark Lectures). Jenny is in Italy, married to Patrick Crosse of Reuters; and happy.

How is dear Kathleen? And the children? And Adrian?

We don't know exactly when we shall be in England this year. It depends on whether Wm qualifies to sit for the real scholarship exam in May.

Should dearly like to see you again. Love from Beryl who is in better health than she was but otherwise exactly as always, thank goodness.

Yours ever

Robert

* including a 400,000 word corpus of Greek myths, for Penguins.

In February Graves finished *Homer's Daughter* and sent a copy to
Ken McCormick at Doubleday, and another copy to Selwyn Jepson
for his advice on how to amend the text to suit the US magazine
serialization market.

10 March 1954   Palma

Dearest Selwyn

Thanks very much indeed for your letter and all the trouble you
have taken. I hope you made it clear to the editor whom you have
in mind that I don't care in the very least what liberties he takes
with the serial version. My version is the hard-cover version, and
the other market is one for which a certain amount of pre-digestion
is obviously needed, and I should prefer it done for me than do
it myself.

About 'I cried': the admirable G. A. Henty[34] never used any
other word than 'said', and 'said' is a perfectly good word in all
cases where the audition and acoustics are perfect and no emotion
is involved. But when, for instance, a hall is full of drunken
Sicilians and their servants, one can't 'say' unless one is sitting at
a table with one's addressee. And as one tells the laundry about
collars on certain occasions: 'semi-starched please', so the occasions
here sometimes demand semi-starched language, sometimes (as in
the Temple of Poseidon) starched, sometimes unstarched as when
everyone is feeling relaxed after the massacre. I shall go over the
typescript once more to consider your points when I get the two
further copies (one for MGM's option, one for Cassell) typed. I
have already spotted about 100 minute, or not so minute,
emendations which I shall get typed in triplicate to add to the
existing copies . . . I am always learning how to suck eggs, and the
sort of criticism you make is extremely useful to me. I have
learned a great deal from Jenny (of all people) about writing – and
I am appropriately grateful. But Nausicaa was a tight little body.
She would have made a very good shore-officer in the WRNS. And
there is always a certain *noblesse oblige* hauteur about her. Now
Eve, she's different. More of a WAAF type.

Well, we'll see what (if anything) happens. Ken McCormick is
currently (as they say) reading the book.

About Aldington. Collins are a decent firm. So are Doubledays
in a Transatlantic way. Ken (I happen to know) rejected the

Aldington book as incompatible with Doubleday traditions and the summary I have seen in *Newsweek* is certainly not very Collins. What seems wrong is the claim to have checked up on facts among people whom he has not even consulted, and the obvious attempt to do a right and left with both barrels at D. H. and T. E. Lawrence. D.H. was fair quarry and easy game, T.E. is also fair quarry but can hardly be brought down by Aldington's extemporized pea-shooter. Also regrettable is the insistence on T.E.'s bastardy in the lifetime of his mother: a splendid woman, who broke her leg at a later age than Shaw and is walking about again, and lost two of her bastards in 1916 in defence of England, and was a missionary in China for many years. In my experience, T.E. was guilty of understatement often in regard to himself, never of overstatement. Disbelieving his account of the interview with George V, I once wrote to Stamfordham and the account which the Monarch supplied was far more comically impressive than T.E.'s. Anyhow, I shall probably be asked to reissue my limited edition *Lawrence*[35] – did I tell you this? – plus an omitted chapter, plus an article I wrote about him and his psychological secret, plus a suggestion of where the first draft of *Seven Pillars* is likely to be found.[36] So it's an ill wind, etc. And T.E., were he alive, would be tremendously amused. But I can't help thinking that Collins ought to sell their interest to Hutchinsons or some even less reputable firm.

Shall now sign off, for a thing I am writing of advice to serious young writers; mostly about how to use the OED.

Love to you both   Robert

I have just had to spend valuable time stink-potting nasty clerical dons in *XXth Century* and *Theology*. Jesus Christ, how ignorant and how dishonest! Joshua Podro and I are collecting all these correspondences for the information and help of Doubleday next June; and maybe to form the basis of an article on the intellectual bankruptcy of Anglicanism.

Secret private and confidential: Just heard from Eric Kennington[37] who has read the Aldington book and given Collins and Smith a bad 2 hours. He has read it and says I am insulted a dozen times (not that I care!) and that Collins are in a hole because of the large investment in 3 years' work by A. who is 'bedridden, sick, penurious, asthmatic and in despair'. 'What are we to do?' babbled Collins. 'Destroy the filthy thing, pay A. and start life afresh' says Eric. Eric is sorry for A.; but none the less will go on making a fuss and rousing T.E.'s friends to do the same. From E.K.'s description it really is a pretty poisonous affair.

Later that month Graves sent Jepson several small additions to *Homer's Daughter*.

23 March 1954   Palma

Dearest Selwyn:

Attached are the spare handkerchief, sponge bag, packet of cigarettes, etc., that Homer's Daughter left behind when she went off to you. Please send them on to her. If she fails to marry that rich American, please send her to Willis Wing,[38] my marriage broker in New York who will advertise in the *Matrimonial Gazette* – I am already tired of this metaphor.

Ken McC. says he hopes soon to have news about *HD*: 'It is a very provocative book.' So I am writing to him that this ill-omened adjective was the nicest of a lot of similar ones sent to Doubleday by their learned University readers when I offered them *Mrs Milton*, because vested interests in Mr Milton were threatened. They turned it down and the pipsqueak Creative Age Press, with no organization and only unkind reviews to help them, sold 20,000 copies. I imagine Professor Tush of Columbia and Professor Bosh of Harvard are bellyaching about Homeric scholarship. But I have taken expert advice and there's nothing in the world *against* my reconstruction; and every nice Vassar girl will feel flattered that she could have written the *Odyssey* herself.

How University professors hate me!

Am busy on proofs of *The Greek Myths* for Penguin. Viking Press[39] got scared because it is in advance of University fashion in the USA (i.e. it treats myths anthropologically and archaeologically, and not as uprushes from the so-called Jungian unconscious) and turned it down. I am not sure what to do with it, because Doubleday have already *The Naz. Gospel*, the *Poems* and *Homer's Daughter* to dispose of. The question is whether to make a mere college text-book of it in the US by giving it merely the narrative part, and omitting the explanation – which would allow it to sell as a commodity – or to publish it as it is as a

127

general book for the general public, and be damned to Professors
Tush and Bosh. The point about the book is that it is the only
one now available in which one can turn up any mythological
reference that crops up in poetry and psychology and get its case
history. Uncle Selwyn's advice needed. Uncle Selwyn will be sent
a copy of the corrected proofs in due course.

I hope the *Times Literary Supplement* prints Joshua and my
letter this week.[40] Not even Billy Graham[41] could answer it. But
I like Billy Graham: the Bible foursquare, and no nonsense about
history, as it was in the days of Good King Stephen or Old King
Cole.

This island is warming up and will welcome you at any time
you please.

Love to Tania   Robert

I have written a really *horrible* thing for *Punch* called 'The
Protocole of Kitsch'.

28 March 1954   Palma

Dearest Selwyn:

I think you had better see what is happening in Garden City,
and read my letter to Ken McCormick. I'm not worried about
the book selling, but I should have liked a cosier relationship with
Doubleday. Ken McC. hasn't committed himself personally; he
merely told me (incidentally to a letter about the Lawrence book)
that it was 'a provocative book' and he would write to me soon.
I at once replied that if he expected Professors Tush of Harvard
and Bosh of Cornell to give a good report on the book, he could
expect on. It would antagonize them madly, but that the book
wasn't written for them but for young ladies who would love to
think that they had written the *Odyssey* in a previous incarnation
– or words to that effect.

I gather that no fish are nibbling in the Serial Sea.

Another trouble is that while I am busy at and enthralled by the
Greek Myth proofs for Penguins (hard cover) Mr Huebsch,[42] who
has a weak heart and doesn't like trouble, has shown the book to
Professors Tush and Bosh (as in para. 1) and they say 'it is most
unscholarly and we can't recommend it to our students'. Meaning
that the sophomores will quote Graves at them, about East and
West African, Irish and Hittite analogues to Greek Myths and

128

get the Anthropology prof. in to support them, and classes will become intolerable. But as there *are* no other books on the subject . . .

I'd switch to Doubledays if I thought they'd behave with any more sense. That again is a *popular* book, and its documentation is elaborate and magnificent and the argument is much too exciting for the Academics.

Love   – Robert –

To Ken McCormick

28 March 1954   Palma

Dear Ken McCormick,

I hear *via* Watt *via* Willis Wing, but not direct from you, that *Homer's Daughter* is not in some of your colleagues' opinions 'of the same stature as *Claudius*', and though 'successfully saleable, not to be billed as of the same calibre'.

The adjective *provocative* warned me that something in your editorial department was a bit off-centre, and I wrote to you about three days ago to remind you what sort of a book *Homer's Daughter* really is.

To enlarge on the subject:

As T. E. Lawrence once rightly observed: 'R. G. was born without a reverse gear' – meaning that he never writes the same book twice. Your colleagues, the product of your smooth-running system, tend to think of authors as dependable producers of a certain repeatable type of commodity. Once, therefore, I have successfully written *I, Claudius* (though they would never have published it themselves, because in 1934 it was a new *genre* of historical novel of which they had no experience) they logically expect me to write an *I, Nero*. As I mentioned in my last letter, they turned down *Wife to Mr Milton* in 1941; but it nevertheless became a popular success.

Now they complain that *Homer's Daughter* is 'not of the same stature as the *Claudius* books'. If they had been publishing in 730 BC, they would have complained that the *Odyssey* could not be billed as of the same calibre as the *Iliad*. *Calibre* and *stature* are invidious words. *I, Claudius* and *Claudius the God* made a big book of some 340,000 words long; full of barbarous late Roman

129

detail. This is a sweet, exciting, early Greek love story of 80,000 words. It is as different from the *Claudius* books as *The Nazarene Gospel* is from either, and the only similarity between the three, apart from my authorship, is that they are all works of historical detection. I didn't just vaguely want to write about Rome; or to write about early Christianity, or to write about pre-Classical Sicily. It was the *problem* of Claudius hitherto mishandled by the historians, and the *problem* of the Gospels hitherto mishandled by the Church, and the *problem* of Homer hitherto mishandled by Classical professors, that forced the books on me. Each book obviously has its different public. This is a story of another new *genre*, and a story for women – almost for women only. Your editors must understand that whenever I write a book they ought to judge it as though it were an imponderable first novel by an unknown author; it will never be the same mixture as before.

If you feel there is a lack of confidence in the book among your editors which will permeate the lower ranks of your great Garden City organization and prevent *Homer's Daughter* from being the success that it could be, please either restore their confidence at once, or else tell me frankly that you can do nothing with them – saying that they are like that, and have to be like that because you like them like that; which would be an understandably loyal view.

In my recent letter (referred to in para. 1 above) I suggested that it would be unwise to expect any warmly appreciative comment on the book to come from any Classics Professors of note. They are all sworn to the untenable view that Homer had a white beard three fathoms long. If that is what has discouraged your colleagues, give the book to any bright Classically unprocessed young woman (plus E. V. Rieu's translation of the *Odyssey*) and ask her if she doesn't instinctively agree with me. And if she does agree, by-pass the Classics Professors.

This is straight from the heart. A reassuring or frankly discouraging cable would keep our personal relations sweet and clean. I don't want to force anything on you, but the few people here who have read the book think it my most exciting novel, and I agree; and if you can't make your staff believe the same you will surely expect me to take it elsewhere to avoid embarrassment in the office.

Yours very sincerely   Robert Graves

Jepson thought Graves's letter to McCormick unwise, but neverthe-less Doubleday published *Homer's Daughter* in an edition of 12,500 the following February. Graves continued to have trouble selling the hardback rights for *The Greek Myths* in America; Viking Press demanded repayment of the advance they had given and Doubleday also turned it down; finally the book (published in paperback in the US by Penguin in 1955) came out in hardback in the US in 1957, published by George Braziller Inc., New York.

In March James Reeves's edition of *The Selected Poems of John Clare* was published and Graves arranged to review it for the *New Statesman* and the *Hudson Review*, and to broadcast on Clare for BBC Radio.

29 March 1954   Palma Tel. 5051

Dearest James

¡Look, we have a telephone!

I have sent for Tibble's *Poems of* [43] and hope that with the *Introduction* and your excerpts I can get by.

Your job is admirably done, Martin and I agree. And how well you write!

Yes: it's a bad world for authors, even the worst of us!

I have dealt fairly completely with St Paul in *The Naz. Gospel*, and would find it hard to get a publisher for a really awful novel about him. Billy Graham wouldn't allow it, for a start.

Tied up with *Greek Myths* proofs and thanks for everything.

Clark Lectures are being specially reduced for me to six lectures in three weeks, not six in six. October. Shall not be over this summer until late September.

I *have* lectured to 2000 Canadians once, at half an hour's notice; voice carries all right . . . But yes, of course, I am going to distinguish the real poets from the factitious ones. The difficulty is that even the factitious ones sometimes stumble on a real line, or even stanza. What I *can* discuss is professional standards – workmanship; models and admirations; class prejudices; subjects permitted, etc. – of a bard-society which is unofficial, unendowed and usually perverse. See?

In haste and love to you all   – Robert –

Why not write to the *Hudson Review* and say that you would

like to review for them, and that I say you are just the guy they need. Joseph Bennett is my contact. They pay quite well.

Also in March Graves received the half-galleys of Aldington's book, sent by Basil Liddell Hart, who enclosed his own notes showing military inaccuracies in Aldington's argument. Graves wrote from Palma to Karl Gay: 'Have seen a preview of A.'s book; a lot of hard work, very nasty, some of the mud will stick.'

To Basil Liddell Hart

No date   Palma

My dear Basil:

You are being as noble as industrious; and I am most grateful for the pre-view of the Aldington book.

I think that, on the whole, it had after all better be published, <u>because</u> it is perverse and sneering and contains all the muck that an industrious rogue could rake together in three years; and should certainly not be corrected or modified by you or anyone else to modify its nastiness but left to its critical fate. A 'debunking' was obviously due one day; better that it should come now, and in its most unpleasant form, while it can be dealt with faithfully by survivors who know the facts. The only objection I have is to the bad taste of smearing Mrs Lawrence, whom I admire and love, before her death. Yet this bad taste will be more damaging to A. than anything else.

I can disprove the bastardy complex: T.E. was not informed of the 'guilty secret' until he was so emancipated that as he told me: 'My mother was shocked that we weren't shocked at her news and that we took it so lightly.' The facts about S.A. are that she was a woman and that I accidentally and honestly saw a letter she wrote him in 1927 signed 'Jehanne' – unless (as is most unlikely) there were two S.A.'s in his life. I only read the first lines, saw it was private and desisted (in 1927 T.E. had asked me to read and destroy all female fan-letters sent him c/o myself; and this was one!).

The facts about his sex-life are, so far as I can make out, that he was made impotent by the flogging at Deraa: I recorded this in print in 1950. Since then, curiously enough, I showed a letter of his to the most gifted graphologist I know – 100% accurate – who came to me in a flutter and said: 'I may be wrong or mad or off-colour, or something, but this writing is that of a man who has been made impotent by some great shock and, instead, enjoys fantastic sexual orgies in his mind.'

About military facts I can't of course speak; my job in *Lawrence and the Arabs* was to condense 7 *Pillars* (in the Oxford version) for Cape to sell, and I had only 3 months to do it in. But all the people I consulted, including Philip, who was in charge of the Turkish Order of Battle and at the Cairo receiving end, testified to T.E.'s accuracy.

About Lowell Thomas – Arnie, a gay young schoolboy (or undergraduate? I forget) stuffed him up good and proper when he visited 2 Polstead Road.

One test of T.E. (as of all people) is the 'fragrant memory test'. The inferior or bad worsen with the years. T.E., for all his internal sufferings and manifest failings, remains a warm, generous, essentially truthful (meaning that he had an Irish twist to his character) friend. All his naughty tricks are forgiven absolutely.

You misread, or I miswrote: my Cambridge job is *next* October, so let's hope to meet. No: Kathleen[44] will never grow old; she has the inner fire. Our love to her.

Yours ever   Robert

In his debunking of T. E. Lawrence, one of Aldington's points was that Lawrence had lied when he said that he had been offered the post of High Commissioner of Egypt; Aldington wrote asking the Prime Minister, Sir Winston Churchill, if the offer of the job really had been made and in reply received an 'emphatic disavowal of this offer' from Churchill's secretary. However, the offer had been made unofficially, and Liddell Hart and others were pressuring Churchill to put the record straight, which he did.

To Basil Liddell Hart

Holy Thursday, 1954 [15 April]   Palma

My Dear Basil:

You are being very splendid still and thanks a thousand times for keeping me in touch with the Aldington affair. It is wonderful that the PM has come through as he has. Yes, I got the half-galleys and read them with disgust.

By the way, I knew John Buchan[45] very well – we were county neighbours – and he had implicit and abounding faith in T.E. If I remember, Buchan was employed in the Intelligence Service, pretty high up and in a position to check facts; *Greenmantle*, though palpably fiction, was certainly a projection of T.E.

Listen: the *New Republic* have come into money and want to blue [*sic*] some of it in an article by me on the Aldington book, if it appears. Presumably some English journal will also want to print this.

What I should like would be permission to mention you as having disproved some of the most specious lies, naming your sources, but not of course quoting the actual text – which would be unethical, since you will certainly be called on to review the book yourself, if it appears. This would be the necessary background stuff to what I would have to say about my own experience of him, and his family, and the way I have come to reassess him since his death – with greater understanding and affection than before, even.

Wm has passed into Oundle, thank goodness, and so will have his first experience of English school life in September. Hope to see you and Kathleen in October.

Have secured an abject apology for libel from the *Manchester Guardian* who let their reviewer, a high-ranking ecclesiast, say what he please about *The Nazarene Gospel*. Joshua Podro and I are about to do the same with the *Times Lit. Supp.* . . .

Love

Robert

The reviews of *The Nazarene Gospel Restored* (published October 1953 in London, July 1954 in New York) were, with few exceptions, very hostile, some to the point of hysteria; reviewers on the whole paid little attention to textual details and avoided serious analysis of the argument, content to denounce the book as 'a farrago of rubbish' (*Church Times*) or complain that Graves and Podro 'reduced the story to the plane of pure history' (*Observer*). The reviewers were mostly members of the clergy ('canons to the right of me, canons to the left of me . . .') and each one was answered by

Graves. In February the *Manchester Guardian* was forced to print an apology for libel in its review and pay legal costs. On 5 March 1954 the *Times Literary Supplement* printed a letter by Graves in reply to an anonymous review (the reviewer was M. J. C. Hodgart of Pembroke College, Cambridge; Graves 'guyed' him in an article in *Punch*, 18 August 1954, called 'Thy Servant and God's'). Graves's letter was 'pretty hard on the reviewer, my God, though unctuously courteous', he wrote to Gay, but the paper printed a rejoinder from Hodgart, who was incensed by Graves's portrait of St Paul (he had described him as 'a Syrian Greek opportunist with no regard for factual truth and mainly responsible for the Christian misrepresentation of Jesus's acts and beliefs') and accused Graves and Podro of 'unethically camouflaging the true text of Galatians 4, 14', which concerned Paul's famous 'thorn in my flesh'. At that point the editor declared the correspondence closed. Graves, however, having rechecked the texts and decided that 'the clergyman in question was using a secondary reading found in the worst manuscripts', demanded the reopening of the correspondence on the grounds that the reviewer's comment was defamatory. The editor refused and Graves therefore instructed his (Jewish) lawyer to begin proceedings against the paper for libel.

James Reeves was now considering writing a critical book about Graves, and in May wrote to ask him how he felt about such a project.

3 June 1954   Palma

Dear my James:

You are very welcome to write about Graves, for whom I have a power of attorney, if you can face the moral problem, which is: whatever you find bad, strained, untrue in my *Collected Poems*, by which I mean the 1947 edition (and in next January will mean the 1955 New York edition which cuts and amends still more), you should have told me about as a friend when it first appeared and suggested improvements; so you censure yourself if you censure me. Ha, ha!

Nobody has ever written a book about Graves before, except myself – that biography *Goodbye to All That* – but the question is whether (so to speak) the fruit is yet ripe enough to pick. Possibly the Cambridge Lectures will ripen it, and my many recent contributions to *Punch*, both of which are obvious signs that I'm going respectable. I should have thought Cassell might be a suitable publisher, but if you prefer Chatto, because of Day-Lewis,[46] why should I care?

It will be an extremely difficult book to write, and if I had to do it for poor Graves, I'd emphasize the clearer view he has gradually been getting of what is his own peculiar line and what isn't; point out that at times he has gone badly astray (e.g. in the *Mock-Beggar Hall* volume) and realized this just in time. He has never, however, I claim, worn anybody else's hat as regards rhythm or diction or where-are-you. Or do I lie? But as censure is morally barred, so is praise; the main point being Graves's forty-five years' obsession about getting poems *right*. One odd thing Graves does is to preserve all the drafts of all his poems; a habit of probably thirty years – no, five more. You see there how it all happens: the only exception being 'Pure Death' which Graves wrote on one of those clever things you buy in railway bookstalls for taking notes on and erasing them again.

But isn't critical work difficult? The vocabulary I mean. Soup-tureenish and cock and hoop [*sic*].

The Fertisan[47] was fine. So sorry about Mary's sister. Have just made a nice historical discovery about Chopin and Sand, and why she hated Majorca so, and feel all set up.[48]

Love
                  Robert

Reeves, however, did not write the critical book about Graves, though in 1960 he did edit a selection of Graves's poetry and prose, with an introduction and notes, for use as a school textbook.

To Basil Liddell Hart

29 June 1954   Deyá

Dear Basil.

Thanks so much for your addition to my Lawrence file; I liked his comment on Churchill, having come to the same conclusion long ago.

Lawrence like Churchill had a devil, but kept it in check remarkably well. It was a humorous devil, not a cruel one. I don't know who Elie Kedourie is who writes in the *Cambridge Journal* but he has missed the point; T.E. was an intuitive, affectionate, Galahad-like man of action who came a frightful crash before his War was over, and is to be judged thereafter as a broken hero who tried to appear whole and make the best of it.

It will be difficult for Churchill to admit his lapse. But it doesn't matter all that much.

Love to Kathleen and yourself.   – Robert –

I shall know this week whether the *Times Literary Supplement* are going to apologize for libel or prefer to be sued. My lawyer has taken Counsel's advice and reports our case is cast iron. It's all due to *The Nazarene Gospel* and St Paul's 'thorn in the flesh'; there was a correspondence which the editor closed on a note of libel and refused to reopen.

That summer Graves met the young writer Alan Sillitoe, who was living in Sóller, a coastal town eight kilometres from Deyá, with his American wife, the poet Ruth Fainlight. Graves was largely responsible for the direction Sillitoe took in his writings by encouraging him to write about his working-class upbringing in Nottingham. The immediate result of this was Sillitoe's first (and some say still his best) novel, *Saturday Night and Sunday Morning* (see page 175). Graves also helped Sillitoe and Fainlight, who both became close friends of the whole Graves family and regular visitors to Canelluñ, with criticisms of their poetry.

26 July 1954   Palma

Dear Alan:

Nice meeting you briefly in Sóller. This is our busiest time of year. Everyone crowds in on us – Relations, friends, acquaintances, arruptrous [*sic*] strangers.

Your poem sounds good, holds together well, but the language has been taken a stage beyond common sense, and that I always regret. A poem should always be able to stand with a dictionary in its hand and swear: 'This is not anything else but this; see pages so and so.'

Once you do violence to common sense there is a danger of ridicule: e.g. pillows raped beyond repair, sounds like the work of a big pimpled boy at a Reform school. And 'green' does not

explain itself with music. 'Green' *may* mean frightening: as in
Greek 'green fear'. Or it may mean 'fresh'; or it may mean *verde*,
erotic.

Love   Robert

To Gordon Wasson

29 August 1954   Deyá

Dear Gordon:

Very glad to hear from you again. Any chance of your being in
England in October? I have yet to deliver those lectures (Oct.
12–29th) at Cambridge and since they have lured me to England
from this island refuge I suppose they'll want to hear something
out of the ordinary; so I shall not spare anyone's feelings. The
great way to keep one's path clear is not to play ball with anyone;
not a good metaphor except for boy scouts but it will serve.

Of course all books on totally new lines like yours take 6 times
as long to write as one expects; but who wants to write books
on totally old lines?

I have eight books coming out, if I count the lectures to which
I will add four or five essays on poetry. *The Greek Myths* (1000
pp); translations of Galván's *Enriquillo* and Alarcón's *Niño de la
Bola*; critical edition of Sand's *Winter in Majorca* plus
Quadrado's two-fisted reply; *Collected Poems 1955*, Doubleday;
Homer's Daughter, a historical novel; *Adam's Rib*, a monograph
on the anomalies of Genesis 1–4 with an explanation of how they
occurred. And to keep myself in cash I have been writing out
family jokes and anecdotes as they occur for *Punch* and that is
already about 35,000 words. Overproduction.

Stevie Smith[49] is a queer, queer girl who wrote a book called
Novel on Yellow Paper and does a lot of reviewing. I met her
once in a park. It is usually either in a pub or park that she receives.

Don't think that the *Times* tiff is over. They are pleading for
more time to prepare their defence – after their incredibly stupid
lawyers, who thought we were bluffing, did not answer our
lawyer's letter 'would they accept service of a writ for libel?', so
he had to breeze into the office and serve it on the editor in person.
We started proceedings because a non-litigious counsel told us
we had a cast-iron case. The other day John Walter the chief share-

holder came to see me; he didn't know of the affair so I told him
and he shook his head and said 'what an incredible blunderer that
fellow is! He could have settled the whole affair amicably in a
moment!'

So we'll see if the case is fought out, or if they will prefer to
settle out of court.

No mushrooms yet this year.

We missed your partner, George's brother-in-law. He was
extremely ill when he came here and the whole visit was a disaster.
George himself is fine.

All the best to you both. How is your son?

Robert

Will restrain my impatience about your book's appearance.
You didn't consult that oracle again at Easter, I suppose?

On 16 June Graves had written to his lawyer, Mark Haymon:

When reading the Bible beware
That you read it with absolute care.
O beware that the Bible
Don't lead you to libel
And scandal in Printing House Square.

In September Graves went, with Beryl, to England to deliver the
Clark Lectures.

To James Reeves

15 October 1954   4 Mortimer Road
Cambridge

Dearest James and Mary

All well. I like Cambridge; so do Beryl and Lucia and Juan. Wm
likes Oundle; so do we. I talked to the sixth form there, after
dining with the Stainforths, on poetry; and it was great fun.

First lecture here a success. Hordes of devoted students turned
away at the door.

Second lecture today.

Last night I answered English Club questions at the Union and
was less nervous than my interlocuters.

The great news is that I consulted the great C. H. Dodd[50] on the textual problems of Galatians which are concerned with the *Times Libel Action* and he found to his astonishment – and my deep delight – that the text which I have been favouring, and which the *Times* regards as hopelessly 'bad', is in fact one hundred years older and far superior to the one they call me unscholarly for not accepting.

So their case will break down and not even (I think) go into court.

When do we see you? We are going back to 108 Clifton Hill on Monday and the phone is MAI 2702. Let's arrange a get-together. I am incidentally mentioning you in my last lecture (with great respect) apropos of Yeats's letter about *Natural Need*.[51]

On October 20th at 10 p.m. I broadcast in [*sic*] HOME service, see *Radio Times*.

We are all well and haven't had occasion to use an umbrella since we arrived a week ago.

Much love   Robert

To Selwyn Jepson

6 February 1955 I guess   Deyá

Dearest Selwyn:

Nice of you to write, just like that, with no particular excuse. I reviewed the Aldington book for *News Chronicle* but couldn't say all I had to say; will expand in a review for *New Republic* – the clue to T.E. was that as a result of the physical impotence and degraded feeling produced by the flogging at Deraa, T.E. had very vivid, waking fantasies (diabolical even) which he could not always control; naturally he was a pure-hearted romantic truth-teller, but the fantasies were evil, especially the power-fantasy. The *general* impression was wholly good; the bad was done in corners.

February is a month I don't like; it's not really cold, but nothing grows, here. And the children usually have flu, or at least one expects it. Ken McCormick is being awfully nice to me, I do appreciate it and sincerely hope that *Homer's Daughter* sells; I'll send you a copy with Jim Metcalf's cover (Cassell) – the Doubleday one is terrible but just what the bookshops like.

Haven't a notion when we shall be coming over; the trouble is

I need a lot of money and haven't got it in spite of all these books and busyness. There's a hope of a set of *Arabian Night* shorts for NBC television; but not a bright one. Meanwhile, I'm doing my 2000 words a day of translation from Lucan's *Civil Wars* in an attempt to make that bogus classic readable (Penguin) and also Suetonius's *XII Caesars*, and occasionally dashing off a thing for *Punch*, who have 4 or 5 things of mine in stock. And there have been three small poems, to show I'm still alive.

Are you ever coming here? Book up before the rush. Glorious sun, and yesterday I bathed – largely to retrieve a valuable ball being carried out to sea.

Irving,[52] of course, never turned up.

I suppose Wendy is frantically busy?

I don't understand if *Zuleika* is being filmed or staged; sounds like merely staged.

This is getting disjointed. As for your book just past half-way – 'Young Man, I pity thee' as Catherine said to Wm Blake – The only fun is the last chapter, and the first; and above all the rewriting which I adore.

Much love from us all to you both,   Robert

In February Graves wrote to Savage, whose sixth (and last) child had just been born.

15 February 1955   Palma

Dear Derek:

Congratulations to Connie and yourself. 'Good stock can't over-breed', and 'every baby finds a welcome' and so on. But I hope Connie can cope!

I forget when I last wrote: nothing much has happened since that brief raid on Cambridge in October; I am publishing those lectures under the title of *The Crowning Privilege* – which is the privilege poets have of being their own masters, unregulated and unorganized, owing devotion only to poetry itself.

Doubleday are publishing my *Collected Poems* (once more pruned and amended) this summer, when I attain 60. The new poems which have not been published in book form in England will be printed at the back of *The Crowning Privilege* (about 12).

Then this week my novel *Homer's Daughter* (Cassell) comes out;

it's about the *Odyssey*. And *The Greek Myths*, 2 vols. (Penguin).
And a shorter *Nazarene Gospel*. Publication date not fixed for my
Winter in Majorca (Cassell) which is an investigation of the lies
George Sand told about this island in 1840. On to *Adam's Rib*, a
monograph on Genesis 1–4. Or for the *Infant with the Globe*,
translation of Alarcón's novel; both these Trianon Press and Faber.
Translation of *Enriquillo* (by Galván) is out in USA (Univ. of
Indiana Press).

So now I am trying to limit production of books which are not
text books; and so busy translating Suetonius's *Twelve Caesars*
and Lucan's *Civil Wars* for Penguin Classics. For ready cash I write
short stories and what *Punch* doesn't take the *New Statesman*
has done, and what the *New Statesman* doesn't take . . . , etc. The
only drawback is that these jokes, which take only a few hours,
are now piling up into another book. The pay-off is that I'm still
only just solvent. [*margin note*: Children's Education, need I
explain?]

At the moment doing a really considered article on T.E.L. in the
New Republic. Aldington is all wrong and bad, but there was
that ugly quality in T.E. (which he's fastened on) needing
explanation and I seem to be the only one who has the facts.

I made my peace (to our mutual satisfaction) with Siegfried
Sassoon[53] at Cambridge. Yes, his poems from 1916–1921 were
superb in their way. He gave me a copy of his recently printed
verse, and to my great relief there was one real poem in the bag.

My libel action against the *TLS* won't come up for hearing until
1955. Their published *Defence* is foolish; they are justifying their
libel by quotation from an out-of-date Greek Testament.

While in England I canned a tribute to Hardy,[54] which will be
put on the BBC any day now . . . (Sunday 20th, sorry!) No, don't
cramp your style by sending me that *Encounter* script,[55] unless you
are doubtful about any historical point. I shall be too embarrassed
to listen; but send me the typescript afterwards, please.

I do hope that Royal Literary Fund award comes off for you. In
USA you'd be simply heaped with them because there are more
awards going than worthy candidates.

We all send love
                                                    Robert

Finally, the *Times Literary Supplement* decided to settle the libel
case out of court; the editor apologized to Graves in an editorial on

22 July 1955 and paid his legal costs; Graves's reading was based on the recently discovered third-century Chester Beatty Papyrus (P. 46) and 'unscholarly to the end they referred to Page 46 of the Chester Beatty Papyrus as though it were paginated!' (to Wasson; 'P. 46' is 'Papyrus 46').

To Selwyn Jepson

3 March 1955

Dearest Selwyn:

How nice of you to write like that! I hope dear Nausicaa heaps my lap with gold from Aethon's sack of Canopus. Claudius was grateful for what I did for him; so were Marie Milton and Hercules and Belisarius. Jesus hasn't been grateful so far, and indeed I'm ashamed to read the Doubleday returns on *Naz. Gosp.*; but maybe something will happen to stir him up again. Unless it's just that I'm a hopeless Gentile. I certainly need a bit of money at the moment.

I wish you'd come here, you and Tania.

Not that there's any absence of intellectual company here, or of drama, or that we're bored in any way; but we wish you were about to enjoy the way things are.

I don't mind photographers. I don't mind anything really, except teatime conversation and queers with great liquid eyes.

Have just written a piece for *Encounter* which combines with *Der Monat, Epreuves* and *Cuadernos* to commission translateable pieces publishable by all – a good racket – because it becomes worthwhile. This is just a statement of the Georges Sand–Chopin set-up here in 1838–9 and what *really* happened – I think I told you about that. Then I have another long piece to do about the Whitaker Negroes;[56] about whom I broadcast briefly in 1953. I now have checked up on them in full medical and geographical and historical detail. They are OK but dying out fast.

Also a long piece about T.E.L. for *New Republic*.

So it goes on.

The snow has melted from the mountains, I hope for the rest of the year.

Love and thanks   Robert

To Karl Gay

16 March 1955

Dearest Karl:
 Have been correcting proofs of 'These be your Gods, O Israel' for Freddie Bateson's[57] *Essays in Criticism*, and beginning work on that piece about *Goodbye to All That* and the year 2010.
 The cold – *catarro* not *frio* – has after all got me; I should have remained in bed.
 Thanks a lot for your long-suffering about *Whitaker Negroes*.
 George Merrill has just asked Beryl and me to lunch with Count von Luckner, the 1915–1918 U-boat hero. But however anti-Hitler he may have been, and however good a European, and however gentlemanly and chivalrous, I think not.
 Some mental trauma prevents.
 Love

Robert

In 1955 James Reeves, who was doing editorial work for Heine-mann, commissioned an anthology of ballads from Graves, who had edited a similar anthology for Benn in 1927.

Graves's Clark Lectures were heavily criticized by several academics and critics, such as Herbert Read and Donald Davie; Graves, however, had been aware of his position in the lectures as something of an *agent provocateur* and so was not unduly surprised.

27 July 1955 Palma

Dearest James:
 I keep no press cuttings, and what Donald Davie may have written about me I know and care not. The book itself will be out in September. What I say may be embarrassing but cannot be disproved. Or can it?
 Have just celebrated a 60th birthday; at least 60 guests were present and Beryl and I had to arrange food, drink and entertainment and policing for all; and transport for many.
 I am too busy for words and in great need of large cash. So collaborating on a TV spectacular script with Will Price,[58] now no longer an alcoholic loss but very bright and lively. Translating, also, *Suetonius* to keep a contract (September); Englishing a most

144

important but ill written book[59] by a leading neurologist on the
physiological aspects of religious conversion and political
brainwashing; keeping abreast of a fantastically large
correspondence . . . Yes September, for a fortnight, we come, all
of us.

I think you'll have to let me do that ballad book *after* September.
Can't before without self-murder; no time to read the headlines
even; and swarms of visitors. It will take a month when I start.
November? OK?

Thurber can be very funny; nice man. Tom Matthews never
writes; or visits.

About Gretl[60] and Alan. Alan promised me last year he'd get on
with the job of Norman's poems. Gretl ought to take steps: a
lawyer's letter if she can't get an answer – because he's after all
inflicting injury on her. I think it's stinking. And no excuse: none.
He wants my introduction expanded or amended. For God's sake
does that take two years? It isn't as if I have objected.

Hot here; I like real heat, it makes my mind work better. I'll
have you sent my *Collected Poems 1955*. Ingrid Bergman wants
to play Nausicaa in *Homer's Daughter* directed by her husband.[61]

Compost in the early morning and the dewless eve. Wonderful
cucumbers this year with Fertisan (advert).

Children fine. Much love to all.   Robert

In September 1952 Graves sent Gordon Wasson a cutting from
a pharmaceutical paper about the religious role of hallucinogenic
mushrooms in Mexico, especially in the hill country of Oaxaca and
the Valley of Mexico. 'In almost the same post' Wasson also received
a letter and photograph from a Hans Mandersteig in Verona empha-
sizing the importance of the mushroom in Meso-American cultures.
Both letters set the Wassons off on their most exciting investigation
so far, which took them to remote hill villages in Mexico where
they took part in sacred oracular mushroom rites, presided over by
a *curandera*, a priestess and healer. In August, Wasson sent Graves
a detailed account of his 'mystical' experience of eating the Mexican
mushroom and this triggered off further thoughts on mushrooms
and their place in ancient religion in Graves's mind. He first of all
linked 'mushrooms' with 'mystery' in Greek, both having a common
stem; then, on the problem of why some peoples are 'mycophagous',
i.e. mushroom-eating (there are two main groups, the Limousin

group – Provence to Catalonia – and the Slavonic group), and others mycophobic, he suggested (21 August):

A new idea: do you not think it possible that mycophoby is perhaps due to a *tabu* on mushrooms because of their oracular *sacredness*, translated popularly into a fear of their poison? I am suddenly convinced of this. Nobody leaves remotely edible food uneaten except for religious reasons . . . That would imply that the mycophagous tribes came from an area where mushrooms had no sacral use.

What fascinated Graves most, however, was Nero's calling mushrooms 'the food of the Gods' – was he coining a phrase, Graves asked, or was he jokingly applying what was perhaps a Greek proverb about mushrooms to the murder of Claudius, whom he had deified after the poisoning? Graves now began to wonder if the hallucinogenic mushroom had been used in ancient divine ritual. He tried out these theories on Wasson, also another guess that Buddha, who died after eating mushrooms, deliberately took toxic mushrooms to ensure immortality or to 'see' the gods.

22 October 1955   Palma

Dear Gordon

I have now had time to digest your account and, when Beryl has finished reading it, will send the typescript back. It makes a very strong impression on any reader.

(By the way, I do hope that you'll publish a cheap edition of the book, without the coloured prints, for the general public.[62] It is of such universal appeal that it would be undemocratic not to make it available in that way.)

Now my comments supplementary to the first letter about 'food of the Gods' (I am most impressed in that context by your Chinese tradition; and grateful for your putting in the bit about Buddha though the name you give the dish does not correspond with the one I passed on to you from Zen Buddhist sources). – Here goes:

You're right about Keats having that capacity for seeing things in the weird romantic light usually known as 'glamour', and which you experienced under the mushroom influence. Coleridge, Shakespeare, Spenser and a few others had it. *Hablando entre nosotros,*[63] I have also had it, fitfully, and poems written in that

146

sort of trance are capable of affecting readers susceptible to
glamour into a re-creation of what the poet saw. With Coleridge
it was very clear, e.g. in the 'Ancient Mariner' or 'Christabel',
when the trance was on him and when it wasn't. Most poets lose
the capacity for the glamour-trance very early; with me it has
persisted as an occasional visitant until now, so I still know about
it. The colours are exactly as one sees them in early childhood
and so are the scents and smells; and to be interrupted, while in
the trance, by any 'gentleman from Porlock' is a horrible
experience. The main difference between the poetic trance and the
sort you experienced (in each there is a strong realization of one's
actual situation, and the critical intelligence is not dormant) is that
the poetic trance comes on because an important statement is waiting
to be made; the images are induced by the need for the statement.
And the freedom of the mind to remember half-forgotten things
(which seems also characteristic of the mushroom trance) is
enlarged by the faculty of choice between the things remembered.
In a poem written under the glamour-trance the mind is working
as rapidly and efficiently as one of those scientific calculators that
grind out an answer, in three minutes, that would have taken a
team of mathematicians 4 weeks to work out on paper: on several
levels at once. Your mind, since you did not come in search of any
answer of a problem, merely went for a visual holiday.

In *The White Goddess* I relate the poetic trance to the ecstatic
worship of the Moon Goddess – a throwback, or revival, or
continuation, of it – showing that there has always been a tradition
linking poetry with Muse worship. The Muses were nine, which
is merely an emphatic form of 3, as in the Triple Hecate. The Irish
Goddess of poetry and the arts was the Triple Brigid. The Akan
Goddess of all the arts is Triple Ngame (she is of Libyan origin –
like Athene who was also once Triple). Talus [*sic*] and Daedalus
and Hephaestus were originally subject to the Triple Goddess, as
Wieland will have been (before Odin's victory) to the Thrice
Three Norns. I am not at home among the Mexicans, but people
tell me there is a White Goddess in Mexico, also a calendar which
corresponds with the Libyan calendar, and the English Common
Law Calendar, and what I have postulated as the Orphic
(Helladic) calendar – namely one of 13 twenty-eight day months,
plus a single day; and four stations of the year – the two equinoxes
and the solstices – but with the 365th day, which marks the

difference between terrestrial and sidereal time, added at the
winter solstice. Thus one gets five stations instead of four, by
separating the 5th and 1st by the extra day.

I would not drag all this
speculation out, were it not
that your Señora used 13
pair of mushrooms, and
also the four points of the
compass, and because you
mention the pyramid. The
pyramid is the three-
dimensional equivalent of
the calendar figure just
given: you simply raise the

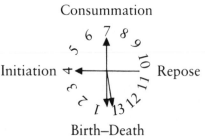

Birth-line into the air above the paper! In kingship rites, the king
shoots an arrow to the four points of the compass, and then one
into the air straight up – in honour of the Triple Goddess, whose
triangle faces you from every side of the pyramid thus sketched
out. So maybe the Trinity is not, as you suppose, an intrusion
into the Mexican mushroom rites, especially as it comes in the
third and most important place: but a memory of the Triple
Goddess – girl, nymph and crone – air, earth, underworld – spring,
summer, autumn – waxing, full and waning Moon.

The Señora's cult was obviously the oldest and purest of those
you mention; but the insistence by Don Aristeo on 7 and 5 and
51, which are *female* numbers (and on 5 times 5), suggests that
the cult was originally a woman's one, and that the men broke
in – as at Delphi, Tempe and Dodona – to break the monopoly.
Until the last few years, women have never broken into a male
monopoly; the reverse has always been the case in Europe since
the third millenium BC, except in times of acute labour shortage.
So where both men and women engage in the same holy task, one
assumes it to have been originally female . . . I wonder whether
Prometheus – to whom 'Athene taught architecture, astronomy,
metallurgy, navigation, medicine and the other arts' – stole not
fire from Heaven, with Athene's help, but the sacred mushroom.
Zeus, you remember, treated him even more roughly than
Sisyphus. The only city with which Prometheus is connected is
Sicyon – commanding the Gulf of Corinth.

Naturally this speculation is all in the air. *But* if you would try

148

it out on the Señora – saying that your friend Don Roberto the poet wanted to know: whether the thirteen mushrooms stand for the thirteen months of twenty-eight days; and whether 5, 7 and 42 are numbers of great importance to the mushroom-gods (42 is a test question); and whether smiths or painters take mushrooms before attempting a difficult work[64] – I would be most interested to know the answer.

Yours ever,   Robert

I apologize for the amount of work I am throwing at you; but you are one of the very few people whose mind works along the same devious channels as mine, and correspondence with you makes me feel less eccentric. Especially as you have a most admirable capacity – and organization, it seems – for checking up on 'fantastic' theories by consulting the best authorities on specialized subjects. And I'm glad you're an American; because that capacity of thought is even rarer in USA than in England.

P.S. Thinking over this problem logically, I have decided that 'the food of the gods' could not very well mean the food of the philosophical abstractions called gods by the 'Olympian', Egyptian and Babylonian priests. Nor could it mean the food that gave one a view of the gods. In pre-Olympian days it was the sacred kings and queens who were the gods: *vide* my remarks on Ceyx in *Greek Myths* (vol. 1, pp. 164 and 165 quoting Tzetzes) and on Salmoneus (vol. 1, p. 222). Mushroom eating would thus be a royal *tabu*; connected particularly with smith-gods? From what is known about Pythagoras, who was a Hellad by race and was initiated into Helladic and Cretan mysteries; and of his successor Empedocles, both of whom were regarded as gods; it may well be that the secret of his peculiar knowledge of divine matters was the *mushroom*. The Olympian authorities forcibly suppressed the Pythagorean brotherhood.

Wasson's reply to this letter has gone astray, but he was very enthusiastic about Graves's line of thought and wrote several times encouraging him to pursue it.

Graves was now busy selecting ballads for the Heinemann anthology, as he wrote to Reeves:

8 November 1955   Palma

Dearest James:

I have been making a selection of ballads from *Child*[65] and elsewhere; and on comparing it with my Benn book of 1927, find that my taste hasn't changed a lot. Now, that book has been out of print for 25 years, and Benn is down the drain (isn't it); so is there any reason for avoiding my former choices? This doesn't mean that I propose to palm you off with a reprint; I wouldn't do such a thing.

Now: please refresh my failing memory. You want how many pages of (I suppose) small 8vo? You want how much introduction? Glossary in margin, I take it? Notes to each ballad.

I am finishing *Suetonius*: the last go-over of the last part. Also will soon help Beryl with her translation of a bull-fighting novel. No other work of haste and I am refusing commissions for reviews, etc., for a while.

E. V. Rieu likes my *Lucan* but complains that I run Lucan down in the Introduction. Haven't I a right to, after months of sharing a shaving-brush and razor with the yellow bastard?

The *Sunday Times* thing about me appeared in the end. Quite decent, as these things go.

Crowning Privilege has made a lot of people cross. Even Martin had his little yap.

We are still not rich, but still have golden hopes, which cost nothing except incidental postage.

Terry Hards[66] sent me some real poems.

We are still bathing. Did I tell you that Cecil Day-Lewis is taking action over Norman's poems?

Much love to you all   Robert

14 November 1955   Palma

Dearest James:

Thanks.

Cecil Day-Lewis got a promise from Alan to send poems and introduction; then silence; but writes to me that he will get them from him or die in the attempt!

No, I will write a splendidly new introduction to the *Ballads* – thanks for the exact instructions. Old E. V. Rieu wrote to complain that I attacked *Lucan* in my preface to the translation –

haven't I the right to do so? Lucan stinks; but it was a new stink and has infected the world since. The ballads don't stink.

. . . .

A verse from a wistful poem of mine written 1916, suppressed 1917, has been used to caption a luscious nude in the pornographic New York *Modern Man*. This provoked a poem from me called 'The Naked and the Nude' which I hope will soon be published somewhere. Quotes:

And naked shines the Goddess when
She mounts her lion among men.

Love and thanks   Robert

According to Graves and Podro, Jesus survived the crucifixion, after having realized (on the cross) that he was not the Messiah, nor was the end of the world imminent and that by trying to 'force the hour', i.e. by trying to fulfil all the Biblical and Apocryphal prophecies made about the Messiah, he had led the disciples into sin; Graves and Podro suggested he admitted his error after being taken down from the cross and soon afterwards disappeared across the border to Damascus; they claimed he travelled widely in the East and lived to an old age, and was buried in Srinagar, Kashmir, by his disciple Thomas Didymus, not later than AD 72. At the end of 1955 Graves and Podro were assembling all the known historical evidence of Jesus's life after the crucifixion for a sequel to *The Nazarene Gospel Restored*, though they offered this book, called *Jesus in Rome*, only as 'historical conjecture'.

At the same time, Princeton University offered Graves a considerable sum of money to lecture, and it was suggested to him that he stand in the coming elections for the Professorship of Poetry at Oxford. He turned down the Princeton offer (see page 153) and after considering the Oxford job, which he would have preferred, he decided against it because it would have been hopelessly uneconomical (as it was, he became Professor of Poetry in 1961, and estimated his loss at roughly £150 a lecture).

In January he finished his edition of the *Ballads* and sent it off to James Reeves.

16 February 1956   Palma

Dearest James:

So glad you like the book of Ballads ... [*margin note*: the test is Gareth and Stella.][67] I don't think I ever called 'Kubla Khan' sexual, but in a long forgotten book *Poetic Unreason* (since suppressed) I believe I suggested that the woman wailing for her demon lover wasn't there just for fun, and that the mysterious stream may have been associated in Coleridge's mind with the approaching birth of his son ... The poem is certainly very lush.

Professorship at Oxford turns out to be worth only £300, not £1500 as I had been told – what a lot of fuss about 300 quid!

Just finished my collaboration with Joshua about the quite decent evidence for Jesus's post-Resurrection life in the flesh – Damascus 36 AD – Rome 47 AD – stated by Paul to be alive in AD 60 – by St Ignatius to be alive and in the Flesh after AD 70 – early evidence in Indian books for his burial at Srinagar in Kashmir close to Tuxua where St Thomas preached – and Thomas is pretty good well historical [*sic*]. Date of death uncertain, but perhaps before 72 AD, since that was the traditional date of Thomas's martyrdom at Chola in India; and Thomas is said to have buried him. It's called *At the Pincian Gate* from a dramatic scene in which he was reported there among the beggars.

We had 16 degrees of frost and Majorcan agriculture has had a body blow.

Love   Robert

On Saturday a Frenchman went ski-ing at Deyá, to the amazement of the locals.

Graves's friend, Ricardo Sicre, was helping Graves with his finances at this time, but as Sicre wrote to Gordon Wasson (23 August 1955), 'The help needed is little as Robert is dead broke.' In the same letter he asked Wasson if he knew anyone in the 'main Foundations' ('Guggenheim, Rockefeller, Whitney, Ford'), or particularly in Princeton's Institute of Advanced Studies, who might help arrange a grant for Graves, who, now in his sixty-first year, was still struggling financially because of school fees, employing a secretary, maintaining two houses and assisting his elder children (from his marriage to Nancy Nicholson). Sicre, however, knew Graves well enough to know that he himself would do nothing about getting a grant:

'Robert, whom to ask help is not his trade, will do nothing. He is not even worried.' Graves heard of the 'plot' and wrote to Wasson:

24 February 1956   Palma

Dear Gordon:

If George Merrill (who has been ill) can't put you up at Easter come to Deyá! Ricardo and Betty Sicre and their family will be there at Easter, in our guest house (Ricardo, I hear, is still pretty sick, despite his overhaul in USA). We'd put you up, somehow; and I'm longing to work at the infra-red pictures.[68] It would be splendid to see you again.

I hear you have been plotting with Ricardo to get me some sort of grant, which is very good of you. That sort of thing never comes off for me, and, indeed, why should it? I'm not in the ball game. Princeton Univ. wanted me to give six weekly lectures this Fall for $5000, but it would have meant being away from home for four months (not six weeks, as I thought at first) and I haven't been away for more than a week since 1939! ('I'd rather sweep the crossing' as people used to say.) This decision doesn't please Ricardo, who thought it would help with the other matter. But I know myself well enough not to do what goes against my conditioning; so I'll have to write a best-seller or something. Nobody gets grants without strings; and I haven't had a string to my name since I left the Army in 1918. I think Ricardo takes my financial predicament more to heart than I do myself; I make quite a lot but he sees me getting older and acquiring more responsibilities as the children need to be educated, and feels bad. He's a nice guy; so are you!

Yours ever   Robert

Best wishes to Tina.

To Derek Savage

3 March 1956   Palma

Dear Derek:

It's always a pleasure to see your handwriting on an envelope, even if I read inside that you've been having a hard and unhappy time. But somehow you survive; and it's nice to have you as a name to quote when people say that there are no honest critics who are good, or good who are honest.

Yes: *Crowning Privilege* was criticism only in matrix (a crystalline rock of personal belief and prejudice), at least the lectures were. The written pieces came closer to criticism.

(O dear, seven books published last year; five new books already finished in 1956 – two long *Penguin* Classics;* a book of satiric short stories called *¡Catacrok!*; a book (with Joshua Podro) about recorded appearances of Jesus in the flesh, after the Resurrection, from AD 30 to 70 AD – glad I don't mean visions, but solid appearances – Christian, Jewish, pagan, Latin, Moslem and Sanscrit documents quoted – not conclusive, but suggestive; a critical edition of *English Ballads* for schools; another book *Winter in Majorca* already out. Three more books projected: one nearly done; one half done. Too many. I also have written some short poems.)

So pleased you have a room of your own. I once had an attic – it was wonderful for poems, and smelt of apples.

Siegfried: yes, too much money. But he didn't settle as a landed proprietor for some time after the War – lived in a Westminster flat and played the piano, also godfather to destitute young actors. He was never really a rebel against society, only against British military stupidity, and joined the *Daily Herald* merely because the Socialists had been anti-War; and for no other reason. True he never really fitted into county Society because of being a Sassoon, a name greatly scorned in good King Edward's day, and more when he died. But he wanted to. I met him accidentally the other day, and he was very glad to greet me; but slipped away into furtive retreat. Besides his homosexual soul-scar, he has an Enoch Arden complex – or so he told me once – and a lot of self-protective dishonesty. He never read Marx or preached Socialism in my hearing.

Herbert Read: another mess. I have always avoided him. And carries Jung in a carpet bag, as the Scots are said to have carried the Holy Ghost, in the Civil Wars, to London.

Beryl and ourselves all well. Tomás, now 3, is terrific; Lucia is beautiful and thoughtful and amusing and recently spent ten days with her big sister Jenny at Rome. No teen-agers here – the step is cut out somehow. Girls; and women.

Love to all   Robert

* *Suetonius* and *Lucan*

154

The Wassons visited the Indian country of Mexico every summer after their first trip in 1953, to study the sacred mushroom rites there. In 1956 they took with them Professor Roger Heim, the celebrated French mycologist (then director of the Laboratoire de Cryptogamie of the Musée National d'Histoire Naturelle), who identified for the first time seven kinds of mushroom used for divination, four of them previously unknown to science.

20 September 1956   Deyá

Dear Gordon:

So glad you're safe back – I had a sense of more than usual drama among those mountains. Poor Maria Sabina's[69] son! That ecstatic face of his (in your transparencies) and her face of maternal love are unforgettable . . . Congratulations on the scientific successes!

You say nothing about your next 'swing' and whether it will bring you here. The first rains have fallen and soon *esclatasangs*[70] will be in the market to remind us of you. When you do come I'd like to ask you about the hallucinatory dreams – whether Heim (for instance) saw only unmodern scenes (as you and Tina and your daughter did) or whether he saw Boulevards, taxis and laboratories.

Ricardo Sicre has been here; and bought a cottage at Deyá, which is nice.

There's a chance of my *Arabian Night*'s film being made in US with Fernandel in the leading part; but I am tired of all these illusive golden dreams, and it's easiest to work hard with my steel pen (not a fountain pen, like my son's; and my father used a quill) on simple books. Today I send off my historical crime novel *They Hanged My Saintly Billy* – about Dr Palmer the poisoner (1856). That should see us through the next few months. Peggy Glanville Hicks[71] the composer is here: making my *Homer's Daughter* into an opera.

I'll give your message to George and Miss Niven. Best wishes to Tina.

Yours ever   Robert

They Hanged My Saintly Billy was Graves's twelfth, and last, historical novel and, as with all the others, he was trying to correct in it

what he saw as a historical injustice; he didn't believe that Palmer
had committed the fourteen murders he was hanged for and therefore attempted to clear his name, and incidentally rescue him from
the Chamber of Horrors at Madame Tussaud's wax exhibition –
but in that he was unsuccessful. He was, however, pleased with his
luck in getting 'a subject on which I can use my detective capacity
and in which all the seven deadly sins parade so splendidly. It will
be a "Book of the" with any luck' (to James Reeves, 14 August
1956).

5 November 1956   Palma

Dearest James:

I do hope that your awful sister Ethyl [*sic*] delivered the book
in the end. I have been giving the children poems to learn from
the proof, and Lucia points out a misprint of *they* for *thy* in the
'Lyke-Wake Dirge', first stanza.

This is to thank you for *The Critical Sense*[72] and your kind words
about my poems in them [*sic*]. I love your castigation of 'The
Solitary Reaper'; but in 'Good King Wenceslas' – perhaps the poor
man couldn't get through the fence and hadn't the right to collect
wood from a Royal Forest. But that, I agree, should have been
clearly said: 'Your forest fence' would have done it nicely.

And Byron's telling the Ocean to 'roll on' was as ridiculous,
surely, as Cnut's telling the tide at Westminster not to – which
you overlooked in your finer analysis of his nonsense. Or was it
too obvious?

I am going (*Critical Sense* in hand) to lecture for a week in USA
next Feb. A woman's college[73] will pay me $1400 for a single
lecture, and $600 is the return fare, and I expect to pick up two
or three more lectures and so pay for the car we need when we
have to give up the present one.

I do think your book is a useful one for sixth forms – teaches
boys and girls the necessary disrespect, and has no nonsense in it
at all.

Am revising *Goodbye to All That* – for publication in
Doubleday's Anchor Books – very badly written, but a good story
when the nonsense is cut out and some of the things restored that
I had to cut out in 1929. Have finished today.

Thank goodness, Doubleday like my *They Hanged My Saintly*

Billy book without any 'Buts'. I am now in a holiday mood, no more proofs expected for a few months and all my contracts completed. Shall write a few reviews and see if any poems are about; and then think up those lectures for USA.

I wonder if you feel as shocked by Eden as we do?[74] Or does it look different in England?

Much love to you all   Robert

You must come to Deyá somehow next year.

Graves told Wasson of his intended trip to America and Wasson invited Graves to stay with him and his wife in their Manhattan apartment, and promised to meet Graves at the airport.

6 December 1956   Palma

Dear Gordon:

How nice to be welcomed!

Actually (as they say in England, on the least provocation) I shall be staying with Alastair Reid,[75] the poet (whom for some reason or other you never met when you were here) and who is arranging the lecture tour for me (with the help of Ken McCormick of Doubledays) and will act as my bodyguard and protector, and come with me to Washington and so on. But I hope to see a lot of you, and if for any reason Alastair can't get the flat he has been promised in February – somewhere warm and central – I shall certainly accept your invitation, and thank you very much. Alastair is a Scot, ex-Naval Lieutenant, for two years reserve Back for the Scottish International Rugby team, is an expert writer of librettos for opera, and like you was the son of a poor minister and brought up the hard way. He commutes between here and New York.

You and he happen to be my only real friends in New York – I mean, to whom I can say anything I like without fear of not being understood – so I hope you'll like him. I'm so glad you'll be about when I come.

Yours ever   Robert

The most exciting result of the correspondence with Wasson was Graves's theory on the nature of Ambrosia, the food of the Gods and immortals in Greek mythology. The following letter was written when the idea first struck him (in bed with a cold – which was when he got many of his ideas); he later developed the theory and wrote it up in one of his best essays, 'Food for Centaurs' (1960).

22 December
Winter Solstice 1956   Palma

Dear Gordon

Reference my letter of yesterday –

About Ambrosia = ἀμβροσια (ἐδωδη) withheld from mortals because it conveyed immortality (*Odyssey* v, 93). It has been identified with the sanscrit *a-mrîta* (elixir of) immortality – the *a* being privative, and the *mrîta* meaning death. But αναβροσια means 'what is eaten up there' or 'food which grows up there'.

Now, Gordon, by this time you know how my mind works; so be patient! The Celtic druids had an early alphabet which they were not allowed to write down (according to J. Caesar), and the Irish *ollamhs* used it (or another like it) by mentioning objects which began with the letter needed, though usually these were given a riddling disguise, i.e. one would not say 'oak', one would say 'royal gate'. All the *oghams* – 150 different kinds – referring to trees, animals, castles, plants, birds, etc., were learned and used by the poetic-initiates. Now, if the nature of ambrosia was the prime mystery in Greece, and it could be communicated to the ἐποπται[76] only in silence, the natural means of doing this would be by food-ogham. And my intuition tells me that what all but the real ἐποπται of the mysteries got was a *symbolical* ambrosia – in the form of a food-*ogham* ambrosia. Unfortunately I haven't got the Classical references, but I know that ambrosia in common Greek religious rites was a sort of sweet mess containing honey, water, fruit, oil, cheese and barley meal.

In those early days there was no ἠ in the alphabet – 'H' was an aspirate – only an ε.

So what about | M | ΕΛΙ
| Y | ΔΩΡ
| K | ΑΡΠΟΣ
| E | ΛΑΙΟΝ
| T | ΥΡΟΣ
| A | ΛΦΙΤΟΝ

In answer to the question 'What do the gods eat?' = τον μυκητα[77]???

I am in bed with a cold and this problem is haunting me. I wonder whether the mouse-feasts which the Israelites were forbidden to partake of *were* really mouse feasts – whether the MY stem common to mice and mushrooms was not the cause of a disguised reference to mushroom feasts. Hence perhaps the mice and the ermrods?

Now, here's another thing. The Greek σκῖρος which meant a 'hardened tumour' (i.e. an ermrod) *and* a white parasol (mushroom shaped – see the Parthenon frieze) gave its name to the month Scirophorion (the end of the Attic year late June early July) which was presumably when in ancient days the sacred king was killed and became immortal – being given ambrosia first. The festival was simply called Τα Σκιρα (mushrooms or parasols) or Σκιροφορια (parasol carrying).

Yours ever

– Robert –

On 3 February Graves left for his first lecture tour in the USA and was not looking forward to it, as he wrote to Martin Seymour-Smith, who was now back in England and who wrote saying he would like to review Graves's next book.

2 February 1957   Palma

Dearest Martin:

I wrote to Frank for news of Jan, and then got your reassuring letter . . . Nice poem of yours in the *TLS*. (Another nice one by James in *New Statesman*.) Why am I writing so small? Probably because at 7 a.m. tomorrow I fly to the States, and am not feeling particularly extrovert at the prospect. But the money's all right, if I can stick it out for a fortnight.

The book I've Englished* is only unofficially so; so better leave it. You can write what you like about *They Hanged My Saintly Billy* when it appears; or about *Jesus in Rome*, and this comes thanking you in anticipation. The first was great fun to write. The second is a mighty odd book.

I have written a bi-millenary piece for the *New York Times* about the *Ides of March*. Get Jan to do likewise, for some paper. Nice subject?

159

Yes, I watched the 'Pope' dog-fight in the papers. But why grudge Davie Pope if he likes Pope? As they say pacifically in pubs: if everyone thought the same what a dull world it would be (even for admirers of Pope).

Look forward to *Robin Hood* . . . Egyptologists tell me that the official Pharaonic records give absolutely *no* picture of the popular cults in Egypt, which appear in literature 6000 years after they are known to have been practised. A sort of parallel to English Medieval records? And nobody will ever admit here (officially) that there's been a strong witch cult in Majorca ever since Jaime's time.[78]

Poor Krebs died: cirrhosis and flu. We miss him; he had not long had a third daughter.

Love to you both   Robert

* Delayed, anyhow.

On his return from America Graves wrote to the Gayes in Deyá:

18 February 1957   Palma

Dearest Karl *juntamente* Rene y Diana:

Safe back. Toscanini's[79] coffin was aboard the plane serving as a buffet for the PAA luncheon trays.

An almost frighteningly successful tour. May have to go again next Feb.

– Saw and did and got everything.

– See you Sunday if not sooner.

– Meanwhile: – enclosed gifts as per list. Diana's bathing dress was the most difficult to get and also cost most, but I wasn't going to be beaten; and so now she'll be the grandest tiger in the jungle.

– Lots of people sent lots of love I forget whom. –

– This morning a man tried to commit suicide on our staircase (the owner of the nearest *colmado*[80]). I broke his fall the second time he tried; Juan's bike did so the first time; the third he was held by Beryl and Salud. ¡But the blood! and Juan's poor bike!; Christ![81]

Love   Robert

They were turning away audiences at the end of my tour. The thing is: one can let oneself go in USA not in England. Details on Sunday.

Graves has admired only four contemporary American poets: Laura Riding, E. E. Cummings, Robert Frost and John Crowe Ransom. He wrote introductions to the British editions of Cummings's *The Enormous Room* (1922), Frost's *In the Clearing* (1962), and the first volume of Ransom's poetry to appear in England (its publication was arranged by Graves), *Grace After Meat* (1924). Ransom, one of the Fugitive group of poets, in turn greatly admired Graves's work (it was he who had first introduced Graves to Laura Riding – see *In Broken Images*, p. 162) and they maintained an occasional correspondence until Ransom's death in 1974. In 1971 Ransom wrote to Graves, 'I still read you in the letters I've saved . . .', but despite an extensive search, only one of Graves's letters to him, the following, has been found.

20 February 1956   Robert Graves
                                                       Palma

Dear John:

Haven't written to you for years but think often of you, and find your name a convenient one to quote when asked 'Who are the real poets?' They are getting fewer and fewer, so please survive!

I can't remember who of the many people it was I met in America this month who knew you; but anyhow the question of your early suppressed poems came up.

I had been looking at *Grace After Meat* and *Poems About God* the other day and comparing them with your *Collected Poems* and wondering why on earth you had cut out so much that still stands up strong and true and well-written. And (whoever it was) X said that you were embarrassed by them, and that maybe if I wrote to you, I could persuade you to put them in circulation again. Is there any hope of that?

I was very much disappointed that I missed you; you had just lectured and gone from somewhere where I lectured – Yale, wasn't it? – my mind is a blur! I should have written to you before I came over. I missed Frost too; but at least saw Cummings.

Yours ever   – Robert –

'X', Ransom replied, was probably Robert Lowell (whose poetry Graves did not like). Ransom was delighted to hear from Graves, but, as to the poems, wrote:

161

The great trouble with those poems which I omitted from the 'canon', they were the ones which seemed muddled and ambiguous in style; they were the 'literary' ones. I didn't like them, and don't. But we'll talk that over some time.

However, they never met again.

To Selwyn Jepson

22 February 1957

Dearest Selwyn:

Just to announce my return full of glory and swag from America, where I had a *succès fou*, probably because I didn't take my tour very seriously so never got stage fright, and avoided cocktails, and had my friend Alastair Reid to do all the phoning and ticket-buying and note-taking for me. I got listed as a cultural missionary and thus brought back all the swag income-tax free. Doubledays couldn't have been more helpful (or grateful) so general euphoria is spreading. I cleared off all my book-writing commitments before flying over; so have now got all sorts of rich commissions, such as reviews for *New Yorker* and work for *Atlantic* and *NY Sunday Times*. Am getting an option on writing a stage version of *Mrs Milton*, and took the *I, Claudius* film negotiations one stage further. I do wish I could get you to gather all the loose threads of this complicated affair together; it's rather like a crime novel now. Jenny knows the whole story and is lending advice. Briefly (between you and me) the main obstacle is Vincent Korda[82] who's a sweet, sentimental, lazy slob and from whom somehow I've got to recover the rights in the film, for secret sale to United Artists, without his knowing that United Artists are interested. He will do absolutely nothing himself, and we have Anna Magnani and Alec Guinness, both champing their bits to get their contracts signed for 1958. I *should* hear from United Artists in a few days' time (Max Youngstien [*sic*] is my contact) and then will have to take action.

Anyhow, see you in April if not sooner and much love to Tania. A wonderful Italian called Gialatti of Mount Holyoke showed me his collection of Dante first editions, and regretted he knew nobody in London who sold Italian rarities. So I said: '10 Orme

162

Square' just like that. Am sending you a *Suetonius* for your shelf.
(Nice book.)

Always   Robert

To James Reeves

12 March 1957   Palma

Dearest James:

Ashamed though I be to ask: could you send us some more QR?
We have got a lot of compost material together – Karl has suddenly
rolled up his sleeves and started scouring the ditches for green stuff
– and want to have a good vegetable garden this year.

I find myself writing an average of 60 letters a week, only very
few of which are a pleasure (as when I write to you, or Sally, or
Jenny) and doing an increasing amount of chores for publishers and
publicists generally in order to support growing family. It's very
difficult to know just at what point I should say: 'Stop before you
become a hack!' Of course if a poem or any sudden new discovery
about anything seizes me, I throw everything overboard which a
real hack doesn't. But do these jobs lessen the occurrence of poems
and sudden new discoveries? And if they do, does it matter? There
are never any more poems than is fated, and most poets stop at
about 27. (You and I have altogether exceeded our time.)

Anyhow we love you both dearly   – Robert –

On 13 April Graves received the Wassons' two-volume book *Mushrooms, Russia and History*, in which they give him full credit for
his part in their discoveries of the exact circumstances of Claudius's
death (the original subject of their correspondence), of the sacred
mushroom cult in Mexico, of the role of narcotic mushrooms in
ancient history and the thesis that mycophobia, the irrational fear
of mushrooms felt by a great part of mankind, is the survival of an
ancestral religious awe or taboo.

Graves was now reaching towards another 'discovery'. The
Wassons emphasized in their book the important link between light-
ning and mushrooms, the widespread ancient belief that lightning
engenders mushrooms and the fact that in Oaxaca the Mushroom
God is also the Lightning God (Tlalóc). Graves then thought of
Dionysus – born from a flash of lightning that impregnated the

163

Underworld goddess Semele – and wondered if he had once also
been the Mushroom God. Perhaps, Graves thought, fly amanite was
the 'secret-agent' which sent his Maenads raging, and his festival,
which took place during the mushroom season and which was called
'the Ambrosia', perhaps originally was a mushroom orgy.

No date   DEYA MALLORCA
[*April 1957*]   until April 24th. Then
                                          108 Clifton Hill London
                                             NW8 until May 20th.
                                                Then back here

Dear Tina and Gordon

1000,000 thanks for the book and for doing me the honour of
so many credits in the Index. It is a *wonderful* book.

You will be utterly overwhelmed with correspondence for the
next few months; so don't answer this. But I have a new lead.
You remember that Dionysus was the god who had 'Ambrosia'
festivals. Well: aren't we fools not to remember that he was the
son of Heaven, πυριγενης (1), born from lightning (1); that the
Titans ate him ceremonially (2); that his intoxication made the
devotees tear animals and people (including Orpheus and Pentheus)
in pieces when berserk (3); and I have already expressed the view
some years ago that DIO<u>NYSOS</u> means the <u>lame</u> God (see Dict.),
not the God of Nysa – LE BOT in fact. That at Argos whose
emblem was a toad, he was called Dionysus the Mystic (4), and
that he was taught mysteries by one MYSTIS himself (5)? That he
had as great a share in Delphi as Apollo (6). That his emblems
were the serpent and the ram (Robin Goodfellow).

Dionysus is at any rate Mycenaean – he is mentioned in Linear
Script B – not late.

But I think that the Bacchic *wine* is a concomitant of the fly-
amanite (as the Curandera used *aquadiente*) not the original
maddening agent; and a disguise or *placebo*?

I wonder whether the taboo on *red* food was put on it to protect
the fly-amanite?

I wonder whether the ceremonial bread and wine (which is pre-
Christian – Essene – see *Dead Sea Scrolls*) was a *placebo* for the
fly-amanite?

I go on wondering about lots of things.

Yours ever affectionately   Robert

(Check)
1/ Strabo xxii, p. 628 (Casaubon). Apollodorus iii, 4.3
2/ Apoll. iii, 5.2; Pausanius viii, 37.3; Diodorus iii, 62
3/ Theocritus xxvi (Idyll); Euripides *Bachal* 1142; Ovid *Metamorphoses* iii, 714
4/ Paus. viii, 54.4
5/ Nonnus *Dionysiaca* xiii, 140
6/ Euripides *Bacchal* [sic] 300.

On 27 April Robert, Beryl and the children drove in their Land Rover to London for what was now their annual visit to see friends, buy books, and so on. There Graves received Wasson's reply, telling him that his wife, Valentina, had cancer.

9 May 1957   108 Clifton Hill
                                                              London NW8

Dear Gordon:
   Beryl and I are appalled by your news, the only mitigation of which is the possibility of a cure – maybe the mushrooms would be able to give you a definite answer? – or do you prefer not to ask the question? Tina is a very strong character and the blow is probably heavier for you and Masha than it is for her; I think when there is real love in a family that is always so. We feel *dreadful* about it.
   I don't expect you to answer any letters I write; but I do expect you to file them in the mushroom-file against the day when we can get these questions sorted out. I think that fly-amanite is the key that fits a number of locks. The point is: that there is a missing element in the whole concept of Greek religion has always been apparent – a practical explanation in terms of a drug or some other direct way of inspiration.
   Thanks for *Saturday Review*.
   Very busy time here, with four children to keep out of mischief and Juan in hospital with a slight operation for the removal of a squint.
   Much love to Tina and Masha.
   Yours ever   Robert

After three weeks in London the Graveses returned to Mallorca via the Silver City Channel Bridge plane for cars. From the airport Graves sent James Reeves a postcard.

21 May 1957   Lydd Airport

Dearest James and Mary:

Just off by Silver City aeroplane with Landrover. It seems odd for Landrover to be airborne. When Robert Frost arrived yesterday he asked me to be the first to see him (after the Embassy folk); apparently attributes his English fame to me! He is exactly as I expected him: wonderful man. When asked what English poets were about, I said Norman Cameron had just died, but you were still about . . . Dear James: please send him 1) Norman's poems 2) the Ballad Book (he says English and American poetry is founded squarely on the ballads and Mother Goose!) 3) James Reeves's poems putting in a note that I recommend 'The Waterfall' and the poem about waking in the morning, and 'The Haystack' and the one about 'more than morning quiet', and 'Greenhallows' to him. Address Connaught Hotel, W1. Charge them all to my a/c. If possible see him . . . It was lovely seeing you again. Looking forward.

Love   Robert

While in London Graves had also seen Basil Liddell Hart.

3 June 1957   Palma

Dear Basil:

It was great fun meeting you and Kathleen again. Many thanks for the cuttings of your recent thoughts about warfare. I find it so difficult to think in terms of long range missiles, now that everything is so secret and the newspapers either do not know the truth or cannot print it, that I had simply stopped thinking about the problem of war, and 'cultivated my garden' assiduously. Perhaps this is wisest.

I am appalled by the gradual creeping *indirect* censorship of all individual thought, on the subject of religion especially, and consider myself very lucky to have been able to build up a faithful reading public and so escape the fetters that bind the non-famous writer. The automatization of writers, in the 'Free World' as well

166

as the Communist World, is a natural trend of economics; few are stubborn enough to resist it.

Yours ever

– Robert –

PART THREE

1957–1963

On 21 June 1957 the Graveses left Palma and moved back to Deyá (though they continued renting the flat until 1982) as William was now at Oundle School in England, and Lucia and Juan were to go to the International School in Geneva.

Apart from *The Hebrew Myths* (1964; with Raphael Patai) Graves did not write any other long prose book from now on; he concentrated instead on lectures, essays, articles, short stories, translations and, as always, poems. He also continued to have show-business 'golden dreams' as he called them, and wasted much time and energy over the next few years working on various ill-fated scripts for stage and screen, and negotiations with producers and agents.

In 1957 his greatest hope was for a film of *I, Claudius*; in 1937 the Korda brothers (who still owned the rights in 1957) had begun filming it, with Charles Laughton as Claudius, but after a series of disasters this was abandoned (see *In Broken Images*, pp. 275 ff.). Now Alec Guinness had expressed an eagerness to play Claudius and, at his suggestion, Graves prepared a film script with Brigid Boland, another friend of Guinness's, to present to the American film company United Artists; Graves and Boland finished the script and, with the help of Will Price, prepared a formal proposal which was, however, turned down.

In December Graves made preparations for a trip to Rome, to spend Christmas with Jenny and Brigid Boland who both had flats there, as well as for an extended trip in the new year to Yugoslavia (where he had unexportable royalty money), Austria and Switzerland; a trip which was to be followed, in February, by another lecture tour in the USA.

171

To James Reeves

4 December 1957   Deyá

Dearest James

Glad you got the record[1] safe. I read the poems too fast, but I think the pace has been speeded up also and my voice made higher.

I am speaking to the Washington ICA in February – in fact, they are my sponsors in USA and my! they *have* arranged a big tour for me. (But if Alastair strings along it should be all right.) So I feel well-disposed to the ICA wherever it grows; and thank you for your tribute to me, in anticipation.

Today I have just finished a poem[2] about walking around a mountain, which I think is so-called typical Graves, and serious; after four or five short jokeish ones. I was wondering whether I had reached my menopause. 'Every poet has good cause, To fear the dreaded menopause . . .' continue, please! Not that it matters stopping, but it is very enjoyable to work on a poem and get it right . . . ¿A?

So now I don't mind doing a light story, as pleadingly asked, for *New Yorker*. The subject will be old Gelat and the Lady Carnarvon divorce case.[3] But I'll have to trick a bit, because the co-respondent of her husband's ex-wife is still alive.

I don't want to work for OUP because they are difficult people, and Cassell now publishes all I offer. The next thing is a book of my new poems and essays, etc.,[4] since *Crowning Privilege* . . . We are now definitely spending Christmas at Rome with Jenny – all of us – and then going on to Jugoslavia, unless we can get *dinars* exchanged for Austrian *schillings* (at whatever rate) and ski in the Austrian Alps instead.

No film news; but I never sniff at options when paid for, and these I have got. Tomás is learning to read very fast. Ygrec's pups are in the slipper-training stage.

I have been doing reviews for *New Republic* and *Sunday Times* (see next issue on *Mont Blanc*) and have now finished four 8000 word talks for USA. It is very wet and wet and wet; how good your 'Waterfall' poem is on the subject!

Love to all   Robert

New York Times have asked me to review South African Campbell's *Collected Poems*; he's dead, so why not?

Roy Campbell (1901–57) was another writer who had spent many years in Spain. On the way back from Spain at the outbreak of civil war in 1936 (Campbell in fact returned for the war and fought on the side of Franco) Graves and Riding met him on the ferry crossing from France to England, and greatly disliked him. Campbell was well known for his translations of Lorca and for his love for bull-fighting (he was for a time a professional lance and bullfighter in Provence). Graves described his review of Campbell's poems in his next letter to James Reeves:

About Campbell's poems: have sent off the *NY Times* review. It was very dry, and I emphasized his boast of being a better poet than Lorca; and hinted that he was as phoney as Hemingway . . .

To Karl Gay, from Rome

23 December 1957

Dearest Karl and Rene: If I lived here I should never get any work done at all, but it is all very civilized and agreeable. We are in the centre of the Ruins beautifully isolated from crowds and trams and with central heating and all complete. We arrived to the noise of cameras whirring and were met by the whole family and a lot of newsmen, and a PAA functionary who whisked us through. We went up the Appian Way past all the tombs (another camera pose here) and have been eating spaghetti and drinking red wine ever since.

Shall be going to Jugland for 3 days with Beryl and Wm and then to *Lech* in Austria from July 5th to 12th (Geneva). Father Christmas has invaded Italy and climbed on a hackney carriage I had to take for want of taxis and insisted on being photographed . . . There's no time for work, Christmas is just on us. *Sunday Times* wants me to do '*Murder of Claudius*' in 2000–3000 words and I'll do that when I get back. Patrick likes the Viscountess story a lot and is giving her to the Embassy lawyer for a check over.

All very well here and Italy is treating me rather as America did, and as England never has and never will.

Tomás is being splendid and was the only child at the Press Club party to thank for his present adding 'Isn't this good luck!' which put him right up. Left my lighter in the plane – what the hell? – There are always matches.

Wish you were here. The Hills of Rome are very low, even the Capitoline one, and one could spit across Julius Caesar's forum with a good wind.

Anyhow much love to all and I hope all has been fine with you 4.

                                                                   – Robert –

Couldn't post this until today. Wonderful Christmas, too much to report – now off for a picnic in Veci. Everyone well. Attended Xmas tree with Ingrid and Roberto happily reunited. They could not come out because of 300 photographers outside like dogs waiting for a bitch on heat – and utterly hopeless – she sent out drinks and sandwiches at intervals but did not appear.

We got the old Pope's general blessing.

After returning from another successful lecture tour in America in March, Graves received a copy of *The Talking Skull*, James Reeves's latest volume of poems.

9 March 1958   Deyá

Dearest James:

What a good book *Talking Skull* is! I'd forgotten, or not realized, how many real poems it contains, and how just your self-epitaph in 'On a Poet'! The 'Celtic bombast' in my own blood applauds your moderation.

The thing to do really, now, is to get a *Collected Selected* book published in America; it may (unfortunately) be necessary for me to write an introduction – 'unfortunately' because you really need none, not that I wouldn't like the job. I don't think that Alastair and I would have any difficulty in forcing it on Little Brown where we have Sam Lawrence as ally.

Love, again,

                                                                   Robert

New compost heap cooking nicely. It's Sir Arthur Bliss. (We now call the heaps after visitors.) Recent ones have been Stephen Spender (rots quickly), Brendan Gill (very active), Gordon Wasson (grows the required fungi), Alston Anderson (black and rich).[5]

Graves was now translating Homer's *Iliad*, in 'the only sensible way', he wrote to Martin Seymour-Smith: 'as if it were an Irish epic, prose laced with lyrics.' (It was published as *The Anger of Achilles* by Doubleday, New York, 1959, with illustrations by Ronald Searle, and in 1965 was adapted for radio by Graves.)

To Alan Sillitoe, whose first novel, *Saturday Night and Sunday Morning*, had just been published.

17 October 1958

Dear Alan:

Saturday Night and Sunday Morning is terrific, we all agree. I knew you had it in you to write a good book but did not expect so good a one so soon.

I have written at once to Doubleday to grab it, unless someone else already has the offer. Doubleday are splendid people to deal with.

Thanks a lot.

Wm is at London University staying at 59 Harrington Gdns with Leslie Horvat.

I am translating the *Iliad* and doing a lot of smaller chores. A Deyá story is coming out in the *New Yorker*. It seems as if *Claudius* will really be filmed this year; at any rate I am being paid for the tail end of my rights in it, most of them sold in 1934. Alec Guinness will be Claudius.

Love to Ruth and yourself from us both

– Robert

To James Reeves, who had sent Graves a copy of *The Idiom of the People: English Traditional Verse*, which he had edited from the mss. of Cecil J. Sharp.

No date

Dearest James:

Thanks a lot for the Idiom Book which deserves a literary pension or something; it is great fun. (I still think you're being naughty about the 'Foggy Dew', but there, I won't bring it up unless someone asks me to review the book, and then only gently.) It really is a fine work and meets a need.

So glad you liked *Quixote*,[6] so do I like *Homer*. Am now ¼ of the way through the *Iliad* and Ronald Searle wants to illustrate my version.

You should get your American *World Writing*[7] check (*Sigue*) any minute now; they have your address and are counting the lines: at 50 cents a line.

'Borrowers' much appreciated.

Only Tomás is still here, and lovely weather reigns.

So sorry about *Talking Skull*, and even more sorry that they talk about me as a sort of mentor. If you had been born first it would have been put the other way about. And anyhow if you had by now published a collected volume, well selected, instead of only contributory ones . . . but that will come and then they'll heap your head with laurels, and we'll all eat a chicken dinner.

Busy writing Homer's lyrics for him at the rate of four or five a week – all the Homeric similes are simple country-themes like the ancient Irish verses in their epics, and go easily into simple stanzas, and are like currant buns in the prose loaf [*sic*].

QR is *Quick Return* and consists of herbs and honey mainly – invented by a crazy but brilliant English woman gardener. Long may she speed dandelions!

Much love to all

Robert

Graves later sent Reeves a list of those poems he thought good enough to include in a projected *Collected Poems of James Reeves*. He also reviewed Reeves's poems on the BBC Home Service.

12 November 1958

Dearest James:

So glad my broadcast helped. About 'Foggy Dew': it is my general principle that the more complicated story is always the earliest in a song or legend; and *a* 'Foggy Dew' being grouped with tunes bearing Gaelic names and others of obviously Irish location such as 'The Top of Cork Road' (which my dad used for *Father O'Flynn*[8]) suggests that it was not imported from England. Anyhow, 'makes a story'!

I have just written to *The Times* who published a note about the underwater discovery of Sir George Somers's flag ship *Sea Venture* between rocks off Bermuda (1609): without mentioning the 'Master, the Swabber, the Bosun and I', who cried 'We split, we split' in Act 1, Scene 1 of *The Tempest*.[9] That was the very ship; Shakespeare got it from Jourdain's book recently published. Isn't it exciting?

– I hope the *Don Quixote del Mar*[10] doesn't do the splits. Alastair wrote (entranced with his 'large canvas') from the Canaries, and expects to make Antigua around December 6th.

We had a fine time in Geneva with the children: staying with some friends called the Foggs: Americans, common clay but extremely warm and generous. We came back laden with new clothes and special Aga pots and pans; no trouble at the Customs, because Diana (who came too) was displaying the hula hula hoop hitherto unknown at Port Bou.

– Leavis[11] didn't attend my lectures either, so you are in good company. A detestable fellow.

I hope you didn't take my list of poems too much to heart; but it should at least be a guide as to ones you are doubtful about. Obviously ewe-lambs are ewe-lambs. I did the same job for Alun Lewis[12] before he died; and he said he was keeping some I had rejected – not because they were good but for sentimental reasons. A nice man he was.

Much love from and to — Robert

In January 1959, Graves visited Israel at the government's invitation, and enjoyed himself there immensely.

Before going he had been asked by Alexander Cohen, a Broadway producer, to write a popular musical based on the Solomon and Sheba story. Graves was becoming disillusioned with the 'golden dreams' of show business, but nevertheless he needed money and this time it did seem to him that something might actually come of it. To help him write the musical he brought his daughter Jenny over from Rome.

To James Reeves, who had sent Graves a copy of his edition of Coleridge's poems (Heinemann, 1959).

10 March 1959

Dearest James

Thanks a lot for the *Coleridge*. Alastair will be here [within] ten days to collect his. We got a fright last week when Ricardo thought that the plane that disappeared off Lisbon had Alastair and Mary aboard – but they don't fly until the 15th.

Jenny was here and we worked for a fortnight, ten hours a day, at the *Solomon and Sheba* musical, and sent it off three days ago, complete with twenty lyrics. I think it's all right. Tyrone Guthrie[13] comes here on the 17th to discuss its stage possibilities; he is directing. I get 4½% (less agents' fees, tax, etc.) of the weekly takings: if it only runs for three days, too bad. If for two years, much too good: I shall have to wear mink bed-socks.

Now writing a piece about Israel for *Holiday* and then for *Saturday Evening Post* about 'Intuitions' for an embarrassingly high fee.

Your Coleridge *Introduction* is damned good, and it is splendid to have 'Dejection' in the original and best form. 'Addition to Shelves.'

Damned cheek of that US reviewer of *Ballads*: doesn't even read the anti-anti-Semite note at the end.

We come over on the 20th – usual rush complicated by my having to spend a lot of time in conference with Alex H. Cohen the Broadway producer. His odd choice of me as the writer of the 'musical' was due to his being a devoted reader of my poems. (Who says poetry don't pay, eh?) And I have to record another long-playing record of poems.[14]

Much love to you all

Robert

19 March 1959

Dearest James:

Always nice to owe you a letter.

Expect you have had a call or ring from Alastair or Mary by now? Hope so.

– You'll be glad to hear that as a result of Jenny's coming here and working with me like a black, we got the first complete draft of the *Solomon and Sheba* musical off to poor anxious Alex Cohen who commissioned it from me (as a wild shot); and he cabled back 'Magnificent, bravo, bravo, bravo!' He said the same to

178

Tyrone Guthrie who is to direct it, and who turned up here the next day to read and discuss it. Same reactions, and a few useful emendations.

We come to London on the 20th not the 26th (sorry for my handwriting) for a fortnight. I have to meet Cohen and his partner – also his Money Bag named Twitchill – and be taken around the shows.

On Ap. 2nd Newington[15] (BBC TV) comes here with his gang, to interview and televise me – did I tell you? – in honour of my *Collected Poems 1959*. The programme will be shown on Ap. 29th when the book comes out (it is a Book Society Recommendation – for what *that's* worth).

As a result of writing so many Lyrics for *Homer*, and for Solomon, Sheba, and their gang, genuine poems are few – In fact only one for the last three or four months, but it's (I think) part of the canon, not an expendable.

Lucia comes tomorrow; Juan stays to ski in Austria and the snow lies thick all around Geneva, so when he goes up to 1400 metres he'll be all right . . .

– The Posada was lovely when we put the Guthries there. There's even a new box-spring mattress on the double-bed: at last! And the upper storey is tiled, in case you've forgotten.

– Antonia very pleased that you're coming. And everyone else too.

– Doing my 'Israel' piece for *Holiday* now. They accept my 'Minorca' one (1000 dollars for 5000 words) and want me to write at random for them too. I do think you should lecture in USA and make useful connexions there. If one stays in England the Americans don't believe one exists. And you aren't an introvert, and you *do* speak well, so . . .

Much love to all   Robert

James Reeves spotted a misprint in the poem 'The Thieves' (first published 1940) in Graves's *Collected Poems 1959* – '*meum-teum*' for '*meum-tuum*'. The poem reads:

Lovers in the act dispense
With such *meum-tuum* sense
As might warningly reveal
What they must not pick or steal . . .

179

16 April 1959

Dearest James:

Meum-teum is really extraordinary – How it could have passed so many scrutinies and proof-readings; and my own eye when I read it from the public platform and into the public microphone, really beats me, I must trace it to its source. Of course I always read it aloud as *meum-tuum*.

There are other similar cases such as Victoria's 'Godless Florin' which left out the DEI GRATIA in spite of scrutiny by all the Mint and Palace officials; and the Wicked Bible which printed 'Thou shalt commit adultery' in the XX Chapter of Exodus; and the *mumpsimus* for *sumpsimus* in the late medieval mass-book quoted by Henry VIII. But this does really stagger me!

We had a five day ordeal of BBC Television types televising me and the family and the scenery for 20 minutes worth of 'Monitor' programme on April 26th. I think they got some nice pictures, which I hope will whet your noble family's zeal for return here.

Just read a remarkably honest and revealing book about Yeats by Monk Gibbon,[16] which justifies all the nasty things I ever said about the man, especially as Gibbon hero-worshipped Yeats almost to the end. *The Masterpiece and the Man* (Rupert Hart Davis). For your *History of English Poetry* the best procedure is to condense Courthope's 6 volumes.[17] I have these here and could bring them if you cable me. Or perhaps you could work on them while here?

Love from us all

Robert

Graves now heard from Alex Cohen, who had modified his initial enthusiasm for the *Solomon and Sheba* script; his partner Ralph Alswang did not like it; neither did Lena Horne, the black singer who was to play Sheba, and Cohen had so far been unable to find a composer for the music. Graves explained the situation to Jepson.

28 May 1959

Dearest Selwyn.

What a good telegram! Yes, of course I agree with you in principle, and have told Cohen, Alswang and go [*sic*], through my agent, that I will do what I can to meet their wishes. But they tell me that they can't 'hook a big theatrical fish as composer' (which means, I think, that the lyrics will have to be scrapped because big theatrical fish expect the lyrics to be written to their music, not vice-versa) until I have rewritten the musical as they direct. This incidentally infringes the agreement, which says that the author shall submit the musical in a reasonable state by Ap. 15th; and they have agreed that it was a reasonable state by shelling out the money then to be paid. By the contract I am not required to rewrite until after the music has been submitted to the producer (in case there's any incompatibility). Now they expect me to rewrite (for nothing) according to Ralph Alswang's doctrinaire views of what a musical should be: Solomon's character must be seen developing, the wives should be given better parts, the mine scene should be scrapped, and the Finale of the First Act should be the Salt Banquet – which makes no sort of sense to me. Also Solomon and Sheba must haggle cleverly about copper [prices], after their Song of Solomon love-making – which to me would be in the worst of taste. They say that in the present draft 'we are kept waiting about until someone sings, like in Opera.' This is simply untrue, and the tone of the letter is so stupid and bloody that I cannot accept it.

The premiere has been put off until Fall 1960, and apparently they're ditching Guthrie. . . . Maybe they're backing out.

So I'm digging my heels in. As would Selwyn Jepson, unless I have mistaken that very reasonable but independent-minded character.

– I have sent Jenny the producer's letter, plus my answer, and asked for her comments. The great thing is to make up my mind, as I *have* done, that I don't mind risking my reputation on a play, but that I won't sacrifice my conscience. Alex Cohen is a sensible man, his partner Alswang, who is a scene designer and whom Alex told that this play was not his kettle of fish, is I think rocking the boat. . . . So I'll go through the motions and see what happens, meanwhile working at other jobs. I am keeping Tony Guthrie informed; he is, I think, solidly with me.

Love –   .Robert.

21 June 1959

Confidential, but of course I needn't really put this in – it's only that I'm such a loose lather myself!

Dearest Selwyn:

You asked to be kept posted. In reply to Cohen's very dictatorial letter, I said that he should come here during his European visit in mid July and rub his nose in the script with Jenny and me, and we'd see how much of his suggested rewriting was valid; but that he'd have to pay Jenny's air fare (I've paid two such fares already for her) and do some hard work instead of just talking; and a cable would oblige. No cable yet; but an offer from Robert Kahn of CBS who has heard (he says) that Cohen is abandoning the project – to find the funds and take it on!

I've cabled Willis Wing in New York to find out what this is worth and (since I haven't yet signed the contract or been paid any money) to be ready to switch unless Alex finds a composer at once and comes here as requested.

Someone in a NY university seems anxious to buy my mss. of poems, etc., for 30,000 dollars, because funds have been put at his disposal by a rich benefactress and I think this is a good idea – avoids estate duty when I die, and tax; and a University is as good a curator of this waste paper as anyone. Wants to have an R.G. Exhibition next May when the University celebrates some sort of centenary. I'll let you know when this is off the secret list.

Meanwhile I have written a story for the *New Yorker* called 'The Lost Chinese' about 8000 words, which I think is really very sad, funny, interesting, etc. But I may be wrong.

Much love and it's such a relief to feel you are behind me.

Love to Tania.   Robert

The New York university was the State University of New York at Buffalo, which had been given money and instructions by a Mrs Lacey to buy Graves's manuscripts. This made up for the financial disappointment caused by the collapse of the *Solomon and Sheba* project, the contract for which was never signed. Graves's further attempts to sell it to another producer were also unsuccessful.

On 2 September Graves went to London for a prostate operation at St Thomas's Hospital. Although the operation went well he experienced some dangerous post-operational haemorrhaging and pain (see his poem 'Surgical Ward: Men'), as he wrote to Alan Sillitoe whose collection of short stories, *The Loneliness of the Long Distance Runner*, had just been published.

[Postmarked 21 September 1959]   Edward Ward
                                              St Thomas' Hospital
                                                   London SE1

Dear Alan (*juntamente* Ruth)

Beryl brought me your letter when she came here three days ago
– I had an operation for prostate, which wasn't as simple as
expected, so she came to look after me. All's well now after a
fortnight here and I expect to be evacuated to above address[18] at
the end of this week, where I'll stay until well enough to go back.
By then Tomás will have joined us.

Tomorrow Beryl's going to Bumpuses to buy the *Long Distance
Runner* (decent review in *Observer* or *Sunday Times*, I forget which)
and another *Saturday Night* to give Sally Chilver, with whom we're
staying again.

It was a teenage summer with the record player going on the
whole time and Wm, Lucia and Tomás, each with a dozen friends,
using the house as a hotel. Juan at least sometimes brought back
fish he'd shot. We missed you at the party when we sent off the
globos.[19]

The only two yachts were Ricardo's which did indeed anchor in
the Cala and the *Flying Clipper* (with 31 Swedish Eagle Scouts
aboard, also Senator Benton and Mr Adlai Stevenson who came
calling at Canelluñ) which funked it.

Am not writing anything at the moment, but when out will do
a couple of talks for the USA in January. I had a bit of luck:
Buffalo University are paying 30,000 (!!) dollars for my poems
mss. from 1910–1959 (I have always kept them superstitiously.
Do the same: the price may go up as the century advances) and
having an R.G. exhibition in May . . .

– I expect I'll be able to drink again soon. Beer. I had an
enormous amount of blood transferred, 3½ times my original
liquid [content], and dear Alec Guinness has sent me four bottles
of hooch to alcoholize the new stuff.

Best of luck with the film. I'm *so* glad you're on the up road,
and am sure you'll never write below your best (except perhaps
when you have jaundice). When I'm well enough, will give my
friends a party and you'll be invited. Meanwhile, if you are in
town and like to come and see me, do! I'm a privileged patient
and have visitors not in visiting hours.

Love to you both   Robert

While in hospital Graves found himself at the centre of another controversy concerning T. E. Lawrence: Terence Rattigan's play *Ross* was soon to be staged (with Alec Guinness as Lawrence); Professor A. W. Lawrence, however, objected to the play on the grounds that it implied that his brother had been a homosexual, and in his efforts to have the play stopped he asked Graves to give his opinion and had him sent a copy of the text. At the same time David Lean visited Graves to consult him about a film he wanted to make (to be produced by Sam Spiegel) based on the life of Lawrence; Lean and Spiegel, who also visited St Thomas's Hospital, wanted the film rights of *Lawrence and the Arabs* and *T. E. Lawrence to his Biographer R.G.*, and also asked Graves to help in an advisory capacity, though the exact nature of his function, and the payment he was to receive for it, were both kept vague. All of this he explained to Karl Gay in Deyá.

13 October 1959
108 Clifton Hill
London NW8

Dearest Karl

Sitting up at a table to write for a change; I have my meals up now, but am glad to be back in bed [usually].

So sorry for all this trunk business, but since I've already warned the Buffalo people that you are sending the trunk 'collect', insurance and all, that's all right! I hope it's on its way by now. You must have suffered a lot of anxiety. Grateful sympathies.

Thanks a lot for cigarette papers and Obispo: via Bert.

Expect us home early in Nov. As I expect you know, Jota[20] seems pregnant, and Beryl wants to be there for accouchment and disposal of.

Tomás is fine.

Please order more coke – Juan Rasca knows where – but preferably in a fine weather patch. Half a ton or a ton, whatever. Please take Maria the best flowers money can buy, and give Juan our condolences on his worry; Beryl had a worse time than I did, really; because I knew the score and she didn't.

I am reading up a lot of books on Virgil sent me (*via* Jim Metcalf, who's had a terrific success with his Exhibition) by dear Kitty.

I forget if I told you – I forget everything – that Hugh Beaumont, the producer of Rattigan's play on Lawrence (featuring Alec Guinness), sent me the text, saying that Arnie (Prof. A. W.)

Lawrence would like my opinion on it. There was something fishy so I contacted Arnie (now returned from Africa, and living on his film earnings and royalties from *Revolt in the Desert*) and he came to see me. It appears that he thought the play couldn't be stopped when he first heard of it last July, and suggested that I should vet it for him and try to make it less disgusting. Then he discovered accidentally that the Lord Chamberlain had told Beaumont that the family if they objected strongly enough could stop the play altogether. He told Beaumont that he and his mother (aged 98) did disapprove. Beaumont tried to keep him to his original position. I made out a full report, which Beryl typed, and he said that it coincided exactly with his views, though each of us had found different monstrosities. So now he's written to tell Beaumont definitely that all is off. Beaumont has now tried to contact me to bring pressure, but I say that I'm in no state to be bullied and the affair is out of my hands.

Anyhow I discussed the Spiegel film with Arnie. Arnie said 'If Spiegel wants to make a sort of Western, that's fine. The public deserve it. But no psychological slants or libels. The trouble is one can't control the script-writer and director.' So I said: 'Who can't? I can. Tell Spiegel you want me to guard the decencies and everything's fine. He's already asked me to help.' 'Suits me,' says Arnie. So now Spiegel and Lean's great anxiety (apparently they had heard about Arnie's objection to the Rattigan play) is solved, and when I see Spiegel on Friday I can bargain from strength. I'm sorry about Alec, but to play a sadistic, vain, unbalanced queer would not have done him any good. Good old Lord Chamberlain. He's appointed directly by the Sovereign, which is one of the great reasons against Republicanism. He knew and admired Lawrence. And there's no appeal against his judgement.

When I see Spiegel, I'm getting Selwyn Jepson down from Hampshire to be my representative – Watt hasn't sufficient subtlety.

This is the main news. Lots of minor stuff about which will keep [*sic*]. Please tell me what was the last credit balance in my September Irving Trust return (big yellow affair) and whether any small white pay-in returns have since come thence. Cash 10,000 pesetas cheque when necessary.

Love

Robert

Back in Deyá Graves wrote to Derek Savage, whose father had recently died; Savage was left a small legacy in his will, though this was being contested.

7 *December 1959*   Deyá

Dear Derek:

Thanks for your two letters. I do hope that things will now improve, and allow you to do more of the work that you alone can do, instead of what *anyone* can do; and that Connie likes her new job.

As for the £100. Please forget it (even if the appeal against the Will fails, with costs). My luck was on a far bigger scale than yours; (though a father's death can hardly be called 'luck', forgive me!).

I probably would have got stuck like you in a rustic economy if T. E. Lawrence hadn't given me a helping hand, back in 1926; and curiously enough ever since his death there's always been something coming from him to help me whenever things got tough: sale of his MSS letters in 1936 for £2000 when I became a refugee; money from *Lawrence and the Arabs* film rights, twice since then: £1000 and £3000 . . .

. . . Musicals and operas *never* come off. Or as good as never. Unless you know a millionaire with a girl friend who thinks she can sing. This is a business world.

I'm so glad to be in touch with you again.

Yours ever   Robert

James Reeves was now editing two more anthologies, one of *English Essays* and another of *Georgian Poetry*, and wrote to Graves asking for his suggestions.

14 *December 1959*   Deyá

Dearest James:

Essays:

There's Addison, and Goldsmith (*The Bee* volume) and Swift, and Thos. Browne, Milton on Divorce[21] and Coleridge and Sam Johnson and Lamb and Hazlitt and de Quincey and James Clarence Morgan (I have all of these) and Nat. Hawthorne and Mark
¡O dear! Twain and Pater's hard gemlike flame and Macaulay (Christ) and

above all Samuel Butler ('Humour of Homer' and other Essays). And *Elizabethan Critical Essays on Poetry* (have those) especially Philip Sidney. And E. V. Lucas. And Robert Lynd. And R. L. Stevenson ('Virginibus Puerisque'). And Oscar the Wily Man.[22] That's over 100 already. And . . . Laura's 'The Damned Thing'. It's not poetry, so perhaps.

Georgians: Blunden,[23] Davies, Delamare [*sic*], Brooke, Flecker, Owen, Sassoon, *Rosenberg, Sorley*.[24] (Ralph Hodgson, 'The Bull'?) (Munro [*sic*] and Squire a *short, short* representation?) Masefield's 'Everlasting Mercy'? Too long. Edward Thomas? Can't read him myself.

Consider F. Cornford? Then omit? Lascelles Abercrombie? ¿¿*Me*??

The point was that the Victorian tradition surviving poetically from the Latinized 18th Century had gone, and so had the borrowings from France (Decadence was French). It was a genial return to the *English* tradition and encouraged by the unanimity of the War. (*N.B.* Housman, Hardy, Doughty,[25] our predecessors.) I can't think in detail about all this but tell me your book needs and you have me at your service when I've finished with Christmas and my US talks and St Thomas's Gospel and all.

Arrange another visit here next year and we'll pour gold into each other's laps.

Much love to all   Robert

I go with Beryl and Tomás and Lucia to England on Jan. 2nd; to USA on Jan. 15th then back on Feb. 1st.

After recovering from his operation Graves set off for another lecture tour in the USA and while there received the Gold Medal (the Prince Drontzkoy Memorial Award) of the National Poetry Society of America. While in New York this time he stayed with Gordon Wasson, whose wife Valentina had died earlier that year.

To Karl and Rene Gay

22 January 1960

Dearest Karl and Rene:

This is the first time I've been alone, alone and alone at last – in the *long sessional* express from Pennsylvania Station to

Baltimore to give my first talk 'Xanthippe' – Ricardo will meet me there and afterwards he and I will spend two days on the farm. Ricardo and Betty have resolved their troubles, thank God: I love Betty, and Ricardo has always been a good friend to me. Ricardo says he's losing his business touch and is slipping, maybe he'll quit while the quitting's good? Jenny has been wonderful as my social secretary. I got my medal last night and had to improvise a 25 minute talk with the broadcast apparatus on and light bulbs flashing. Fortunately I feared nothing, as Jenny was there, also Robert Frost, the only other unconventional person in the room – the SERT room at the Waldorff [*sic*]. I did not lack for words or jokes. Frost and I had a lovely time together. With Beryl's permission I am eating mushrooms – in crystal form to the accompaniment of the tape record of the real Zapotek priestess. Jerry Robbins[26] of whom I have seen much asked me to explain the paintings in the *Women's Mystery* house at Pompeii, because he wants to do a ballet of the Mysteries. So I said: 'Bring them along and look at them when we eat mushrooms together.' A fourth character was needed for our 'pad' and the ideal would be a serious, unflighty, warm, beautiful young woman – of whom I know only one in NY, namely Jess McNab of the Metropolitan Museum who gave me that predynastic [sickle]. So she'll be there. We will all concentrate on the Mysteries and see what we can *see*. That will be Jan. 31. On the 27th I am going to be part of the Ed Murrow 'Small World' TV programme talking across the continent to Philip Wyllie ('Mommism') and guess bloody who else and pop your eyes when you turn the page – Dr Carl Jung in Zürich![27]

It will be rehearsed and taped and cut, etc., so that should be OK.

I can't begin to tell you all I've seen and suffered, but I've kept very well and always got in my half hour's rest. Spiegel has paid up, Buffalo pay up on the 31st.

– Saw Alastair yesterday for a moment. Dog-tired after an all night train ride from the W. somewhere. We gave him whisky and a photograph of Jasper.[28] The Wests also were present.

– Tell Alston that *New Yorker* thanked me profusely for me introducing him to them and want *stories* – if possible without infringing the family sex taboo. He's made.

– Had a funny evening at home the other day – meeting of

Bankers with our Mr Marples (Transport Minister) to persuade him that American interest in the Channel Tunnel was large and realistic. I much admired Marples's handling of the talk – the best Tory high-up I've ever met.

Am arranging a Deyá lunch on the 30th with Ann and Esteban, Cindy,[29] Len Lye and a lot more. Have a useful typescript from Joshua about St Thomas.

I do hope the snow hasn't turned serious. Here it is around 30–35 degrees, and the houses are so warm I feel strangled.

Love

Robert

I meant to say, Karl, thank you for all your letters and enclosures. You are splendid at your end.

This train makes my handwriting even worse than usual.

Love to Diana and Julie.

Saw my first New York play *Gypsy*. Great folklorical interest. (It stank!)

Will be back in London on Feb 1st Monday; Geneva Thursday 4th. Palma: Sat. 6th. OK.

On 31 January Graves ate pills made from the Mexican hallucinogenic mushroom *Psilocybe Heimsii*, in Wasson's East End Avenue apartment, while listening, in complete darkness, to the Zapotec *curandera*'s invocation to Tlalóc, Mexican god of mysteries and lightning. The experience had a profound effect on Graves, who considered himself to be literally eating 'the food of the gods', and he described his almost mystic visions fully in his essay 'The Universal Paradise' in *Difficult Questions, Easy Answers*.

He wrote to Wasson as soon as he returned to Mallorca.

7 February 1960   Deyá

My dear Gordon:

Thank you ever so much, and ever so much over again for your kindness to me and Jenny: crowned by the kindness of Jan. 31st. That was not merely a red-letter day but a day marked with all the colours of a celestial rainbow.

One result is that I am now able to see pictures in my mind far more clearly than I did before: the mushrooms seem to have broken down some sort of barrier between thought and vision – not completely yet, but noticeably.

189

I have no doubt at all but that the mushroom should be restored among Europeans and people of European descent to its original (presumed) position in religion: first of all as an initiation ceremony to religion at puberty; then as a heightening of the marriage rite; finally as a *viaticum* – so that when the door of heaven opens one really enters and sees those one has loved.

Jerome Robbins's remark was one with which I concurred wholeheartedly: 'Why reserve these drugs for the mentally sick? They should be given to the mentally whole. Especially to poets and artists.' I'm glad you liked Jess; she's pure gold.

I have heard of a man being given the psilocybin treatment at Los Angeles – at 100 dollars a treatment – 14 treatments. But when I heard that he had seen himself as a Samurai warrior, and again had the experience of a return to the womb, I felt that the drug was in the wrong hands – I suspected that the doctor who was present with a notebook was wishing the visions on him, just as Freud and Jung's pupils dream the dreams expected of them by their masters. And one should not be given the food of the gods unless in a state of grace.

– Jenny suggested that she and the rest of us should write out our experiences with an introduction by yourself . . . I think I was the only person to notice that you alone did not reveal your vision; and I understood why. We were neophytes; you were an adept and we weren't in your class. But I could at least see that you were in a state of grace, and also that you saw things indescribable: your face glowed like Moses on his descent from Sinai.

When one has had this experience everything else seems dull; except returning to Beryl and my family, which was better than ever.

On the way across France to Geneva by Swiss Air Tomás remarked: 'I wonder why that propeller isn't going round?' The pilot also noticed this odd phenomenon – it was a 2-engined plane – and hurried us back to London. The air hostess broke two coffee cups in her emotion.

Much love to Masha and yourself. Beryl and I shall be coming over early in May and making the Buffalo ceremony the finale on May 15th. I hope that will mean that Masha and John can see us here; and that we can stay a while with you.

Dr Engler sent me a Christmas card. Good! His address is: Dr

Engler, Almirante, Panama. ('Almirante' seems to be a town or village.)

If as I imagine the *priestess* is the original mystagogue, not the priest, she will have been Semele, Dionysus's mother, in the European rites; her child is a God but she is very much his mother. Laughs and plays with him. – I feel that *we* as well as the Indians should have expert *curanderas* too: women with the necessary [   ] balance, humour, courage and discretion. There *are* such about. [   ] nothing with their talents.

Yours ever affectionately

Robert

To Alan Sillitoe and Ruth Fainlight

10 February 1960

Dear Alan and Ruth:

Your letter reached us when we had already come back from our brief raid on civilization; Beryl was actually in Hampstead, while I was in New York, Washington and Baltimore. What a pity!

I am fine now and got through my talks and readings without disgrace.

Now I'm about to translate the plays of Terence, and collaborate with Dr Raphael Patai (of the University of Jerusalem) on a book of *Hebrew Myths*: besides the occasional story; and poems.

There's to be an exhibition of my books and manuscripts at Buffalo University in May; the total number of books I have published is around 90 (with collaborations) and with pamphlets, etc., it comes to 114. On Jan. 21st I was given the National Poetry Society of America's gold medal; Beryl said she was ashamed of me, but it was my only way of seeing Robert Frost again. He came up especially for the ceremony.

I'm helping Sam Spiegel with the Lawrence film which will be made this year in the Middle East (the same team as made the *River Quai* [sic] with Marlon Brando as Lawrence).[30]

I think that's enough literary shop. I tried to suppress *King Jesus* but the publisher and booksellers wanted it in print. Factually it is superseded by *The Nazarene Gospel*; but it has a certain haunting quality and given that it represents itself as written around 90 AD is perhaps justifiable; for by then the original story would be

forgotten and there is evidence in the Gospels that the story I tell
was believed by some at that epoch.

How are you, Ruth? Heartburn and lassitude? Never mind! See
John 16, 21.[31] It is very cold here at the moment and flu is
sweeping away (temporarily) whole households.

Love to you both   Robert

In February Graves won the Foyle Poetry Award for his *Collected
Poems 1959* and for *The Anger of Achilles*; he invited Reeves, who
had sent him his choice of poems for the Georgian anthology, to
the award ceremony in London.

No date

Dearest James:

Hughes, Richard,[32] was not original: he drank deeply from my
poisoned chalice.

Flecker: not bad. The one about the 'Gates of Damascus':

Take to Aleppo filigrane
And take thee paste of apricots
And coffee tables botched with pearls,
And little beaten brass-ware pots;
And thou shalt sell thy goods for thrice
The Damascene retailer's price
And buy a fat Armenian slave
That smelleth odorous and nice!

Memorized. It always amused me.

I don't like your R.G. selection, but then I don't like R.G. of that
period. I'd choose: 'A Boy in Church', 'Ghost Music', 'John Skelton',
'In the Wilderness', '1915', 'A Dead Boche' – faute de mieux.

'Lost Love' was about myself.

Sorry about 'The Bull'. I like it still, as I used to like my old
nurse; but doubtless you wouldn't find much in her now, were
she alive. But I'm loyal.

'Desolation Island' was *South Georgia*. I guess Harvey's dead by
now. What the hell was his real name? I forget.[33]

I have the Doubleday agreement signed and sealed for the
Ardizzone book;[34] so I guess Cassell won't lag far behind. I do
hope he'll get on with it now. Please tell him; I haven't his address,
I find.

I suggested you for a nice lunch at 1 p.m. at the Dorchester when I get this £250 prize on March 3; I hope you'll come. That evening we have a fork party at 108 Clifton Hill: if you can come, let me know. You means both of you.

I go back on March 4 after 36 hours of Britain.

– Love –   Robert

In a review of a book by J. B. Priestley in the *Observer* (14 February 1960) John Wain incidentally dismissed Graves's Clark Lectures as an instance of the 'absurdly eccentric in criticism'. This remark followed an earlier attack by Wain (also in the *Observer*) 'in the name of orthodox literary opinion', on all of Graves's criticism, an attack which an Israeli journalist called 'a murderous onslaught' when he interviewed Graves in Tel Aviv. In reply to the journalist Graves said:

By John Wain? Yes, I know him. He was my guest in Mallorca. He was once one of the Angry Young Men but has since ceased to be angry and decided to support the Establishment. I, as you know, am not counted among its supporters. I have made a blot on my copybook . . . I live outside England, which shows that I do not 'belong'. In fact, I am doing my best to disappoint those who are anxious to bestow titles and positions of honour on me [in 1957 he had turned down the CBE]. I had great difficulties in dissuading King Fuad from honouring me with the title of Member of the Order of the Nile.

Wain, who in his own poetry is considerably influenced by Graves, first went to Deyá in 1956 ostensibly to 'apologize' for misquoting a line of Graves's in the title of his recently published second volume of poetry, *A Word Carved on a Sill* (the title comes from Graves's poem 'End of Play').

After Graves wrote a letter to the *Observer* on 19 February (titled 'Shouting Vague Judgements') in complaint of the 'absurdly eccentric' remark, Wain replied that he admired Graves's work so much that he never missed 'an opportunity to praise it and try to win it new readers'. At the same time, he found his criticism 'aggressive and unbalanced, often showing a repulsive ungenerosity about poets he happens not to enjoy (is there any justification, e.g. for his description of "poor, tortured Gerard Manley Hopkins" as one of the "lesser idols now slowly mouldering"?).' He went on to say that when a poet of Graves's standing tells an audience of students that

Yeats was a fraud, Pound an 'ignoramus who didn't get his Latin verbs right' and suggests that Skelton is more 'interesting' than Wordsworth or Milton, then it becomes the 'duty' of a 'responsible' critic to try to disentangle the poet from the lecturer. 'This I have consistently tried to do.'

Graves wrote again to the editor of the *Observer*.

5 *March 1960*

ECCENTRIC

Sir:

I haven't yet got an apology from Mr Wain for parenthetically writing me off as an 'absurd eccentric'. He replies:

So far from making the remark *en passant*, I am referring to the body of critical work that has already been done. Or does it have to be done afresh each time?

'The body of critical work' apparently means his own essays about me, which he expects all *Observer* readers to have handy on their shelves. Yes, it should be done afresh on this occasion, and I'm afraid I'll have to do it myself.

Mr Wain challenges my phrase 'poor tortured Hopkins', and accuses me of 'a repulsive ungenerosity' in not enjoying his poems. That is easily answered. Though I know few poems in English so tortured as some of Hopkins, I was the first modern English critic who called attention to his poetic excellence. Yet my praise, in 1927, was this side of idolatry; and if I reported in my *Crowning Privilege* that the exaggerated Hopkins cult of the Twenties and Thirties (when almost every young poet was writing Hopkinesque) had begun to wane in the Fifties, the justice of this remark can be statistically proved.

I did not call Yeats a fraud, though I strongly suspected him of worse than fraud. Mr Monk Gibbon, in his memoir *The Masterpiece and the Man*, has since confirmed these suspicions. What I did write was that Yeats developed a brilliant verse technique but found nothing worth saying of his own; so he went out like an indigent countryman with no sheep to shear, and collected strands of wool from the hedges and brambles of other men's fields. Mr Wain is at liberty to call Mr Raymond Mortimer,[35] who holds the same view, an equally 'absurd eccentric'. I also quoted Yeats's letter to Sturge Moore[36] in which he says that he prefers the violent expression of error to reasonable expression of truth; and hope Mr Wain does not admire Yeats for this trait.

Nor did I toss off any irresponsible statement that Ezra Pound got his Latin verbs wrong. In 'Dr Syntax and Mr Pound', a careful critical comparison of Pound's Propertius translation with the original, I showed that his Latin was distinctly below O-level in *all* parts of speech. Mr Wain had better not challenge me on this point. Latin grammar is hardly a subject to fool about with.[37]

Nor did I imply that Milton and Wordsworth were 'less interesting' than Skelton. I had written a 150,000-word book and several long essays on Milton; and the equivalent of a short book on Wordsworth, finding them both remarkable characters, and digging up new historical facts about their lives. Skelton I had treated at far less length; but when, in 1923 [*sic*], I published the first popular selection of his poems, this led to his being taken up in a big way by scholars – as they have all in turn admitted in their prefaces. And, though I don't use 'more interesting' as a critical term, I certainly love him best. No 'responsible critic' will deny that Skelton's poems are at least infinitely more various than those of Milton and Wordsworth, both in subject, metre and diction; and that he enriched the English poetic vocabulary far more than either poet.

I do hope that Mr Wain will let the matter rest at this point. I thank him for his admiration; but wish it had been otherwise expressed.

Yours, etc.

Robert Graves

In 1960 Tom Matthews wrote the first volume of his memoirs, *Name and Address* (for the English edition of which Graves wrote the blurb), mostly about his years as editor of *Time* magazine and his final break with its owner, Henry Luce.

22 April 1960

Dearest Tom:

Congratulations on your splendid book; I confess I didn't think you'd ever get down the *Time* story on paper so utterly objectively and decently.

– Most grateful too for your not trying to put down the Schuyler story in full: one that couldn't be told intelligibly and fairly in cold print. It would have to be told from all angles: but two are incommunicable; and for myself, I prefer to let it go into the bottomless gulf where Laura knowingly cast herself, and into which she nearly dragged me and, indeed, all of us.

– We are alive and free, and I hope you are as happy as Beryl and I are, and Alan.

– I thought you pulled your punches (ever so slightly) about Bishop Old Golden: his selfish offensiveness was just a bit worse than you hint. But to have said more would have been unfilial. (Lucky Melchizadek!)

Just preparing for our US visit (May 4th–18th), and crowded with children on vacation.

Love   Robert

I recognized Schuyler's sweetness; I saw his wild rages; I was shocked by something you do not mention – his cynical dishonesty in business affairs.

How and Why

How and why
Poets die
Is a dismal tale.
Some take a spill
On Guinea Hill,
Some drown in ale.

Some get lost
At sea, or crossed
In love with cruel witches,
But some attain
Long life and reign
Like Popes among their riches.

In May, Graves returned to America, with Beryl, for ten days to lecture and give poetry readings. While there, on 6 May, he, Beryl, Esteban Frances and Gordon Wasson took psilocybin pills (dragées) prepared synthetically using Professor Albert Hofmann's technique at the Swiss drug company Sandoz AG, Basel (see page 216). Before, Graves had taken the pills specially prepared from the mushrooms themselves, but this time, with the synthetic pills, there was no sense of euphoria and although the psychic effects, for Graves and Wasson at least, were considerable, they were confused, unlike the experience of clarity and perception under the influence of the mushrooms, and hard to remember afterwards. All were disappointed in the drug which, they agreed, was no substitute for the mushroom and which had considerably unpleasant after-effects.

8 May 1960

Dearest Karl:

All well. The news will keep till I arrive, but you'll be interested to hear that the synthetic *psilocybin*, as opposed to the extract of the real mushroom, is all wrong: a common vulgar <u>drug</u>, no magic, and followed by a nasty hang-over. We had to use the synthetic because someone had pinched the real from Gordon's icebox.

– Seeing Wm Morris[38] and J. Robbins today about the *White Goddess* film.

– My brother Dick is for it, I'm afraid; a similar complaint to Damian's. I saw him in London Clinic looking very haggard.

Lovely weather. Temp about 75 F.

Have fixed up Company papers.

Love

Robert

I've told Doubleday that I'll leave the *Terence*[39] in the original form; I'll get it typed at an agency and then edit it with your help – am wholeheartedly in sympathy with your feelings on the subject; so don't think I'm not.

Spent five hours with the Buffalo man yesterday discussing mss. points.

The *Observer* published Graves's reply to John Wain and the assistant editor, Charles Davy, wrote to Graves that Wain had wished to respond with a Latin tag, but that the editor thought too many people would not understand and be irritated by having the unintelligible quotation 'thrust upon them'. The quotation was from Propertius, *Elegies*, Book Three, I, 13–14:

> *Quid frustra missis in me certatis habenis?*
> *Non datur ad Musas currere lata via.*

Which, literally, means:

Why do you vainly compete against me with loosened reins?
One is not given a broad road on which to drive to the Muses.

This, obviously, did not please Graves, but on 27 April Wain himself
wrote to Graves from Florence, where he had gone on a Somerset
Maugham travel grant, saying it was hard to see what expression
Graves's face was wearing 'behind the impassive mask of public
controversy'. He had, however, detected a note of genuine pique in
the second letter and was very sorry that this was so. He went on
to say, 'I had always assumed that your criticism was written as a
kind of joke,' that in *The Crowning Privilege* Graves said 'in so
many words' that he was out to provoke people. 'Well, you have
provoked me, and I regard it as little short of a duty to combat your
critical opinions and stop them from gaining too much ground
among the young and credulous.' Not *all* of his critical opinions, he
then corrected himself, 'merely the obviously outrageous ones'. And
by 'a body of critical work that has already been done' he didn't
mean, he said, his own articles in the *Observer*, but 'the consensus
of opinion among people with an interest in the subject'.

Back again in Deyá, Graves wrote to Wain. (The letter was typed
and the following version is based on the carbon copy.)

8 June 1960   Deyá

Dear John:

Congratulations on your Maugham grant!

Your letter was forwarded to me at Buffalo, missed me when it
arrived there a month ago, and has. come back here by second-
class mail! I'd have answered it at once, otherwise, as I do now . . .
In private and public controversy I use the same face, not a mask;
and I write to the papers in this severe way only when I feel that
I have been unjustly treated. Your idea that my critical writing is
a sort of private joke surprises me. In a preface to the Clarke [*sic*]
lectures, I did write that they were addressed to the passions; but
meant that the analytic Cambridge school of criticism, by a failure
to address the passions, misled people into thinking that certain
poets who provide interesting analytical problems for students must
be poets of high rank. That I am 'out to provoke' people is
untrue; it is true, however, that I don't mind sticking my neck out
to express an unusual opinion, if I believe it to be true.

I regret in a way that the *Observer* published that last letter of mine, because it ousted one from one J.G.F. Potter of Cheltenham who made the same points rather better than I did. He wrote, among other things: 'It is surely obvious that the influence of Hopkins, paramount in the Thirties, is negligible today,' and 'Mr Graves's other opinions which Mr Wain deplores are not so much arguable as demonstrably correct . . .' and 'Mr Wain's remark "I admire Robert Graves's work so much that I never miss an opportunity to praise it and try to win it new readers" must have made those readers blink a little who recalled Mr Wain's review in your columns a few months ago headed "A Package Deal".'

My own feeling is that you don't take nearly enough trouble over your reviews. They might pass muster in an unrehearsed TV interview but though undigested thought in talk is pardonable and even welcome, it shouldn't occur in writing. In the Hopkins context you missed, and still miss, the point: which was *not* where Hopkins should rank as a poet, but whether he remained an 'idol' in the middle-Fifties. I think it's curious that you try to sell me Hopkins when, but for *Modernist Poetry* (1927), you would never have heard of his excellences.

Also, I think you have come to regard yourself as a public representative of some 'consensus of opinion', some literary constituency which gives your remarks a rather tinny microphonic timbre, and bloats your personality. If you continue like this, you'll end up as a Garvin or a Gosse;[40] and you're better than that, really . . . And I fear that you've nailed your personal shirt to a mast (or masts), and are so shy of lowering it again that you won't examine the soundness of the hull.

I remember once, when you were here descanting on some poem or other, fetching the book in from the library and confronting you with the plain text; I think you seldom really *read* what is before you to find out exactly what has been said.

I am always pleased to be rapped over the knuckles if I have made a factual misstatement; it teaches me modesty, of which I stand in dire need. But you must be about the only critic who keeps up the old gag of: 'Mr Graves doesn't really believe what he writes; it's very good fun but wholly implausible' – which I thought had died out about fifteen years ago.

Forgive this straight talk (Proverbs 25, 11–12[41]), and don't account me an enemy; you know that I'm not malicious, which is what 'enemy' implies.

Yours ever affy.   Robert

They did not in fact become enemies and Wain visited Deyá again in 1979, to interview Graves for the *New York Times*, and afterwards wrote a poem, 'Visiting an Old Poet', expressing his deep and genuine affection for Graves.

That autumn Reeves was preparing his own *Selected Poems* for the press and Graves wrote to McCormick of Doubleday suggesting he publish the book in the USA.

12 September 1960

Dearest James:

I wrote to Ken McCormick of Doubleday about taking those sheets. Hope it comes off.

Quote me as saying: 'I know no other living English poet who can compare with James Reeves at his best; and even his worst is defensible, as Coleridge's was.'

We are going off on Friday, arriving on Sept. 24th (128 Kensington Park Road, W11).

Beryl paid the woman who cleaned the Posada.

John Betjamin's[42] [*sic*] nostalgic 'Summoned by Bells' occupies 11 full pages of the *New Yorker*. That finished the *NY* for me. Goodbye, fat friend!

Have just got my Cassell selection made and typed; also my *Collected Poems* 1961 (Doubleday).

Packing up. The sea is still warm.

Love to all   Robert

I wish I had noted that misprint in *Collected Poems*. It worries me.

In 1961, as W. H. Auden finished his term as Professor of Poetry at Oxford, Graves was elected in his stead, defeating Enid Starkie and F. R. Leavis. He was granted an MA by decree, in order to be qualified for the post, and permitted to give the three annual lectures one after the other in the Michaelmas (autumn) Term, as Auden had done; thus it would mean only one trip a year to England, instead of three.

Between 1952 and 1959 Graves had no 'Personal Muse', but in the summer of 1959 'the Goddess' appeared again in Deyá, in the form of a young Canadian girl called Margot. Although at first Graves tried to 'resist', he was soon drawn into what he later termed 'the process'. James Reeves was visiting Deyá at the time and told Graves bluntly that he was deluding himself. In a poem written at the time ('Symptoms of Love') Graves himself wrote:

> Love is a universal migraine,
> A bright stain on the vision
> Blotting out reason.

He realized that his behaviour was 'unreasonable' and was fully aware of the criticisms which could be made about him, but the situation, he claimed, was 'unavoidable' and true love begins with a blind innocence which has to be experienced and recorded.

It was of Margot he wrote in the poem 'Between Moon and Moon':

> In the last sad watches of night
> Hardly a sliver of light will remain
> To edge the guilty shadow of a waned moon
> That dawn must soon devour.
>   Thereafter, another
> Crescent queen shall arise with power –
> So wise a beauty never yet seen, say I:
> A true creature of moon, though not the same
> In nature, name or feature –
> Her innocent eye rebuking inconstancy
> As if Time itself should die and disappear.
>
> So was it ever. She is here again, I sigh.

However, in May 1961, just before Graves was due to leave for another lecture tour in America, Margot suddenly 'ran off' with Alastair Reid. Graves's friendship with Reid had been strained of late anyway but this came as a severe blow to him.

To James Reeves

16 May 1961

Dearest James:

Just off to USA for ten days: returning via London for two days 26th and 27th to see Lucia and Wm and so on.

Saw your letter in *The Times* which gave me your new address. All well here: Jota has four pups by Erroll Flynn's widowed prize poodle. No rain, but plenty of water through the pipes.

Am on an Aviaco plane for Brussels via Barcelona: haven't been to Brussels since 1912 – sent there to learn French. Thence by Pan American. Arrive New York at 9 p.m. which is really 2 a.m., if you get me. There I read poems, the new ones, plus some newer ones, completing the series, to three audiences in Pennsylvania, New York and Washington, and address the American Academy and Institute on – well, the word is *Báraka* – it means all sorts of things in Arabic but is whatever makes a poem a poem – holiness, rapture, love, virtue. (From the word *Barak*, lightning.) Then I've got to see Fred [Freendly] about a TV narration in Greece in August when I go to see the *Homer's Daughter* Opera (am taking Lucia), and Decca Co. about a recording, and Bill Morris about the *White Goddess* film – though I think that won't come off without a miracle – and Jerome Robbins about a ballet; and am taking a new book to Doubledays (my Terence translation), and will see R. Patai my collaborator on *Hebrew Myths*, and stay with Len and Anne,[43] and buy a transistor radio and waterpistols for Tomás – and so on and so on.

I am well and have lost about a stone of weight and swum every day. This ridiculous professorship makes me feel like a prize cat at a show: i.e. it means nothing at all. Am still Robert. Have been judging the Newdigate Prize and arguing with my fellow judges for its award to the only poet out of 32 – as opposed to the most genteel rhetorician phoney.

Beryl and I will miss each other a lot these ten days – no, twelve – but it's worse to be left behind than to go, I always find. She was a week in hospital having varicose veins straightened out last month. Tomás is fine.

There's a lot more news which won't go into letters: rather horrible, but no damage done – discovery of treacherous

behaviour in an old friend well known to you. I don't invite
guesses. Anyhow, being more perspicacious and less credulous
than I you wouldn't be surprised.

If you are in financial straits – I'm not – so let me know. That
ladderage must have set you back a lot.

Love to you both and all   Robert

Back in Deyá Graves wrote again to Reeves.

29 May 1961   Deyá

Dearest James:

So relieved that money is all right again. Have had a terrific time
in America, and saw Lucia and Wm and Sally on the way back.
– Can't tell you the treachery story by letter – but Beryl and I
were equally surprised and horrified by its Satanism and devious

lying: a close friend of yours and mine. Anyhow: no $\begin{cases} \text{hearts} \\ \text{bones} \end{cases}$

broken. And probably Mary will say: 'I always warned you. Do
you mean to say you *trusted* him?', etc.

My first Oxford lecture will be on the 20th Oct. in the Playhouse.
Have to buy a gown and cap: about thirty quid, isn't it?

Have written several more poems, including one beginning
'Beware, Madam, the Witty Serpent' – which will make the hair
rise on some lovely necks. I know you did not like the *Observer*
lot;[44] but why should you? Too highly charged or too personal
or something . . . The 'Surgical Ward: Men' is in *More Poems*. I
am also publishing a small limited edition of *Reconsiderations*:[45]
old poems mostly amended. Wonderful what the excision of bad
lines will do for an old poem. Printed by the Marlborough College
boys.

If you ask for a *Poems 1961* I'll have you sent one.

Love to you all   Robert

That summer Graves wrote his first Oxford lectures and his own
part in an Esso-sponsored television programme, 'Greece: The Inner
World' (telecast in the USA on 19 April 1964), as he told Martin
Seymour-Smith, whose edition of Shakespeare's *Sonnets* was soon
to be published.

22 June 1961

Dear Martin:

Thanks for writing. I'm so glad things are better with you and Janet. We're fine. Wm finishes his geology course at London University this month, and then intends to go to Texas to 'play oil game'. Lucia also finishes at the Lycée Français – doesn't intend to go to a University[46] but will pass the exams to show she isn't cheating.

– Funny to think of Miranda at that age! Tomás is fine. And Juan is practising throwing the javelin at Geneva.

– This Oxford job involves me in too much correspondence: I go up in October. They have given me an MA by decree!

– Tom pulls his punches a bit – and has carefully avoided all mention of me, because the real story is about Laura Riding and he couldn't face it. But it's good about *Time*.

– Sonnets? James said nothing. (He's done my 'O-Level Graves Anthology' and I find it full of awful misprints; nobody can read proofs these days but it's not *his* fault.) I hope the book sells.

– Terry is the same true Terry still, and his poems still come out drop by drop.

I've been plagued by poems lately: one of these awful periods that come every seven years or so, and sear the heart while gilding the name. But all's well. Deyá is still Deyá, Beryl is wonderful, we have a Landrover and an Abyssinian cat, and two poodles. The garden has never been so fruitful.

In August I go to Greece to do a TV programme for CBS on Greek Myths: have to pretend I have been there before!

Have just done a Terence translation and am busy on *Hebrew Myths* and the Oxford lectures.

Love to you both   Robert

Love to Frank when you write.

On 20 June, BBC Radio broadcasted a centenary programme on General Haig in which Graves and Basil Liddell Hart both took part; however, both their contributions were 'mutilated', and only four sentences of Graves's were used out of a twenty-minute statement by him of his views on Haig. Liddell Hart and Graves were the only critics of Haig on the programme, almost all the other contributors being either devoted friends or subordinates of the general, and the result was, in Liddell Hart's words '. . . an oily stream of adulation mingled with trivialities . . . to the exclusion of any serious critical discussion of Haig's career and performance . . . I have never felt more inclined to vomit, and emigrate, than after listening to the BBC effusion . . .' Graves too was extremely angry, and joined Liddell Hart in his protest.

10 July 1961

Dear Basil:
  Those four sentences of mine were, I am sure, the mildest they could single out of the scores I recorded!
  – The only way to make a really effective protest would be to get a short news-interview with ITV. My old friend – your old friend, too, I think – Geoffrey Cox is head of the news service and would, I am sure, be delighted to arrange such an affair – especially if you could get Hankey[47] or anyone else newsworthy to support you. It is one of the most disgraceful exercises of Privilege I have come across for years, and deserves exposure by the rival organization.
  – You can quote my letter if necessary . . . My main point was that the Cult of the Horse and the Cavalry Man, though not so absurdly evidenced in World War I as in the Crimea, was responsible for the unnecessary deaths of hundreds of thousands of British soldiers and for the economic debilitation of Britain which reduced her to a second-class power. And that Haig the Cavalry Man *par excellence* was rightly associated with Poppy Day because he was the chief sower of poppy seed, and 'sowed with the sack'.
  David Woodward obviously hated his assignment, but he could not control the BBC censors.
  Yours ever   Robert

Graves, aged sixty-six, was now at the height of his fame. His Oxford lectures over the next four years were to be very popular (students even came from Cambridge to hear them) and, with his poems, were extremely influential on a new generation of poets.
  In the summer of 1961, as he wrote the first three of his lectures, Graves was in an optimistic mood. He began now to concentrate on the 'process', on living out the myth of Poet and Muse. Margot

had been a disappointment, and in one of his lectures he delivered 'a message to would-be Muses': 'A poet may . . . be mistaken in his Muse; she may prove unworthy of his continued trust. I have written about this too.' In his poems Graves maps out in detail his explorations of the Muse's 'secret land', and although Margot was to return before long, Graves now realized that, for the dedicated poet, whatever might happen to his personal, living Muse, the Goddess 'abides'. This he explained in the poem 'In Her Praise':

> This they know well: the Goddess yet abides.
> Though each new lovely woman whom she rides,
> Straddling her neck a year or two or three,
> Should sink beneath such weight of majesty
> And, groping back to humankind, gainsay
> The headlong power that whitened all her way
> With a broad track of trefoil – leaving you,
> Her chosen lover, ever again thrust through
> With daggers, your purse rifled, your rings gone –
> Nevertheless they call you to live on
> To parley with the pure, oracular dead,
> To hear the wild pack whimpering overhead,
> To watch the moon tugging at her cold tides.
> Woman is mortal woman. She abides.

To Tom Matthews

5 August 1961   Deyá

Dearest Tom:

I'm so sorry you had that bad turn about Wm. The news of the Jan Mayen disaster[48] gave me a shock too, although I knew he was safe: I have never really got over David's death at the same sort of age.[49]

. . . .

Our dinner, yes; I hope to show you some new friends of ours. End of October will be fine. In England Oct. 15 to Dec. 5th or so, accommodation not yet fixed; maybe London.

Have no desire to meet Laura and Schuyler myself – 'that bird's dead' as the saying is.

So glad you liked the love-poems. There's another batch (as I say) and something new is happening in them.

I'm writing my third and last lecture now: on the 'Personal

Muse' – the most interesting and difficult subject I have yet
attempted. I know a good deal about the Muse now, and am able
to separate the mythic from the personal better; I feel now that
I failed Laura no less than she failed me – not that I blame either
of us. We were premature.

Lots of love to Martha   Robert

To Selwyn Jepson

29 August 1961

Dearest Selwyn:

What has happened to you? In happy retirement? Liss[50] = Bliss?
I miss your neat handwriting. Pray: write!

All well with us. I have just been with Lucia to Greece: for the
first time since – sometime before the Turks got there. It is the
livest [*sic*] place in Europe, I find. Delphi, as I expected, stinks.

– Have written a lot more poems: am plagued by what makes
poems happen. They seem to be all right; the hair stands on end,
now and then. I wish I did not feel so alone in my profession; but
where are the others? There *must* be some, somewhere.

– My stock is rising geometrically; and everything of mine being
paperbacked – including a 100,000 edition of *Jesus in Rome*! Sn
Jn has a lot to do with it. It is nice not to think about money and
write only what I want to write. Thanks, pal!

Wm got his geology degree and has just gone off to learn oilgame
in Texas with my friend Jake Hamon. A pity. I was just getting
to know him.

Principal interest now is a study of how to live by intuition – as
you and I do – and always keep on the beam. It seems to me the
most important problem of our time, even apart from the specific
need of the poet, painter, musician, etc. An anti-intellectual,
wholly personal one.

I am very well and euphoric. Lucia's finished her education:
got the needed A levels for university but doesn't propose to go
there . . . Have written my three Oxford lectures, which will be
given at the Oxford Playhouse; maybe Wendy will provide a nice
backdrop. Funny: a bit more than a year ago I thought I'd finished,
but seem only to have started now. Age is all illusion: one of the
worst.

Saw Jenny in Rome. She takes on too much, and loses interest in all the buns in her oven: lets them burn.

Love to Tania and yourself   Robert

Nice US cutting about my new *Collected Poems*: 'Famous Author Turns to Verse'.

In October, Graves went to Oxford. James Reeves continued to attack Graves's 'Muse' theories, claiming they were not new at all, merely a modernized form of the medieval concept of courtly love.

[Postmarked 23 October 1961]   108 Clifton Hill
                                                       but as from St John's
                                                                     College
                                                                     Oxford

Dearest James

As I warned the Univ. authorities, 2000 came and there was room for only 650. The ones that got in were mostly rubber-necks and 1st year medical students – a bad audience. Never mind.

– Tonight I lecture the London Jews on their Myths (will be reported in *Times* tomorrow) – have I a nerve?

– Am behaving with extreme courtesy and have a close hair-cut and a brand new gown and hood.

– So nice to think of Lucia looking after Stella: you can be fully at ease. Lucia knows what is which at Madrid.

– Apart from a great number of new poems (which the *Listener* will print and which must be carefully distinguished from those of Petrarch, etc. – not being *Courtois* at all) and the *Terence* translation, and a *Trojan War for Children*,[51] and these Oxford Lectures, and a few chapters of *Hebrew Myths* I have been remarkably unbusy these last few months.

Having a wonderful holiday with Beryl here. (College Rooms; a Charles Addams flat on Boars Hill; and perpetual week-end quarters at Sally's.)

Will see you soon.

Much love to you all   Robert

To Selwyn Jepson

31 October 1961   St John's College
                                                                   Oxford

Dearest Selwyn:
   I was very pleased by what you said on the phone yesterday.
The question of intuition and how it can be enlarged into certitude
by long practice and sticking to personal principle seems, I agree,
to be the only really interesting one these days. The humour of
the situation is that it can't be organized or intellectualized or
exploited in any religious or political or scientific way. All that
can be done is for the people who work and think that way to
recognize one another; and to realize that their inter-awareness
increases the sense of certitude. It is very much rarer in men than
in women, because so few men are free of commitments to
organized opinion; but I know four or five, collected down the
years.
   See you soon.
   Love to you both   Robert

   Now that all the organized forces of mankind have grown so
weak because of a total lack of moral certainty, the few people
who are free to follow their own sense of certitude become the
more powerful in the matter of directing their own fate by what
seems like magical means.
   Have written a lot of new poems lately.

In America Graves had seen a copy of *Truth Is More Sacred*, a
recently published book by Herbert Read and the American novelist
Edward Dahlberg (who in 1959 had together written an article on
Graves and T. S. Eliot in *Twentieth Century*) containing several
antagonistic and libellous remarks about Graves. After Graves
returned to Deyá in December the book was published in Britain,
and he replied to a letter about it from Martin Seymour-Smith.

20 December 1961   Deyá

Dearest Martin:
   I am very glad to hear that things are so much better with you
again, and really wanted to see you but everything was against

it: sheer pressure of work at Oxford. Will do so next October
when we come over. This time it will be with Juan and Tomás;
and Lucia hopes to go to St Anne's, if she can pass the entrance
exam.

I saw *Truth Is More Sacred* when it was published in America,
and let it go: a dirty damp squib left over from last year's wet
Guy Fawkes' night. But England is different and I am writing to
Watt asking him to let his lawyers read the book for libel and
act accordingly. Dahlberg was here five years ago: behaved
disgracefully and was mortified that I did not accept him at his
own valuation. Read is a bloody fool to get mixed up in that; but
he seems vexed with me for my piece about him as an 'Eminent
Collaborationist'* – the reference being to his alliance with crook-
psychology, though a self-styled poet – and I suppose owes me a
kick for my plain speaking.

As usual I am publishing too many books. In 1962 there'll be
Oxford Lectures (3 public and 3 ordinary); *Terence's Comedies*;
New Poems; *The Trojan War* (juvenile); and a privately printed
More Deserving Cases of revived and revised poems I suppressed
and which have been pleaded for. Then there are various paperback reprints. But though Wm is off our hands (geology-man
doing 'oil-game' in Texas at the moment) Lucia, Juan and Tomás
still demand expensive educations, which keeps me fixed to my
table for 10 months of the year. No films of mine made yet, despite
so many options. The only exception is *The Golden Ass*!! – the
money-boys to whom someone sold the idea hadn't heard of
Apuleius, but had heard of me, so I was cut in on it. The film
will be made in Spain this coming Spring and I get 1½% of the
takings.[52] Isn't it odd? All those attempts to make *Claudius* have
come to nothing . . . Now I'm working at a *Hebrew Myths*; like
Greek Myths.

The village is very much the same. So, oddly enough, is Oxford:
surprising. The Vice Chancellor; the Merton Prof. of English;
various other professors; and two or three Heads of Houses were
undergraduates with me and made me very welcome. And I met
several undergraduates who had something *to* them.

It is embarrassing the way my stock has soared in the last two
or three years, but I am doing my best to treat it as a joke; which
in Deyá is easy. I am also a little embarrassed by the spate of
poems forced on me by what is called personal preoccupations,

meaning really a new vision of Anatha–Isis–Caridwen–Belphoebe. But they were all undodgeable so there I am landed with them and by the end I think I got through to something so old that I [*sic*] reads like new.

My love to Frank and your mother. And lots to you and Jan.

Robert

Bob Schon died the other day; a mixed up but decent man and we owe him a great debt because he started us on the compost racket. You should see our garden now!

*(Steps)

In January James Reeves sent Graves his poem 'James Son and Spicer', a light-hearted but haunting poem about a totalitarian-like invisible control and terror of individual conscience.

16 January 1962

San Antonio and a big bonfire in the village.

Dearest James

Your poem is very good indeed. Have just been judging the Sacred Poem prize for Oxford – 14 entries, an usual [*sic*] number, but word has spread that since the 20 guineas haven't been awarded for eight years the Kitty now amounts to 160 guineas, which will buy all sorts of things – from a portable font to a summer holiday with a beautiful model. Nearly all of them are lousy: the entries I mean, though limited to MAs or is it MMA?

That's why I am especially pleased with 'James Son and Spicer'. Takes the goo out of my back teeth. I hope the firm prospers.

– Having got off five books to the publishers I am now back at work on *Hebrew Myths* and enjoying the routine and the fun. One of them was 32 new poems. The sequence has probably ended. I think they're all right in so far as poems ever are, but I also think Zulficar Ghose[53] [*sic*] exaggerates. Glad to be rid of them.

– Got to know Stella better: she shines. Lucia is staying here mugging up the Spanish Classics for another fortnight. Stella gallantly pretends not to mind. Beryl phoned to her yesterday.

Much love to Mary and all.

Robert

In 1962 Reeves's anthology of Georgian poetry was published.

211

25 February 1962

Dearest James:

Did I thank you for *Georgian Poetry?* I meant to. You have done a very good job indeed and I was glad that *The Times* accorded you a leader on the news page! Yes, of course, Lascelles Abercrombie was one of the pillars, but he crumbled. So did Freeman and Shanks.[54] Bill Davies and Walter Delamare [*sic*] come out the best, I think. My poems are awful, but I don't care, really, for history's sake.

No recent news from Madrid.[55] Working with speed and pleasure on *Hebrew Myths*; no poems except joking ones for the last two months. Marmalade making. Swimming whenever there's sun and no wind. Tomás entranced by guitar lessons.

At Oxford in the Autumn I think I'll discuss technicalities, more, especially the question of rhythm which has been relatively unexplored.

Alastair's in Hampstead with Margot. He's cut himself off from me with a goodbye letter based on the odd and unfounded charge that I have vindictively told people that he owes me money! Which is how his mind works, I suppose. He has told people that he's going to conquer London; but seems pursued by ill luck of his own making. I can't be either glad or sorry; but my friends refuse to see him, and he's consumed by self-pity, I hear. What Margot's at, I don't know. She doesn't write to me but cultivates my friends still. It's good to be back at work, especially in this early Spring.

Wm returns in June and hopes for an oil job in N. Africa or even Spain. Yancy Lye[56] (who's going to share our cottage in the summer with Stella) wrote us a terrific account of her part in the Paris riots. I love that girl: so quiet and solid and still English.

Tom Blau the photographer was here and is doing a set of pictures of me for the *Daily Herald*. He also offers Juan a job learning the trade in his headquarters, says he sounds exactly the non-academic lone-wolf type whom he needs! We don't yet know Juan's reactions; but to get out of 'A' levels with our approval should delight him.

Much love to Mary and all –   Robert

In his next letter (12 March 1962) to Reeves, Graves wrote:

The usual thing is happening: after a period of intense emotional strain in poems, the clever easy ones are coming out by way of change: a sort of after-birth, and like the afterbirth full of vitamins, proteins, etc.

Early in May, Graves had passed on information to Gordon Wasson about mushrooms in ancient Greek sculpture, which Wasson said he would 'study in detail'.

30 May 1962

Dear Gordon:

I'm glad you are as interested in Charles Morgenstein's finds as I am.

Idries Shah will be here on June 14th. He has *not* been to Afghanistan – he thought of going only to sell some land, but he has got a big advance on his 'Sufi' book so that's not necessary now. I heard from him the other day that he's got new exciting information for you about the mushroom-eaters. Isn't it strange how I seem to act like a lightning-conductor for these things on your behalf? I don't believe in coincidence, only in a scientifically inexplicable serendipitous nexus of thought between a few people who are aware of certain problems and recognize one another as of that sort.

I'm glad you are taking Hofmann with you; he sounds all right.

My word, your moneyed colleagues of the Stock Exchange *are* nervous these days: seem anxious to cut their own throats by defeatism. I have just read that account of the Incas by Garcilaso (Orion Press); what a wonderful book: I suppose it's the crowning instance of defeatism in all history.

We'll be in London, not Oxford next fall – I'll just commute there. We must celebrate your arrival worthily.

My interest in hallucigenic [*sic*] mushrooms is mainly historical. Having once had that experience of a full use of the imaginative senses, I don't really want it again. It certainly has heightened my poetic powers by making me aware of sound and colour and texture as never before since my late childhood. But as a child of 11 and 12, I now realize, I did have the same spell occasionally, including the sense of 'knowing everything': and the mushroom experience was a reminder of its reality. The spell includes everything that is usually known as 'being in love' – 'the lunatic, the lover, the poet', the child and the mushroom adept of the Mysteries are 'of imagination all compact'. *How to preserve it* is the problem of most importance.

Yours ever –   – Robert

Graves first met Idries Shah in January 1961, when Shah was visiting Mallorca in the company of Dr Gerald Gardner, Director of the Museum of Magic and Witchcraft in the Isle of Man. Shah wrote to Graves, from a Palma *pension*, asking for an opportunity of 'saluting you one day before very long'. Shah, then thirty-seven years old, was already the author of various books on 'the diffusion of magical practices' and was currently engaged, he wrote, on a study of ecstatic religions which included experiments in mushroom-eating.

Graves and Shah soon became close friends; each, it would seem, was deeply impressed by the other. As he has done with other young writers, Graves helped Shah with his work and encouraged him to write an authoritative exposition of Sufic thought for Western readers and to make available the relevant basic materials for its study. The first book to come out of this was *The Sufis* (Doubleday, 1964), which had a long introduction by Graves, who described the author: 'Idries Shah Sayed happens to be in the senior male line of descent from the prophet Mohammed,[57] and to have inherited the secret mysteries from the Caliphs, his ancestors. He is, in fact, a Grand Sheikh of the Sufi *Tariqa* ("Rule") . . .' ('But this is misleading', Graves wrote to an American friend, 'he is one of us, not a Moslem personage.')

Most of what is written about Sufism is contradictory and confusing to outsiders; Shah's 'version' is highly controversial, partly because it steers away from Islam or contact with any religion, towards a sort of spiritual humanism and the 'experiential realities' of all religion through direct contact. Their 'secret' lore, which cannot be popularized or explained in book terms, can only be, Shah claims, understood through experiencing it with a Sufi master. Graves describes Sufism, in Shah's terms, in the introduction (though Shah himself shies away from restrictive descriptions or labels): 'The Sufis are an ancient spiritual freemasonry whose origins have never been traced or dated . . . Though commonly mistaken for a Moslem

214

sect, the Sufis are at home in all religions . . . [but are] bound by no religious dogma however tenuous and [use] no regular place of worship.' Graves never 'became' a Sufi, but he did recognize himself as one who shared their peculiar habits of thought and certain innate gifts; he saw himself, in fact, as a 'natural' Sufi: '. . . the natural Sufi may be as common in the West as in the East, and may come dressed as a general, a peasant, a merchant, a lawyer, a schoolmaster, a housewife, anything. To be "in the world, but not of it", free from ambition, greed, intellectual pride, blind obedience to custom, or awe of persons higher in rank – that is the Sufi's ideal.' He summed up what Sufism meant for him in practice in his earlier letter to Selwyn Jepson, on 29 August 1961: 'how to live by intuition and always keep on the beam.' This now became Graves's overriding concern.

Sufism also fitted in perfectly with his dedication to poetry, as poets, he wrote, were traditionally the chief disseminators of Sufi thought and 'earned the same reverence as did the *ollamhs*, or master poets, of early medieval Ireland, and used a similar secret language of metaphorical reference and verbal cipher. Nizami the Persian Sufi writes: "Under the poet's tongue lies the key of the treasury." '

Many of Graves's friends did not share his high opinion of Shah nor the excitement which contact with Sufism brought him – such as James Reeves who thought his new ideas on 'oriental philosophy' 'barmy', and said so. Gordon Wasson, however, was, according to Graves, 'in seventh heaven over Idries's mushroom secrets: ancient Arabia; Swat; and Persia . . .'

In June 1962, Wasson wrote to Graves about his latest mycological theory, on the identity of soma, the legendary divine intoxicating drink celebrated in Vedic hymns and poems, which, like its Greek counterpart ambrosia, had never been satisfactorily identified (current theories suggested it was a barley beer, or perhaps cannabis). Wasson suggested that one of the species of hallucinogenic mushrooms, *Stropharia cubensis Earle*, which is closely related to psilocybe and grows all the year round, but only in hot countries and only in cow pats, was soma, and that the cow is sacred in India because its excrement carried the sacred mushroom. The fact that mycologists studying in India have never recorded sighting the *Stropharia* was, he wrote, suggestive that voracious gathering of the mushroom had completely wiped out the species from the country. Wasson ended his letter by inviting Graves's comments on the theory, but warning of the dangers of this idea being pirated: 'I beg you to keep this idea between us . . . do not even tell Idries Shah . . . '

He also invited Graves to accompany him and Dr Albert Hofmann, the Research Director of Sandoz AG at Basel, to Mexico that summer. Hofmann had achieved international fame in 1943 by accidentally absorbing (probably through the spores of the skin of his fingers) a tiny amount of a drug which had a very powerful effect on his mind and which he later identified as lysergic acid diethylamide – LSD-25. Wasson and Heim sent Hofmann samples of the hallucinogenic mushroom from Mexico and from them he isolated the pure chemical called psilocybe (which Graves had taken in New York in 1960 – see page 189) which, it was hoped, could be used, along with LSD-25, in the treatment of mental illness.

10 June 1962

My dear Gordon:

I like your Soma theory. It sounds very possible, because cowpats are controllable, and there are no wild cattle in India. But how does the cycle start? Does the cow eat spores accidentally, when grubbing for grass near cowpats? And what of the Moslems in India? I suppose they imported no cattle. I have a silver coin dated about 200 AD with a sacred cow on it: from the Indian occupation of Afghanistan. I suppose they exhausted all the *Stropharia* there, too. But it certainly is odd, isn't it?

– I wish I could come with you to Mexico but can't. I'm indispensable here. I wish I were Wm's age; I'd make myco-ethnology my trade.

– I think the importance of the hallucinogenetic [*sic*] mushroom is in informing people of the full visual and sensory powers of their imagination, so that they can afterwards use it to better purpose. With me, the experience certainly broke down a barrier which had been raised in my mind since I was about twelve and had had a vision of the same 'knowledge of good and evil' which the mushroom gives one. There has been a new dimension (or whatever the word is) to my poems since that date. I feel that *psilocybe* should be given once, with full precautions, at an initiatory rite instead of that dreary episcopal 'confirmation' of the Anglican Church.

— This makes one look at sacred cows with a new eye: there's that mysterious story of the Cow Io in my *Greek Myths* (56) where she is connected with a number of places including India, and Mycenae (which seems to have been a mushroom centre as I remarked in a recent letter) and with the mysteries of Demeter as Cow, through Triptolemus and Celeus King of Eleusis. It's a terrible mythic muddle, but refers to the spread of a moon-cow cult, or might it be to the *soma* cult. In other words: when Demeter sends Triptolemus in his serpent chariot to give mankind the secret of bread, is it really the secret of sacrificial bread containing mushrooms that he's taking? Bread had been in use since 6000 BC.

— Is it possible that when the real *soma* became unavailable they gave *placebos* in place of it, such as milkweed. (The *OED* gives HŌM for *Soma* and if you turn to HŌM, identifies it with *Asclepias*, and if you turn to *Asclepias*, identifies it with '*milkweed*' or '*swallow-wort*'. And if you turn to 'Swallow-wort' you find that it's *Vincetoxicum officinale* also called 'Tame poison'. It is possible that a toxic *placebo* might work by suggestion.

Love to *Wm.* I'm so glad you have invited him. He's more magic in him than he lets appear [*sic*].

Yours ever   Robert

Love to Masha and warm wishes to Maggie.

. . . .

16 June 1962

My dear Gordon: *Exciting News!*

You won't believe me but it's true: Idries came here yesterday and, at the end of 24 hours' talk about poetry and other important things, came to mushrooms. He says he has an Indian cousin, whom he has sent as an undercover man to study this subject on your and my behalf in India among the Brahmins, impersonating a Brahmin himself.

(*) *Soma is still made* from *Stropharia*, in cowpats ritually offered to the Gods, and the urine of the priest who has eaten it and gone into ecstasy is drunk by the lesser devotees as 'cow's urine'.[58] Idries told me this without any prompting and says he's *not at all interested in publishing the material himself*: it's a friendship's offering to you and me. It was only when he had told me

217

everything that the cousin reported that I felt empowered to read him your letter. He said: 'How brilliant of Wasson to come to this conclusion by intuition! Tell him that we already have a man in the field.' I gather that this cousin is under some obligation to him: the Afghan Shah family regard the Indian branch as not quite up to standard, but make use of them. He sends you his best wishes.

I hope you feel as happy about this as I do. Idries's address is c/o us for a month.

Yours ever   – Robert –

I can suppose only that the Brahmins have hogged all the *Soma* in India and kept it growing only on their private preserves.

Idries's father, the Nawab, has reminded Idries that SUMA is the name of a tree-fungus in Afghanistan (where some of the Vedas were written).

Wasson was indeed happy at the news, if a bit 'astonished' or bewildered (as the tone of his letter implies) by the extraordinary coincidence. He elaborated on the theory and again warned Graves to be discreet. Graves replied (25 June):

Presumably the Brahmans have their own private temple herds. How clever of them to have kept the secret so well so many centuries!

– The Brahman still gives his urine to the faithful; I think I told you this.

– No, of course I won't tell anyone. Nor will Idries.

. . . .

You'll never get the Brahman's secret acknowledged: it was stolen by Idries's cousin as Prometheus stole fire – *perhaps the same sort of fire?*

Wasson, however, was to take the investigation further and came to believe that soma could not have been the *Stropharia* mushroom after all (see page 283).

In August Graves was reconciled with Margot, who returned to Deyá. James Reeves was the only one of his friends to criticize Graves openly; he disliked Margot and still thought Graves was

218

deluding himself. Graves felt the need to justify himself to Reeves, by now the longest known of his close friends and still one of the very few contemporary poets whom he could admire.

17 August 1962

Dearest James:

Stella was sweet, and we'd miss her even more but for the great tide of people who come surging up to the door and expect to be royally entertained ... Kingsley Amis[59] and his family are at the Posada: I wanted to see what he's all about, so let him do a piece about me for an American glossy. He's very sane, very decent, has a generous heart, and a sense of vocation: which is saying a lot.

. . . .

– Going over *Hebrew Myths* (a pretty strong book: 120,000 words) for the *seventh* time and starting my *Oxford Lectures*. Much behindhand.

Margot is coming here next month, after a silence of eight; she is no longer with Alastair who now accuses her of ruining his life (I hear from people who have seen him lately). But he was warned ... The strange thing is that I can find nothing to reproach Margot with, and owe a great deal to her, and that all the family, including Beryl, remain deeply attached to this strange, primitive being. She's been on her own for about three months, clearing her mind: though unpredictable, she's neither irresponsible nor evil and I now expect a lot from her in a constructive sense.

This is private for you and Mary ... I don't in the least blame you for mistrusting her, of course; nor have my feelings for her ever been *amour courtois*. . . . The fever has ended, I hope and believe; but the bond between us remains.

Anyhow: see you this autumn.

Much love   Robert

26 August 1962

Dearest James:

Thanks ever so much for the poems. I take 'A Kind of Love' personally: and am grateful for the last line.[60] It's a lovely poem. They're all good Reeves, which is praise indeed.

The only criticism is that there is an echo from Graves's 'To Bring the Dead to Life' in 'It Would be Wrong'.

> See as they see
> Speak as they speak

which people will pick up unkindly not realizing how much *you* the rest of the poem is.

About Margot: such things are incommunicable and it's nice that you don't like some of those poems, because you're the only dissident voice of any consequence (except Alastair's, who tried to persuade her that she was having a bad effect on my poetry, and quoted you!) and this has removed the curse of general praise. Also, the whole course of the sequence is what matters: love begins with a blind innocence which has to be recorded. Anyhow: to be undignified is to lose one's self-respect, and forfeit one's family's respect. Neither of these things has happened and the whole family, from Beryl down to Tomás, are solid in their love of her . . .

. . . .

My grey hairs are inconsequential (though it is hard for people to see that) because this isn't a love-affair in the usual sense: so many strange, far-reaching events have already sprung from it. If I told you them in a brief news-summary you'd think me bonkers or put it down to coincidence: two of them are even world-headline-news politically. I know *generally* what it's all about, but can't predict particulars; all I mean is, don't worry about my dignity. All's well; we don't disagree really, you and I.

– I love your 'Precept': perfect Reeves.

– I think that you should change the adverbial *y* of *pointlessly* because of the stronger *narcissistically*.

Thank goodness I'm not a demigod.[61]

Amis: his vocation is writing cleanly and truthfully. Trying to keep clear of the Mess and racket. One has to swallow a peck of dirt, but he swallows as little as possible.

Am getting my lectures ready: on poetic technique. One is on *Vulgarity* in technique.

[Unsigned]

That autumn Graves was back in England to give the Michaelmas term lectures at Oxford. These contain some of Graves's most interesting pronouncements on technique in poetry and on the dilemmas faced by the 'dedicated' poet. In the first lecture, 'Some Instances of

Poetic Vulgarity', he talked about the poet's predicament of being limited to writing poems only occasionally, when properly inspired: 'The writing of true poems happens so unpredictably that the poet is beset by the temptation to write when not in the mood. He may think that this can be induced by withdrawing to a glade, or a quiet, book-filled study, or by violent adventure among corsairs, alguazils, barmecides, and their modern equivalents. It cannot be.' He then set out, in general terms, his own solution to the 'main problem', of 'how to maintain the gift of certitude': '*Always to be in love*: that is one recommendation. To treat money and fame with equal nonchalance, is another. To remain independent, is a third. To prize personal honour, is a fourth. To make the English language one's constant study, is a fifth . . . Yet lightning strikes where and when it wills. No one ever knows. It is easy to take up a pen at random and plead: "I'm just keeping my hand in". But nine-tenths of what passes as English poetry is the product of either careerism, or keeping one's hand in: a choice between vulgarity and banality.' The italics are mine. Graves was gradually moving towards a position where he felt that to remain 'poetically alive' he had to be in love, hence his growing concern with the 'living Muse' and with consciously 'routing' his 'journey' (see page 232) through the realm of the White Goddess. By thus deliberately exposing himself to the vicissitudes and anxieties of romantic love he hoped not only to maintain his poetic inspiration through old age (he was now sixty-seven) but to maintain it at an even more intense level than before. It was a 'process' that was soon to absorb all his attention and though he never forgot that 'lightning strikes where and when it wills', he flew, as it were, his kite in every thunderstorm.

Back in Deyá Graves wrote to James Reeves, whom he had seen in England.

19 January 1963

Dearest James:

So nice to hear from you. No: I don't know who wrote those lines. I certainly didn't, though the spate of poems continues. In fact I have enough for another book; but won't publish unless privately lest I flood the whole Common Market. Yet they *seem* all right.

– It was such a relief having that long talk with you along the roads of Lewes, and finding that nothing was wrong between us.

– Have done a lot of work since I got back including a piece about 'Witches' for *Esquire*, a tidying up and rewriting of an Oxford Lecture for *Horizon*, the introduction to Idries Shah's *Sufi* book. Now I'm doing my MIT Boston lecture on Poetry and Science.[63]

– We recovered the lost *Man Friday* with great joy, so if the other miscarries, or is delayed, lessons can go on. We can always use 2.

– I'm glad about the Ballads. I think it's a useful book for schoolchildren.

Have been asked, as Prof. of Poetry, to recommend a Nobel Prize winner for 1963! All sorts of cracks occur to me, but I think I'll just remind them that Robert Frost is just still alive.

As for Bedales:[64] all schools are bad, but this seems better and out of the Bradley rut.

Lucia's safely back at Oxford, and Wm in the Sahara. We have too many oranges here and too few potatoes.

Love to you all   – Robert –

Graves published *New Poems* in October 1962 and wrote again to Reeves, about a review of the poems by G.S. Fraser.

29 January 1963

Dearest James:

Thanks for the *Men-Friday*.

Good old Sir Walter:[65] I said just what you did about him. He really meant it all, or most of it. But I think Tottel[66] was justified in his titles. G.S. Frazer[67] [*sic*] wouldn't be, if he misinterpreted that birthday poem which means precisely what it says: praise not reproof. I hope you were only joking about this.

I wrote him a letter about the review, but didn't post it because it was intended only to clear my own mind about those poems. He criticized my self-identification with a lion. I happen to have been born on the first day of Leo, to have lioncels in my armorial legacy, and to be descended from William the Lion of Scotland. The lion is the Love Goddess's mount, and lover, and in the poem about 'Inkidoo and the Queen of Babel' (a straight translation of

222

the Gilgamesh Epic) the Lion (*Enkidu*) complains of his treatment by her. Enkidu was conscious of his difficult situation. So am I . . . Elsewhere I call myself a bear.

The 'naked hurt' is part of the story; which has not yet ended, and I'm embarrassed by a great many new poems which should be printed in volume form this autumn – but maybe only privately. Naked hurt healed long ago.

Your small boom: it's not surprising to me. The poems stand up. *Theirs lie down.*

Schools are for different sorts of boys. Knowing Tomás well, I am sure that Bedales will be better than any public school. He likes work, and wants to get on; unlike Juan or the usual Majorcan boy.

Love to all   Robert

Graves's confidant in his dealings with the Muse was Idries Shah, who also became, perhaps unintentionally, Graves's 'adviser' on both the spiritual and practical implications of his experience of the Goddess. Indeed, reading Graves's correspondence at this time it seems as if he stood between the good angel, James Reeves, telling him to behave himself, and the bad angel, Idries Shah, encouraging him in his pursuit of the 'impossible' (sometimes even to the point, one suspects, of Shah telling Graves just what he wanted to hear – as if he felt that to do otherwise would have been pointless).

In March 1962, Shah told Graves in a letter that in the Margot affair he saw 'what might be called an organic process in human destiny . . . working itself out. Like other organic processes, it is susceptible to inner and outer impacts.' He continued: 'I wish I could find a more comely word for it in English, as this is a Sufi term and I want to use it. I find more and more in your poetry . . . ' Graves adopted this Sufi term, though was warned by Shah not to 'force' the 'process'; Shah drew on the example of the man who invented 'Radio communications systems' but who had to wait, before he could construct a receiver, until the vacuum valve was invented. This principle, Shah wrote, holds good in life too: 'I had to "wait" to do this book [*The Sufis*] until I met you. And then it was arranged by you, and everything was right. This mechanism, or whatever it is, must be working where M. [. . . .] and the whole thing is concerned. Some things have to happen before other things, which are "waiting", can happen. If this is so, we cannot ourselves do very much until the situation is ready for it.' For the moment, at least, Graves heeded him, even if Margot still was not behaving quite as Myth dictated.

23 April 1963

Dearest Idries:

Moyne[68] came visiting and said you had sent him! I like him: he's dead honest and one of the few really rich men with a real conscience. Went down for a swim with him. I think we both parted happier.

– My large handwriting is evidence of my euphoria: it varies from day to day, I can only suppose in sympathy with M. in New York; but tonight it's what the barometer calls *beau temps*. It's only natural that this process, or whatever you call it, should take a long time, and be subject to all sorts of delays and pains. Because the world is in a sick condition and we are all somehow infected, against our will, even if we think we are whole in mind and soul and body. But I know now that the process has started: there is too much evidence of it; and M. is as conscious of it as anyone, even when she seems to be retarding it. If she were not right, I would not feel so uplifted as I do; but she needs that meeting between the three of us. If you could write her a short note saying how happy you are to hear that all is absolutely all right again between her and me, it would help perhaps. (But not if it seems forced.) She needs evidence of your trust.

Love   ·R·

At the beginning of May, Graves went to America to deliver his lecture, 'Nine Hundred Iron Chariots', at the Massachusetts Institute of Technology. He put the poets' case to the scientists there and explained to them the role of the Muse in the poet's life:

Almost every poet has a personal Muse, a relationship first introduced into Europe from Sufi sources in Persia and Arabia during the early Middle Ages. She embodies for him the concept of primitive magic; and even if an occasional poet divines the Muse's existence from other poetic work and from natural surroundings traditionally associated with her immanence – such as mountains, woods and seas – his sense of possession by her is real enough. Once the Muse takes individual form, she remains absolutely free and in control of the situation. The poet–Muse relationship can never be a domestic one, nor need it be sexually consummated, since despite all the

224

symptoms of romantic love, it belongs to another order of experience – which, for want of a better term, we must call 'spiritual' and which is usually characterized by remarkable telescopings of space and time and by cosmic coincidences. These coincidences are not wondered at because, though rationally inexplicable, they have clearly been created by the power of thought. To enlarge on such phenomena would lead me into tedious anecdote . . .

Margot was also in New York at the same time as Graves, and at first all seemed to be going perfectly, as he wrote to Reeves.

2 May 1963   as from c/o Wasson
1 East End Av.
New York 21

Dearest James:
   Thanks for poems: splendid! Stella was sweet . . . I am now at MIT having fun with the technologists; back on May 16th to Deyá.
   – I think you should be invited over here to lecture and will get it into motion, if I can.
   – As a matter of record: I have never been so happy in my life as now: all the unhappiness of three years has peeled away. I wrote a poem two days ago beginning: 'Not to sleep all night long, for pure joy . . .' which is one of the few poems of utter happiness ever written. There's 'Sally in her Alley' [*sic*] and 'Fain would I change this note' [*sic*]⁶⁹ and the tear of pure delight that ran down heaven's cheek, and Bill Davies's rainbow and cuckoo; but this is mine, and may it excuse all the dark ones!
   Very much love to you all   Robert

   I am so infinitely glad I had that walk with you; and that what I said has proved true in fact not merely faith.

Reeves was unconvinced and thought that nobody *could* lie awake all night through pure joy. Graves's 'euphoria' was, anyway, soon gone.

6 May 1963   Plane NY–Boston

Dearest Idries:
   My euphoria was short-lived – I found that Margot, who greeted me with every evidence of perfect love, had been concealing a

relationship not only from me and you but even from Phyllis. He is young, sweet, honest, industrious: a rich successful New York Jew in show-business, utterly captivated by her. She is living with him in his apartment here and I was told of this only after her passionate assurance that everything was absolutely all right and that she was doing a cure on him. Now, there are two things wrong here at least, besides Margot's concealment of what if it had been *right* we would both have welcomed: one is that he's [scared] of her especially since he read a poem I wrote about her:

> She is no liar, yet she will wash away
> Honey from her lips, blood from her shadowy hand,
> And dressed at dawn in pure white robes will say,
> Trusting the ignorant world to understand:
> 'Such things no longer are; this is today.'

And the other is that he started talking to me of his ineluctable Jewish inheritance and admitting in effect that *he was not a real man* but a born coward. This was terrible to me and I could not conceal from Margot my knowledge that he was a wholly outside character: that he would never be brought into our magic number. He realized that something like this was in my mind and grew furious. For a moment she decided never to talk to me again, but recanted; however she has not seen me since. This gnawing sense of something that has gone wrong, despite Margot's taking on the Goddess role and talking with beautiful truth and clarity about it, has made me suffer again from that sorrow-pain of the solar-plexus; and I have lost ten *kilos* (22 lbs) since I first became aware of her own sense of guilt (when she was at the Savoy with this man and unable to tell me the truth).

So I have just written her a letter telling her of what you told me just before we left. About using her infallibility as a Goddess for other ends, and the danger of losing *báraka* and her whole being. Maybe that was an error; but I owed it to your sense of truth.

– What more can I do or say? He is an innocent who has strayed into a furnace and begun picking flames as if flowers; when he realizes, he will be scorched to death. Margot thinks no ill of herself but only of me for displaying my true colours in his company.

Until this incident (May 4th Saturday in case you were aware of it) I have [*sic*] been filled with such a sense of joy and eloquence that the effect I have on the MIT professors is frightening. But now I'm on the plane writing to you, the one person I can commune with, I know that I must go on and speak in Her name, ideally; for She abides whatever becomes of her priestesses.

Báraka Báraka Báraka   R.

On his last day in New York Graves was again reconciled with Margot to the point that 'left her fundamental truthfulness and love in no doubt'. However, she continued living in New York and Graves, although still preoccupied with 'the main problem', was now resigned to 'delay' and waited for her return to Deyá.

Another outspoken critic of Margot and the situation was Gordon Wasson, who had now retired from banking and planned to spend several years in the East, mainly in Japan, studying mycological traditions there.

While in New York Graves had stayed at Wasson's flat, where Margot and Cindy, Graves's future Muse, had engaged in a 'mock fight' during a 'Deyá party'. It was after this visit to America that Wasson, who also thought Graves to be deluding himself and said so, became more distant in his letters to Graves.

31 May 1963   Deyá
                              Private

Dear Gordon:

      . . . .

I don't see why 'several years' should pass before we meet again. I am often in London and NY, etc. You sound as though you were going into a monastery! We might even meet in Afghanistan!

The 'electrical pad' was worn out. One damps its contents with water and it serves as a hot-bag. Throw it out.

Don't worry about me and my loves; they follow an ancient mythical pattern and sustain me as a poet; and oddly enough, if money is taken as a criterion of 'are things all right?', the answer is a very favourable bank balance, whatever the disbursement. Margot is not my Mistress, but my Muse.

The three poems I wrote in your apartment will I hope bring it luck: it was wonderful being able to return there to the atmosphere of real friendship from that Cambridge Hotel.

227

To understand women one must love and trust beyond all reason (especially if they are Irish or Mediterranean) and expect no reward except a certain wisdom, and an occasional lowering of the curtain which tells you how utterly dependent on your love and trust they are, and how intensely they feel about you, however wayward they seem. *Amor vincit Omnia.*

Yours ever affy.   ·Robert·

PART FOUR

1964–1972

In the summer of 1963 Graves wrote his Oxford lectures and in one of these, 'Intimations of the Black Goddess', he gave an account of his poetry over the last three years when for the first time he had 'ventured to dramatize, truthfully and factually, the vicissitudes of a poet's dealings with the White Goddess, the Muse, the perpetual Other Woman. Whatever may be said against her,' he said, 'she at least gives him an honest warning of what to expect – as it were, tying a poison label around her own neck . . . ' He then talked of the Muse's evasions and broken promises, of her ruling the poet 'with a whim of iron' and of how, if he remains faithful, 'she will choose a lover from among his friends'. Though the poet's friends may descry his Muse as a vixen, a bitch, a bird of prey, 'he is pledged to accept what he would refuse from any other woman; and suffers most when she uses the light of glory with which he invests her, to shine in an anti-poetic and even criminal world. Is she, in truth, his Muse, his love? Or is she acting a part with sardonic humour? His test will be: which gives the greater pain – belief or disbelief? Many poets break under the strain . . . '

Graves was always fully aware of the criticisms against his behaviour and against his Muses, and struggled perpetually between belief and disbelief. In this he was, undoubtedly, a Don Quixote rather than a Don Juan, but in his pursuit of Dulcinea he was, also, his 'own' Sancho Panza.

In 1964, he was again in that state of optimism and wilfully blind innocence which, he said, characterize the beginnings of love. In the same Oxford lecture he records his new hope, but giving the Muse a new name, that of the White Goddess's 'mysterious' sister, the Goddess of Wisdom – 'Call her the Black Goddess'. Black, because of the Sufic tradition of wisdom as blackness. Graves, however, had doubts that Margot could ever fill the role of the Black Goddess,

231

who offers 'certitude in love', and talked to Shah about rerouting his 'journey'.

No date   Deyá

Dearest Idries:

Everything is in confusion here: shortage of water, workmen in every room, no electricity. But Beryl and Karl are being heroic and I am struggling with the problem of 'Poet and Muse';[1] have discovered that the Greeks knew about it and took a pessimistic view: that the White Goddess is fated to spend some months of the year coupling with a serpent and eating corpse-flesh, and that the poet when he tries to get her back permanently on earth from those infernal joys will have suffered so much from his previous experiences of her that he will lose confidence and at the last moment fail.

– The real point is when and how the White Goddess who walks impartially between good and evil (evil, being as you say, nothing, delay, ambiguity, irrelevance, cleverness, cowardice, insensitivity, a draining of *báraka*) will become the Black Goddess of Wisdom. Her previous experiences entitle her to be so, if she wants: the purely Virgin-Mary–good woman does not understand the temptation to delay and eat corpse flesh.

– I trust that this personal case which is beautifully illustrative of the principle will be decided here in a month's time: if it can't be, then patience, and I will have to re-route my journey with your help. In New York she was on the brink of a decision; but seems now to have fallen away again, perhaps to a further point than before. Cindy and Ralph[2] are greatly concerned by this: especially as Cindy has come to a decision about ranging herself with *us*, and being all that she can be; and she is a wonderful girl, and very close to Margot, and shocked at what Margot has been recently doing to herself and to me. Cindy writes that Margot's main preoccupation, she thinks, is how she can possibly face Beryl, with whom she has broken a sacred bond.

Crazy letter from Christopher Hills[3] [*sic*] in answer to mine rejecting his pretensions. He now claims to be a Sufi and says he could, if he wished, levitate his letter to me instead of mailing it! Poor Isla[4] has been unable to come here: in hospital at St Charles's Hospital, Ladbroke Grove, and in great pain.

Love to you both.   ·R·

Margot, however, remained in New York, and Graves decided 'to worry about her no more'. On 20 May he had written to Shah: 'I can't see an alternative to Margot, not even E—— ...' and again in June: 'E—— may be arriving any day; but I resist the temptation to think of her as an alternative, though I am completely at one with her in thought and feeling – nor would she accept the Vessel role unless M. resigned of her own free will as being unable to undertake its responsibilities.'

Margot did resign ('that's all over', he wrote to Wasson in January, 'but I am grateful to her for being so true to mythic pattern') and Graves found his alternative in Cindy. However, unlike Margot and Judith, Cindy, who later changed her name to Aemilia, aroused intense suspicion and dislike from all those closest to Graves, who saw her as a highly unsuitable Muse, as someone, in fact, with whom Graves would not normally have associated. James Reeves was now not the only dissident voice who thought Graves was hopelessly misguided in his new attachment.

Graves explained the situation to Selwyn Jepson.

No date
St John's College
Oxford
(part of the time)

Dearest Selwyn:

One of these things: the natural discrepancy between poetic and historic reality. As you know, I'm fated to be a poet: and the nearer I come to what I really mean, the greater the opposition from those who love me in another sense altogether; such as my immediate family. And even those who refuse to take sides, do so really. It's no fun for anyone. But I can't let go.

And this is not another Margot – though Margot was splendid in her cool self-destructive way, and able to look after herself.

. . . .

– Aemile has too good a heart, rather than too grudging a one, is about 8 years older than Margot, and Mexican-Italian-Basque. Makes no plans, has lived for several years in Greenwich Village, from hand to mouth: numerous talents, no careerist ambitions, an extremist, no children. Is embarrassed, annoyed, surprised, and infuriated sometimes by finding that she and I both get sick and paralysed and psychosomatic whenever we try to break this fatal bond between us – which is rarely sexual and then only because one can't cheat the body, and which has to do with a common huge compunction to think in a region of thought where practically nobody else visits. Her contribution is a fantastic delicacy of moral judgement though few people know about this.

– This is just to explain what's been happening. *You'll* love her at once – but Tania will be more cautious. So I don't think you'd better invite us down! It's very difficult for Aemile to find a harbour in London, and she doesn't know it as she knows Paris or NY. But manages somehow. Future unforeseeable.

– The new poems are all they should be; but this can't very well be offered in mitigation of what seems to others shameful behaviour on my part – Beryl of course doesn't agree with the judgement but she and Aemile can't meet on sisterly terms having nothing in common except what divides them; and the same basic goodness. I have to keep the two lives separate, which is difficult. And both women behave blamelessly, which allows me to make no choice.

Love to you both   Robert

I was terribly grieved about SMITH.

Have been rewriting *Much Ado* for L. Olivier and K. Tynan.[5] But in Elizabethan language, just to help Shakespeare out, where nobody has the least idea what a line means and the laugh gets lost; not in modern English.

On 17 January Idries Shah's *The Sufis* was published by Doubleday in New York.

18 January 1964   Deyá

Dearest Idries

The Sufis is terrific. I regret the absence of an index, and your being too considerate of my time: if I had read the proofs there are scores of small, foolish, inessential points I could have put right.

– It doesn't matter really, because it's all there, and nobody who is troubled by such uses as '*different than*' deserves to read it! I am so proud in having assisted in its publication. Most interesting to see the press reaction to it.

– Heard from Emile [*sic*] in Mexico, where she has found a great family of long-lost cousins: splendid people. And is now on the way back to NY. Sounds at her best.

– I am sending *The Sufis* to Emile and Sally, who will need it most urgently.

– Bill[6] returns to Deyá in the middle of March.

– Have written some poems which I know will make sense to you.

– Will spare you ordinary local news; all is well and *báraka* abounds.

Much love to you both and my deep respects to your father.

Robert

The Sufis is a reminder of my enormous ignorance about so many essentials that I wonder that you treat what knowledge I have with respect: but 'the heart is true' at least, you know that, and I learn every day.

Beryl has just taken it to Palma to read at the *Indigo*.[7] The drum rhythm will probably stimulate her understanding of it: and this is not a joke.

Shah accepted Graves's criticisms and defended himself by saying that the disorganized, 'scattered' or 'undulating' construction of the book was deliberate, as what he was trying to show was how easily misunderstood a 'formulation' could be and how 'systematizing' distorts. This Graves accepted, though he was still disappointed by the quality of the writing (see page 240).

On 4 February he wrote to Shah:

I have been reading and re-reading *The Sufis*. Everything in it seems very familiar I suppose because (as Emile wrote when I sent her a copy) your voice can be heard behind each sentence. (She's magnificent and getting on with her painting after her Mexico visit.)

– And the deliberate unliterariness of the book is, I see, necessary. To show that you are not *selling* anything. At first it disappointed me: professionally – as if I found the village carpenter using an out-of-date and awkward hand adze instead of an electric plane.

– I have been thinking of my own poems in terms of the Sufi ones. The spirit is the same, when I am really inspired, but the terms of reference are very different. I have to respect the long

English and Latin and French histories of the words I use; not Arabic roots. But the theme of love is both personal and religious in the Sufic sense, and always (now) more consciously so.

Shah replied that if he had wanted to project a personal image, or make a plausible case for Sufism, he would have done 'a suitable processing job on the material, making it both more acceptable and "better written".' The Sufis' aim, and his in writing the book, was to decondition people, and prevent their reconditioning.

He also wrote about his own problem, which was being accused of trying to assert himself; if he said things about himself which he knew to be true, people regarded it as 'boasting, because of their social conventions'. Many people came to him for help whom he knew would never benefit from anything he said and the best thing he could do for them was to make them think 'that they have of their own free will arrived at the conclusion that I am no use to them.' This problem continued to oppress him, and several years later he wrote that, having avoided publicity or cultism as much as possible, he still hadn't escaped charges of being a 'would-be guru. How interesting that one can never establish bona-fides, yet remain potentially vulnerable at the caprice of anyone . . . '

In February Graves's daughter Jenny became suddenly ill and died while visiting friends in England; the news came as a great blow to Graves, who had become increasingly attached to Jenny, though as always in such a case he restrained himself from expressing his true sadness.

To Idries Shah

10 February 1964

Dearest Idries:

I got a mysterious telegram from Taroudan which seemed to come from you at a hotel called Gazelle D'Or. It evidently didn't.[8] I wrote to thank you!

– I expect you know now that Jenny died: of cerebral haemorrhage on the day before you wrote. I couldn't come to the funeral because, for the first day in four years, I had no passport – it was in Barcelona at the US Consulate!

In my letter (which won't get to you) I told you that I was converted to your way of writing that book, and how good it is: and asked, well, not exactly to be *forgiven*, but to be understood. It was an impossible book to write; but you did it. You had to *say* and *not to say* at the same time; which does not go with clear writing. My hope is to say things so clearly in poems that only a few people understand them. Prose is different.

I do wish you and Kashfi were well. We all are, here. I suppose you have no plans?

– I don't think anyone would accuse you of self-assertiveness. One has to know one's value, capacities, and limitations. On the contrary I feel that you hide almost too much – but then you must be even more sought after than I am by cranks, phonies and the greedy – and I have an enormous barrage of them.

Poems are by-products of *whatever-it-is*; but I find that they also serve to light up *whatever-it-is* in other people. This is a very strange and humbling experience, because the light passed on comes as a gift unsought, not fabricated by oneself. I would not dare to claim myself a Sufi: but I believe I can now recognize the essential quality in others.

Well . . . I am off to NY on Feb. 22, back on March 4, via Madrid [*margin note*: ¡*inshallah*!]. I don't know yet where I'll be staying but your sister will find me a pad somewhere. She is happy again and painting. I told her not to be hurt by your silence. She will be coming back here with me.

– I asked you about the *spinning-top* as perhaps being a Dervish metaphor for the centrifugal force that focuses a man on a point: even (if a gyroscope) on a taut wire; and I quoted the *Aeneid* as showing that Bacchic devotees also whirled. And did you know that one Herr Windervogel points out the Doomsday Book to be compiled on Moslem principles?

– Am very much with you in spirit and so is Emile. Bill returns here in March, midmonth.

– Jenny was a *good* woman, but dissipated all her energies of honour and love to little purpose; I couldn't get through to her about this.

I don't *worry* about you two; I know that there's some sense in this accident of illness, which time will reveal. But I am sad about it all the same.

What other news? I bought a 12 roomed ruined house at Deyá

opposite the Museum; on an impulse. Wm (who was here for two days) approves . . . I hope you'll approve my new poems. In English one doesn't use those ROOTS but one uses the entire history of every word from its first coinage through all changes and shifts of meaning: that is where the *bárakat* [*sic*] lies for us.

Can I do anything for you? I enclose a letter that may interest you. Somehow I'm not sure of this man despite his credentials.

Love to you both. Keep warm.

Love from us all   Robert

P.T.O.

Jimmy Metcalf has discovered that a great part of the complicated Celtic decorative motifs came from the reflections of several round mirrors arranged in a group: he says that two motives

 and

are often occurring and seem to have some mystical significance. Since the mirror is a part of the Greek Mysteries, and since I sense a connection between them and Sufic mysteries, I thought I'd consult you. The date is the 1st centuries BC and AD.

I would never criticize Mo.[9] I trust him wholly, and feel that he is under a great strain from taking on so much of other people's anxieties.

I have no system myself (I have always repudiated systems), only principles.

Love again to you both and all.   –R–

Shah's 'sister' in the letter refers to Cindy ('Emile') who had made both a pact, or 'vow', with Graves, witnessed by Shah, and had been 'adopted' as Shah's spiritual sister in a solemn ceremony.

No date

Dearest Idries:

No: never got a letter in NY. Emile and I have been saying that a feeling of your absence was the one cloud on our horizon. I had written to you at least five times.

Anyhow: you are well. And you send love to all.

But no news of Kashfi's sickness. May we assume she is well? Or of your plans for coming here.

There is so much to say that can't be put into letters. Emile is here with us. We passed through Madrid (where I saw the Minister about the eternal subject of breaking the deadlock of the Jazz Club's keeping open until 3 a.m. This is for Lucia and Ramón. We are up against Vested Interests, but think that all's well. I wouldn't do anything like that for myself, only for near-and-dears). We have had extraordinary experiences of the strange healing power that seems to affect people when we enter a room together; it is a sobering experience, because we can't claim to know how it happens or even to take credit for anything except the strength of our personal bond.

I am not undertaking any writing or other jobs now. Have too much to do already. You will have heard of Jenny's death. She and I had agreed that I should write out *as story*[10] the *Solomon and Sheba* play we had worked at together. Now I feel I must do that at once as her memorial. But the story is so very close to all that I have been thinking about, with Emile and yourself, about the ideal relations between real man and real woman, which the present ethical set-up delays and distorts, that I want to make it not only as good as I can make it, but as close to your own traditional Sufi thought as possible, and approved by Emile who has been thinking hard of late. I am certain that the Moslem legends of the Solomon–Sheba relationship are of the utmost importance.

The Crusades are merely of historical interest and I seem to have grown out of history.

News: Juan is happy again to have passed his exams. Lucia comes here next Sunday. Our dear old dog, Ygrec, died. In New York I had wonderful audiences when I lectured, and made friends with the top-ranking, wildest and therefore shabbiest-looking jazz musicians.

Emile is here for a few weeks only, then goes back to NY to show her mother the World Fair, then here again in May. I'll leave this page for her to write.

Meanwhile much love.   R

The Sufis had a poor initial reception in America and sold little, despite Shah himself contributing a considerable sum of money towards additional advertising (an action Graves thought ill-advised). Graves wrote encouragingly to him, however, and reverted to the subject of the quality of Shah's writing, which remained a disappointment to him.

21 May 1964

Dearest Idries:

I'm sorry you're off to Morocco because Emile had invested 70 dollars to go by way of London to see you! I have cabled for her to come straight here and now she'll miss you. She got hung up in NY with her mother.

– I'll be in London on June 25th unless you're not there, when I'll come back. Don't put yourselves out. These meetings have their own timing.

– I'm not surprised at the slow start of *The Sufis*, because you took care not to make it read like an advertisement for a new World Religion; and *scattered* rather than set out plainly. The Doubleday salesmen, whose job is to persuade provincial bookshops to order the book, will have made nothing of it: not having had the advantage of hearing your voice which carries most of your truth in its inflexions. The *craft* of written communication, whether one scatters or writes directly, consists of not letting the reader's attention stray from the subject under discussion, except at well-defined breaks. This was what I tried to tell you last year, but I think you misunderstood this *craft* of writing for the *art* of writing, which is a different matter: an oratorical trick of selling shoddy ideas as though they were true.

– The *craft* is a means of avoiding confusion and boredom and atmospherics and fading effect and short circuits: by the *order* in which words are placed. Also by the avoidance of unparallel similarities, and changing synonyms for the same subject; mixed metaphors; repetition: all of which can be safely used in speech because the magic of the voice excuses them and you can correct any misapprehensions when you see that what you say is not being carefully followed. Various facts of immense interest to readers in *The Sufis* are thrown away by deliberate unemphasis. When you *talk*, these facts are given in a sort of *sotto voce* because you know, and we know, that they are unimportant in comparison with the principles of love and honour and wisdom which

240

accounts for them. In *writing*, these facts should be used to rivet the attention of the Western reader: who will then be ready to listen when you give first their historical setting and then their spiritual meaning.

– So I don't think that Doubledays are acting otherwise than can be expected of them. They are puzzled by the book, they expect others to be puzzled, and the book falls off the usual conveyor-belt. There's no Louis Marin at 575 Madison Av., NY 22!

– Now, so long as you aren't worried about sales, that's all right. Books are published and fall flat (as several of mine have done) but then have a slow underground life and eventually spring up again vigorously. A book, *Seven Days in New Crete*, which I couldn't persuade Cassell to keep in print, is now going to be made (or so it seems) into a Broadway musical!!!![11] *The Nazarene Gospel* is out of print, but in a year or two it will (I believe) be on every paperback bookshelf.

The Sufis is a marvellous book, and will be recognized as such before long. Leave it to find its own readers who will hear your voice spreading, not those envisaged by Doubleday.

– I have been thinking very hard about a lot of things lately, and especially about the *process*: you'd be enchanted with the new spirit of Deyá of which Bill and Jacky (because of you largely) are the most shining distributors. Mary Allan is here for another ten days and is wholly with us: what a clear atmosphere surrounds her. My new poems – well, you know how it is – but one or two have that durable quality which poems have when all irrelevances are omitted. 'Durable' does not necessarily refer to the future but is a quality of compactness and certitude; which comes from my love for Emile. Although on the everyday level she's unpredictable and even scatty, on the durable level she's as firm as a rock; so I don't worry about how and what and when.

Love to you both.   Robert

Despite what he said, however, the 'what and when' were causing Graves considerable distress. Graves's expectations of the Black Goddess had been high – in his lecture he said that she 'promises a new pacific bond between men and women, corresponding to a final reality of love, in which the patriarchal marriage bond will fade away . . . ' With Cindy cast in the role, however, the Black Goddess soon became a cruel parody of Graves's ideal. His friends now became impatient, seeing the case as hopeless; Shah now lost all interest in the affair and was reluctant to offer any more support or advice, and Graves became irritated after receiving a 'kitchen sink letter' from him.

2 July 1964

Dearest Idries:

I was grateful for your letter because I misread it: your quotation from Saib of Isfahan I took for a telepathic comment on my distress about Emile's silence not yours; and when I got a letter from her by the same mail, I found it apposite and cabled it her as your blessing.

– No: I don't want news-letters or formal letters about *The Sufis* book, which is of little importance to us compared with the things that rule our life. I am a poet, not a literary man; I am grateful for gifts of love from you, especially the dagger and the Afghan carpet, but I am not a collector of coins or arrowheads – how can you think it? You say nothing at all in your letter.

– Where you found your school is unimportant compared with what is taught: and every choice is always the wrong choice. It decides itself.

– I have recently decided to cut out of my life everything that is no longer alive and sound; it will be a long process. 'Popular demand' is the voice of the dead, I agree. If I go to Oxford it is only in case there are a few live people there; I went there as a young man and have a debt to pay. Soon it will be paid.

Emile is in great distress, and if you had stood by her as was your duty as a brother you would have saved her and me from a great deal of pain. (Hypothetic case: ruled out.) She was dead serious on a certain memorable occasion and speaking with utter truth: as you knew at the time. I hope she will soon be back here. You do not mention her in your letter, though you discussed her with William.

– To me the most important problem in the world is the fateful relation of woman's being to man's doing and I have myself learned more from her on this subject than from anyone else in the world. So could you. Beryl is pure affection, regularity, honesty, single-heartedness – these are the qualities of history which means they are woman's complaisance of a man-directed world; not a direct aid to the process which you envisage and which Emile painfully understands.

All this sounds as though I were criticizing or reproaching you; but I am not. Nor am I demanding anything from you. I am directing your attention not to a *priority* – priorities can be arranged alphabetically or in temporal sequence – but to an immediacy: a dangerous gap in your garden hedge. I no longer have any ambitions or desire for money nor any of the usual motives. All that means anything to me is poetic truth of the most uncompromising sort, which is not a moralistic truth but a personal one of man–woman: the broaching of a new estate. You are a physician rather than a poet.

It's a pity that the airport strike did not occur earlier to redirect you to London; I counted on your being there. But at least you saw Beryl and will see Ralph.

Love and *Báraka*   Robert

You answered my letters without answering them; silence would have been better.

Mo has been very good to me.

Two weeks later Graves reread *The Sufis* and wrote again to Shah:

Rereading my recent poems – they appear to be simple love poems but are all concerned with the central problem of wisdom through love, and the true relation between the poet and his beloved, and the miracles that love can perform by an overflow of personal love into the world of friends. The poems are intensely concentrated.

Our Birthday Play[12] is a murder mystery: among the suspects are a couple of Goofy Sufis (Bill and Wm) whose caricature you would like. But they do point at the murderer by obscure hints.

I feel very close to you again from being laid up with a twisted back and reading *The Sufis* undisturbed. Am not doing any ordinary literary work; in fact, I intend to stop that sort of life now.

At the beginning of October, Graves and Beryl prepared to return to Oxford, as he wrote to Tom Matthews.

6 October 1964

Dearest Tom:

There was a note in the papers about an injury to my knee – not important – but I have since had an operation for a cyst on my elbow which got me down for a while. I'm all right now and swimming again.

– On Sunday we go to England by car, the slow way, and will be at Oxford until December. On the whole an unpleasant summer, no rain, too many visitors, and Beatles records all the time. Plagued with poems; that seems all right when they say what I really mean (as they have) but it is always a painful experience, and my destiny, I guess.

Talking at Oxford on verse craft as opposed to poetry.

I wish I hadn't lost your letter. I'm sure it had some news in it that I should have commented on, but it came when I wasn't really myself. Anyhow: I am so glad that you are getting married to someone I really like – not that I didn't like the other two – and can count upon to treat you well.

Much love   Robert

Wm will be up at St John's by now, doing his archaeology course. Fear this will miss you. We come back here before you return.

P.S. Found letter: had mentally suppressed the Laura–Schuyler news. *Dawn in Britain*[13] was his King Charles head, back in the thirties. Poor lexicographer!

As for Laura's preoccupation: my view is that one can achieve a command of one's language by continually thinking about it at all historical levels and in all social gradations. But to write poetry one must *love* and keep one's spiritual integrity; and the miracle is beyond comment or explanation. Even Laura can't destroy what she once wrote: even though she tried to suppress her love poems to me and Allen Tate.[14]

To Selwyn Jepson

7 January 1965

Dearest Selwyn:

Thanks a lot for returning the poems; they are the price of blood, as you see. I try to take care of myself, but in fighting off routine and falsity, I get involved with manic depressive genius and people either without heart, or with too much, or with hemi*-schizo-phrenes.

– But I always know where I am; if only on a bridge I cannot see, going over a canyon; I feel it under my feet.

– Hallucinogens are good stuff for fiction: one can direct one's mind, if practised, almost anywhere one pleases in time or space under a reliable drug. On the other hand one can be very suggestible under the drug, and be diverted or cheated in one's search.

– There's a *Psychedelic Review* published somewhere.

Don't know *African Genesis* – but I read little these days.

Much love to you both.

Have had three days of nose bleeding – most uncomfortable but almost as purging as a poem – also a long delayed letter which makes sense.

Love from us all.   Robert

*A non-scholar would have written *semi* and goofed.

At this time Alan Sillitoe and Ruth Fainlight also adopted Cindy as their 'spiritual sister', which Graves saw as a hopeful sign of her 'coming through'.

18 January 1965

Dearest Alan and Ruth:

I eventually heard from Aemile in Paris: recovering from things after a three weeks' silence. She's probably in New York now.

– It was lovely to hear that she had enrolled herself as your sister; and that by signing with the Byzantine ring I gave her I was, she says, a witness.

– A corner has been turned at last and I think now I understand exactly what's remained unsettled between her and me; I'll be seeing her next month in New York, I hope. If so, I'll stop and see you in London.

– While in London she couldn't face writing to me; which made things horrible.

– Anyhow, we find that our bond resists even atomic explosions. Like the beer on Christmas Island.

– All well here, though I've been pretty low for weeks until just the other day.

245

– The Swedish Academy asked to have my recommendations for the Nobel Prize. For Aemile's sake (and our own) I named you. You haven't a chance; but just for the fun of it, I hope you don't mind.

Much love to you all three   Robert

I wrote a note to Edna.[15]

Graves was driven to distraction by Cindy's capriciousness, her long silences, evasions and 'ambivalent behaviour', followed by sudden propitiations and ecstatic outbursts of love and belief in her role as the Goddess. His health was being affected and, perhaps for the first time ever, his work. His poems at this time lack their normal power and honesty and he stopped writing prose almost entirely, as there was now enough money coming in to support the family and he needed to 'think out' the problem without any other distraction. The only solution he saw was to get away from his normal life and be alone with Cindy for a while, who now wrote contritely and lovingly, making Graves hopeful again.

In February he went to New York to see her, and from there wrote to Karl Gay. Having stopped writing books, Graves realized that it was not only uneconomical to keep his secretary, but that Gay, now aged fifty-three, would do better for himself by getting another job while he was still young enough. Nevertheless, the following letter came as a shock to Gay, who, although he knew of Graves's intention never to write another long prose book 'with which to burden us both', had not earlier been led by Graves to expect dismissal.

No date   c/o Brooks
                                                          9 Gay St
                                                      New York 14

Private

Dearest Karl:

My life is so changed that I don't know how to write, really. I was expecting you to send me the *Luna de los Perros*.[16] What happened?

– Now it's a month, and on March 15th I have to go out (because I came in on a wrong visa) and return as a tourist. I'm going with Aemile ('Cindy') to Mexico for a fortnight. Difficult for me to mention her name to you, because though you at first liked her, her friend Ralph insulted you, so you sheared off; and perhaps had other reasons. Anyhow, our fortunes, hers and mine (as you must have realized) are curiously linked together. She perhaps represents 'danger' to you, and if so I don't blame you; but she and I have got so far on in thought together that there's no going back; and if it were a simple love-affair I should agree with everyone that I'm a fool. But it's not that in the least. Patience! ¡*Calma*!

How this will affect my life in general I don't yet know; but we are each on the other's hook and any attempt to unhook causes psychosomatic trouble.

Anyhow, I expect to be in Deyá next month; and discuss things with you. I am not going to write any more books and there will be plenty of money available (from sales of MSS, etc.) – to provide you with capital if you want to work elsewhere, either in Spain or England . . . It has been a bit of a cloud that in the Village your friends and mine were always so distinct, though the long tie of friendship and real affection has always been unbroken between you and me. Don't worry; just think well of me and consider *yourself* and your family. There's no hurry! An epoch has ended and what comes next is bound to be good if we realize that we are all in each other's hands, in a way.

Tomorrow I see Cohen about *Solomon and Sheba*, his next project. I am well and alert.

– Much love to you all   Robert

From Mexico Graves wrote again to Gay.

14 April 1965   as from
                                                   9 Gay St, NY
                                              where I'll be soon

Dearest Karl:

I wanted the typescript to work on here. But I'm not really sorry you didn't send it. It's unimportant!

I have done no writing, except a poem or two, and have no plans for writing: seem to be beyond that. Impossible to explain. Nor is my preoccupation a love affair but something so way-out there's no definition possible. It ends my literary life. What happens next I'm waiting to see. I'm returning to Deyá alone.

It would be untrue to say that I've turned mystic. Nothing vulgar like that: only an extraordinary awareness of reality and a sort of prophetic and therapeutic possession. Sane as ever.

– Don't be cross, continue to love me, and accept the change for your own sake.

Love to you and the whole family   ·R·

My life at Deyá was beginning to stink. I had to get out and think.

Graves returned alone because in Mexico the situation reached its climax and Graves reached his (almost) final disillusion in Cindy's attempts to be the Muse.

Back in Deyá he wrote to Ruth Fainlight, who, with her husband Alan Sillitoe, had by now become very close friends of the whole Graves family.

3 May 1965   Deyá

Dearest Ruth:

I have been back from Mexico, where I left Aemile, a fortnight now.

It's difficult to know what to say about her except that she went wild and behaved scandalously, and I came quietly away and that if (as motor-cyclists say) she can get out of her 'roll' and back on the highway, it will be a miracle.

– Nevertheless miracles occur . . . At least I saved her from running off with a delinquent young enough to be her son (easily).

– My joy at her adoption of you as her sister last Christmas was tempered, when I found that ——, whom she had wholly rejected but invited to Sonja's as soon as I left her, and who is a *perdido*,[17] had been witness of the ceremony. It was some weeks before I even knew she had taken him back – despite her protestations of whole and enduring love for me. Now he's got another girl, I hear.

– Omar has confidence in Aemile's eventual recovery, so I cannot abandon my love for her. She *was* coming here for the summer, but two things happened: Wm got married and cabled me to Mexico for the Posada which I'd promised Aemile. Aemile had gone off to a place where there was no mail, and did not answer my letters

248

when she returned and had decided to marry another, rather sweet man (but another *perdido*) – who promptly went off elsewhere with someone else's wife . . . So I cabled Wm letting him have the Posada. I also wrote and told her what I'd done.

Eventually I got a vague, but most loving letter, which showed she hadn't even troubled to pick up my letters from the PO; so that's how it is, or isn't.

– Back here, the sun doesn't shine as usual; but the roses are in full bloom.

– She may still be in Mexico because I left her wads of cash among the group of American expatriates always high on pot – not that I have aught against pot – or perhaps in California or perhaps NY. Spin a coin, or several coins, for an answer.

Much love to you both and to Nimrod.   x R x

Beryl still wants to go to Russia with you. She's splendid as usual. I have had to dismiss Karl and compensate him with half my small fortune! But he's still around.

I think this letter is fair; but of course private except to Alan. And if Aemile recovers, forget it all.

On the same day Graves wrote to Shah about the 'paradox' of being in love: one's spiritual powers are strengthened, but so also is one's 'readiness to accept and pardon and even applaud actions from the loved-one that would seem vile if performed by anyone else – I suppose as one takes one's own follies for granted – and thus to feel close to people from whom normally one would shrink in disgust. In Mexico you'd hardly have recognized me.'

Graves, however, was not rancorous and did not yet (though he soon did) give up all hope for Cindy, as he wrote to Shah in the same letter:

. . . she must hurt herself a great deal more before she escapes from her bush of thorns. I realize that you must have a sense of her eventually coming through, or you would not have originally accepted her as you did. She does *know* in a fantastic way, but fails to relate her knowledge to practice: wilfully, for some hidden reason. Perhaps so do I.

Nevertheless, he was now less disposed to her sudden 'reforms' and reconciliations, as he wrote to the Sillitoes some time after his return from Mexico and on receipt of a letter from her 'encouraging me to get up and out': 'I tell her that I'm no Tolstoy to die at any railway station.'

That summer Graves was seventy. He wrote to James Reeves, who was compiling a collection of 'neglected' poems.

21 July 1965

Dearest James:

'Muses' Garden' – Robert Graves – no, Robert Jones.[18] It's a good song, I agree; but contrived, like nearly all of that lot.

– Neglected poems? The Irish and Scots have a good many. See Padraic Colum's[19] anthology of the 1920s and John Buchan's of the same. 'Bruadar and Glynn and Smith' (1) and 'A Dublin Peeler Once Went Out' (1) and 'Kissed Yestreen' (2) and 'Happy the Craw' (2). And there's W. Y. Tyrell's[20] 'O What Will the Man Full of Sin Do?' published in 1919 or so by *Poetry Bookshop* as a broadside. Emilia's speech in *Two Noble Kinsmen* Act 1 Scene III obviously by Shakespeare is one of my lovedst poems of all. I did not realize her name was Emilia.

– Tobias Hume's 'Fain Would I Change That Note' (*Elizabethan Song Books*) is one of the few happy love poems.

Yes: 70 on Saturday and I am going to do nothing about the birthday except read 'Poems Written at Deyá 1929–65' to a select audience. Aug. 2, Lucia's wedding, is the big day.

Yes I know more than I did what it's all about: namely the impossibility of reconciling the solar with the lunar calendar, though every few hundred years (if one is lucky to see it) a full moon exactly coincides with the Summer Solstice: or almost. Those coincidences are all that really matter; plus the refusal to die while still alive, or to fudge and fluff when seized by a poem. Or to pity oneself, or deny oneself faith in the coincidence.

Loving True, Flying Blind

How often have I said before
That no bland 'if', no 'either-or'
Can keep my obdurate male mind
From loving true and flying blind?
– Which, though deranged beyond all cure

250

Of temporal reason, knows for sure
That timeless magic first began
When woman bared her soul to man.
Be bird, be blossom, comet, star,
Be paradisal gates ajar,
But still, as woman, cleave you must
To who alone endures your trust.

Congratulations to Juliet. I'm glad Stella is with the Shahs in Turkey. She'll learn a lot.

Much love to Mary and all –   Robert

P.S. My new poems are in a new region of craziness; by the way, while selecting a new *Collected Poems 1965* I think I found the Margot-period ones which you would have omitted; and omitted them.

. . . .

Karl takes a job in USA in September; meanwhile he does not talk to me, having decided that he never apologizes for egoistic rudeness; and I, that I need apologies for such.

In October, Graves went to Oxford for his final term as Professor of Poetry.

29 October 1965   108 Clifton Hill
                                         NW8
                                         MAI 2702

Dearest James:

Did not recognize [Gatter] at Oxford but he revealed himself from behind his Newgate Fringe and all was well.

Beryl goes to Russia for 3 weeks on Nov. 9th, and I then move to Oxford.

It would be nice to see you again. 'Nice' = exactly right.

In revising my *Poems 1965* I did leave out four or five of the Margot ones – probably the ones you suspected at the time.

Lectures, my last, are getting very unlecturelike. They must elect an academician in my stead next Feb.

Did you hear I'd been robbed of £10,000 by my income-tax-saving company? It's all a great joke.

Everyone well.

Much love from Beryl and me   Robert

In the elections for his successor Graves supported Edmund Blunden, who had been a friend of Graves in the twenties but who argued with Graves, as Sassoon did, after the publication of *Goodbye to All That*. Although Graves thought that Blunden had been 'dead' as a poet for many years by then, he supported him mainly to show that on his side all past differences were forgiven. Blunden responded with an apology for his 'editorial' attitude towards *Goodbye to All That* in 1929 and 'begged' Graves not to 'finally condemn' his war poems; Blunden was both 'moved and gladdened' to be in touch with Graves again (see *In Broken Images*) and in February he was elected as Professor of Poetry.

The income-tax-saving company was International Authors, a Swiss company run by T. W. C. Roe; he helped writers domiciled outside of their own countries to avoid taxation by buying their copyrights from them and then paying the money, received through the company, into the authors' bank accounts. However, Roe was arrested in August for passing forged 100-dollar bills, and the company was investigated and found to have no funds. Graves's money, over $30,000, was lost irrecoverably, but his main concern now was to recover his copyrights, as he explained in a letter to Karl Gay (15 October), who had found a job as Curator of the Poetry Collection at the University of Buffalo. The loss of the money affected Karl directly for he was due a large sum of 'redundancy' money after eighteen years of working for Graves.

Dearest Karl:

You got away just in time: money-wise I mean. When I can repay you, I will – BUT

Not only have I been robbed of 30,000 bucks but I can't get any new money in because it legally still has to go through International Authors, although this company has no funds and its sole director is in jail and unable to sign anything. Can't even make new contracts; Int. Authors has the sole right.

This is the same in US and UK. My Swiss lawyer is prosecuting Roturman the parent company, and Selwyn Jepson thinks that he can get secret gen on where Roe stashed his cash. But that will take months. Meanwhile, we have *no* money here and old bills such as from Valenti (three years unpresented) for building the Extension, have come in; and the Bank won't lend me more. And the manuscripts haven't sold and the letters that have[21] aren't paid. Have inexportable money in England to pay for my lecture tour, and for Tomás's school, and for Antonia's course in computers. So, patience! My US bank balance is 55 dollars 9 cents. Until the Swiss Court have prosecuted Roturman and got back my copyrights, at least, there seems no chance of money – by the way Graham Greene[22] is in on this with me and so is the Estate of T. H. White, and Parkinson the Economist of Parkinson's Law!!

In September 1966, James Reeves's wife died; she had also been a close friend of Graves since the thirties, and he wrote a letter of condolence to Reeves immediately on hearing the news.

16 September 1966

Dearest James:
    There's nothing to say really – we have only just heard the catastrophic news – except that we all love you without the least reservation, and know you will face the blow with your usual nobility; and that Mary will always be with you in that extraordinary way that women have of surviving death and remaining the moral mainstays of their surviving families. It is a common and lovely phenomenon.
    – No particular news except that Lucia is expecting in February and that it's been a quiet summer and that I'm coming to England very soon for a gall-bladder operation and hope to see you before or after. I may be at Sally Chilver's, or at the Sillitoes'.
    – Give all our loves to Stella, who has become a really great person of late – a change difficult to explain or assess – and to the other children, whom we don't know quite so well.
    – Write a poem: that's the best way of concentrating your mind when it's whirled around by dark clouds but is still burning golden inside.
    Always   Robert

In October, Graves had his operation and while in hospital (St Thomas's, London) began translating into English verse the *Rubaiyyat* of Omar Khayaam; Omar Ali-Shah, Idries Shah's brother, provided Graves with a literal crib of a twelfth-century Persian manuscript, called the Jan Fishan Khan manuscript (after Shah's great-great-grandfather) of 'uncontradictable authority' belonging to the Shah family. Most scholars accept that Edward Fitzgerald's famous Victorian translation is highly inaccurate, full of mistranslations and his own inventions, but both Graves and Omar Ali-Shah went too far in their respective introductions in attacking Fitzgerald, as well as 'so-called' Persian scholars and the authenticity of (then) accepted manuscripts, and in claiming too much for their own manuscript and Omar Ali-Shah's credentials as a poet and a scholar of classical Persian. They set out to break the Fitzgerald myth, which 'persists in academic circles to this day', that Khayaam was an atheist epicurean, and to show that the *Rubaiyyat* is really a deeply religious poem (or collection of poems) by one of the greatest Sufi poets and teachers.

To be entrusted with this task, wrote Graves in his introduction, 'was the greatest poetic compliment I had ever been paid'. In a letter to Shah from hospital he wrote:

I am getting on very well with the *Rubaiyyat* – and am both proud and humble that Omar has entrusted me with the task of making the translation read poetically in English. Omar Khayaam is terrific when one gets behind Fitzgerald. But that the divine love he felt for his friend from Shiraz was comrade love, without the least hint of bodily love, disappoints me. I had hoped it was love for a woman and would give a precedent for my impossible love for Aemilia and hers for me, which cannot be divorced from bodily love – but which I believe our ancestors of 35,000 years ago (if the Sufis are right) whom we call Adam and Eve first discovered and which has lapsed for so many millennia.

From hospital he also wrote to Selwyn Jepson.

23 October 1966
Stitches out today

Dearest Selwyn:
I finished the poem enclosed. Then I got a confused letter from Aemilia in Mexico, saying how happy she was and why did I deny her such joy in her renewed and marvellous ——, and so on and so on. First letter since September 28 when I phoned her and she failed to confess the truth.

So I had to write – Sally was here and agreed – that our
outstanding accounts could now be settled – she could keep all
that I had given her, though she would not now be wanting the
Deyá House (for which payment is not yet made) and which I
would reserve for her friends – I didn't say 'former friends' but it
amounts to that – that if she was ever in great trouble she could
ask me for help and it would be regarded as a further gift from
the past. . . . Her frequent returns to —— had always been
conducted with deceit and cruelty to me, and followed by later
loneliness. That I believed in miracles, but not in *that* sort; nor
had she given me the least evidence of any change in him. On the
contrary, her timing of this default was particularly cruel; as she
must have known.

All very quiet and definite.

– It's sad: for her, especially. The end of a vision of truth – until
she extricates herself from hell, as she eventually will. But if ever
she wants to come back, it will be I who directs her; and as a
teacher not as a husband or whatnot.

It had to come to this of course.

Love to you both   Robert

I'm all right.

See you Tuesday. What about your FONE?

To James Reeves

No date   as from:
                                                       The Far House
                                                              Liss

Dearest James:

This is your black period of poetry: *black* signifying 'wise', not
'gloomy'. Quite a new region; also the rhythms are more
characteristically yours than at any time for the last twenty years.
One of the only tests of poetry is: 'could anyone else have written
it?' and it's not so much a question of *diction* as one of personal
rhythm. Paradoxical, that you should achieve this at this juncture,
but there it is – now you must learn to love yourself more (it took
me a long time even not to dislike myself)[23] and, damn it, you
are loveable.

Am going out of Hospital tomorrow with an interesting 6-inch scar on my chest – looks like I'd been fighting a Mexican. To Liss, with the Selwyn Jepsons now. Then Deyá; America; Deyá again.

Much love to Stella and to yourself always   Robert

To Selwyn Jepson

14 November 1966   Deyá

Dearest Selwyn:

I'm glad John Hammond is over his crisis. So is Robert Graves. Off on Friday . . .

So glad you have that copy of my poems – I've mislaid my own – at Liss or Clifton Hill and have had to restore it from early typescript.

In doing this I have altered:

I face impossible feats at your command
Astonished at
              to
Resentful at[24]

which is more honest.

I had a gay note from Aemilia in Mexico, on the back of a heartbroken letter from my friends Jim and Jo with 'Letter follows'. But I guess that she hadn't yet got my letter of resignation.

All well here. The new house is being tiled below and installed with 'the necessary offices', and the arch being cut out upstairs in the main room. Then I'll get that chimney made to draw, and build a garden and a gate in front. What fun one has with sad old houses, restoring their pride.

Much love to dear Tania   Robert

X ← for Tania

My USA address (Nov. 29–Dec. 6) is c/o J. B. Brooks,[25] 9 Gay St, NY 10014. But will be at Fred Higginson's[26] on the 21st Nov. if you have need to write.

After returning from his lecture tour in America, Graves wrote to Shah.

16 December 1966   Deyá

Dearest Idries:

When asked to preface a translation of St John of the Cross[27] I used the invaluable index[28] to *The Sufis*, and found what I wanted (in addition to a recent pamphlet by James Dickie [*sic*] on Spanish-Moorish poems).

But I was ashamed to find that I had not taken in what you wrote there about Omar Khayaam; which of course has added immensely to my perception of the poem, though not contradicting it in any way. (It is strange how one is not ready at times to *read* what is before one; until one day it hits one.)

In fact, the impact of the original on me at St Thomas's was so great that I might have qualified as a disciple of Khan Jan-Fishan Khan himself, had I been humble enough!

– It is strange that the poetic principle which I have always formulated for my moral path should correspond so closely with Sufism: and it is an Irish tradition to combine poems of love with satire and sudden violent contrasts of attitude.

– The famous early Irish poem *The Madness* of Suibne*[29] ('Sweeny') should be translated into Classical Persian, where it belongs. The Sufi influence is unmistakable.

I wrote to you yesterday c/o Omar, not knowing your Clifton Hill address.

Much love   Robert

*Ecstasy really.

After writing his 'letter of resignation' to Cindy in St Thomas's Hospital, Graves had found his final Muse, a young English ballet dancer called Julie, daughter of his friends George and Joanna Simon. Graves, however, though remaining 'a true poet pledged to death and death again in the Muse's house', was no longer obsessed by the 'process' nor torn by anxiety and melodrama, and, although his last Muse provided him with the romantic happiness and unhappiness necessary for the writing of poems, she did not torment him as Cindy had done. In the foreword to *Poems 1965–1968*, which contains the final poems to Cindy and the first ones to Julie, he wrote:

Once more, my theme is metaphorical of experiences which, as in Classical

Persian poetry, transcend ordinary physical circumstances . . . When I sent
Love Respelt and *17 Poems Missing From Love Respelt* to the printers I
twice deceived myself into thinking that this particular poetic battle had
ended; in each case another charge was needed.

Now, I can withdraw my forces a while and see whether 'Respelt' should
have read 'Mis-spelt' for the battlefield seems deserted for a while. Perhaps,
though, in Theocritus's words, misquoted by Coleridge in his introduction
to 'Kubla Khan', 'And henceforth I shall sing to you even more sweetly?'

'Who knows?'

To Ruth Fainlight

17 December 1966   Deyá

Dearest Ruth:

I forget when I last wrote. I have been back about a week. The
lecture tour was wonderful – I was never at a loss for a word
and everyone welcomed me as I have never been welcomed before.
And I saw half Deyá – especially Esteban and Ralph – and came
back feeling well at last. Yesterday I swam in the cold sea from
the hot rocks. Getting back into some sort of routine, making
jam, cracking nuts, answering letters and so on. And feeling
free. . . .

I saw a letter from Aemilia to John S—— with whom she lived
before ——'s day. [. . . .] John is a wonderful man and says he
knows she will one day recover her integrity. Meanwhile, she
complains of her drawing that her colours are all right (as she
told me) but her forms don't correspond. I had already told her
that only a reintegration of her character could do that. But the
handwriting of the letters, which were an attempt to say she was
blissfully happy, was very uneven and uncertain; and I smell
violence on the way, but can do nothing . . . Today as I write, I
feel a great appeal for help from her; but I can do nothing, except
have no hard feelings about her.

– I met Margot in NY and asked what she was doing and she
said: 'Voluntary nursing at St Vincent's.' She hadn't known
Aemilia had been a patient there! Margot will make it too, one
day. . . .

– I feel all right myself, but dreadfully sad for Aemilia, especially
as —— makes himself disliked wherever he goes. He is her worst
punishment, and according to a NY girl (whom she knows well)

258

she has always been reproaching him for not working and not behaving like me. But can find nobody else who corresponds with her demonic ups and downs.

– Have spent a lot of time getting the new house in shape: it was originally an act of love for Aemilia, now it's for the sort of friends who used to stay at the Posada before it became William's. It was once a tower, then was called Ca'n na Susaina; so I'm calling it the Torre de Susana. It should be all ready by January. It will sleep five comfortably.

. . . .

Oranges ripe, roses still blooming, narcissus in flower. Lucia and Ramón and Tomás will soon be here. Ava Gardner[31] is coming after Christmas: she and I are very close to each other. It's nice not being in love with her. . . . Juli writes to me regularly. She's so cross with herself for forgetting the Indian Dance engagement with Sonja and you. Our love for each other is very strange: she has never lost her virginity. Of course there are two sorts of virginity – the physical and the spiritual. She has kept both. I have tried to keep the spiritual sort all my life so her feelings for me are a great blessing and are what helped me to get out of my combat-shock in hospital; and what sustain me now. Let anyone call me a dirty old man who dares.

– The world is still beautiful.

– I long to see you and Alan again. This is really a letter for him too, but it is easier to write clearly and openly to one than to both: especially to you as a woman; and American at that. One has to know America to understand Aemilia's background. I find that as a child and girl she had to conceal and be ashamed of her Mexican blood: now the swing is in the other direction. But she can't face the real Mexicans, and prefers a Gringo resort like Puerto de Vallarta, where one has American-style food and housing, to the real Mexico where I wanted to go with her.

– Any further news of your expedition to Crim-Tartary, as it is called in *The Rose and the Ring*?

– My money situation has eased, and soon will be cleared up wholly. (I made 5000 dollars in my trip, for a start.)

– I love you both dearly, and Nimrod as much as he will let me. I do hope Ina is still with you.

– Did you know that James Joyce was a schizophenetic [sic]? It began half-way through *Ulysses* – a sort of Van Gogh schizz at first – and ended in *Finnegans Wake* in LSD type disintegration. He died in a catatonic trance; his psychiatrist was Bleuler of Zürich who said he was the only case he knew of a schizo who could combine his practical life with his fantasies.[31A]

– Happy Christmas and New Year and repeat 'love, love, love' – as in the last para but one.

Always   – Robert –

Love to Edna and all – I have written to Sonja.

One of the young poets whom Graves helped most was Terence Hards, whose first volume of poems, *As It Was*, Graves had himself published as a Seizin Press book in 1964 and written a foreword to. Hards (who has published little poetry since) was one of Graves's regular correspondents at this time.

26 February 1967

Dearest Terry:

We are six weeks ahead of you, Spring-wise, with apricot blossom and daffodils and St Brigid anemones. – But all the same I do love winter aconite.

– Put your book where it won't get *damp*. I have people ready to pay up to £15 for copies of my early books which I couldn't sell; but most of them got forgotten at the back of damp garages, etc. It must have paid expenses, for I got no bill!

– Glad something new is happening to you. Publication makes a watershed.

A lot of new things have similarly been happening to me; at my age, it isn't usually done. But I am always in love, which is what makes the pendulum wag on the wall.

Had my gall-bladder taken out just before having to go to US to lecture. It all went very well. That was Nov.–Dec.

Judith turned up last year from Paris – I didn't recognize her (quite different features). When she told me she was only 32, I did a swift calculation and called her a liar – but she explained that she had called herself 23 when she knew us and was only 17!

– I am helping my friend Omar Ali-Shah translate the original 12th century mss. of Omar Khayaam. It is a *wonderful* poem, believe it or don't, and nothing remotely like FitzGerald's [*sic*] version.

I am in favour of these new Universities, particularly Leicester and Kent. Don't let Clodia waste her talents on an Elder One, as I did –

Love to you all, including 'Father' if he's still around. I still preserve my 1895 penny he gave me.

Always — Robert

Shropshire, that's a nice county. 'Shrop' means shrub or scrub or low bush.

In 1967 John Masefield, the Poet Laureate and Graves's old landlord (on Boars Hill near Oxford in the early twenties), died. During the following weeks Graves was often mentioned in the press as a likely successor to Masefield.

To Ruth Fainlight

23 May 1967

Dearest Ruth:

Beryl will write about possible gifts to Russia:[32] with the greatest envy of Alan. Weather has been horrible: cold, damp, low but no rain; and a two days' sirocco, but still no rain. Better today: no fires in the evening and a clear sky: Beryl has bought a Jap telescope of 60 diameter enlargement.

However the TV team have been very decent and, I think, got the *interviu* they wanted. *Baleares*[33] much impressed by the honour to Mallorca. I think the programme will run to 50 minutes. So many people say I should be Poet Laureate if it weren't so creepy a job. I think it should be honorary, and though Royal in the sense of the Astronomer-Royal, or the President of the Royal Society or the *Regius* professor of Greek, not attached to the Court; but the incumbent should do – what Ben Jonson did – remind younger poets of the principal responsibilities and craft of poetry.

The Times tried to steer me that way by inviting me to celebrate Chichester's[34] return. I am too old a soldier to be caught. I cabled that 'Honoured, but Chichester, however gallant, is not my bowl of toddy'. No: no poetry conferences. I have already refused 4 (four) this summer including the world one at Montreal. I have written to Ted.[35]

O, yes, I *had* read Freud in 1917 but I also wrote a votive poem in Greek anthology style:

Dolor, analyst of souls
To the Graces hangs up here
His shrimp-net rotting into holes
And oozy from th'infernal mere
He hangs his [gift] around with cress:
Lush harvest of the public cess.

Yes, darlink, we miss you all! So does the Tower which looks pretty bad now that the masons are mending the well – full of public cess from above – and the rooms dusty with the sirocco with the masons busy at the entrance building the two levels: for car and garden. But the other garden is splendid now, with a stairway up from the steps and everything squared off.

I forwarded a letter from Aemilia to Idries the other day: good sign if she can mend that fence.

Deyá not filling up much yet.

Joyce has rented a cottage and the foolish old mother of Fat Miguel Bufat expects me to pay: some hopes!

Busy, busy, busy: and it's whitewash time! Ca'n Quet[36] has 18 guests and borrows blankets fom us. I'm pretty well again.

. . . .

Have swum three or four times: 'Russian' swims (*rush in*, and rush out again: joke).

I expect to flip over to London and read part of my poems with Isla in the Abbey when I know the date.[37] It will be a Tuesday – but which? I hope I see Alan before he goes off.

A big hug and abrazos to Alan and love to all I love: beginning with Nimrod.

– Robert –

To Idries Shah

2 August 1967

Dearest Idries:

. . . .

It will be wonderful when you come over; and (repeat) how fortunate that you didn't come over sooner!

Juli is here with her family; she has been turned out of the Royal Ballet School on various pretexts, the truth being that she is too good a dancer and too independent-minded for a Prussian drill-school. I am helping her write a long piece about it:[38] because the same attempt to militarize any so-called art or craft is found everywhere in England, including the medical schools; and it is only in writing and to some degree in painting (but in painting there are the galleries to fight) that real work can get accepted despite academic pressure from schools, universities and critics. I'm fortunate to be my own master.

I expect the Khayaam proofs soon and am enormously relieved that the King's Man[39] and your father are not unpleased with my version of Omar's literal translation. To me all that matters is justice to Khayaam's ghost; and the blow that is being struck by our friends against the Ring of so-called Sufi experts and Persian scholars is well-timed.

– I am enormously grateful to him for his help in my recovery at St Thomas's; and so to you and Omar. I was allowed to keep my blue hospital bed-jacket; and I occasionally wear it for sentimental reasons.

Like Juan, I have made a new start, since Aemilia's defection. A return to the gentle age of innocence, with most of my problems solved. In 1931 I planted an agave here; and not until this year did it flower, shooting up a 20-feet stem with flowers that were in full bloom on my birthday and that dripped honey by the pint over the steps leading to the grotto.

Much love to you all   – Robert –

I am very close indeed to Juli, but publicly she keeps her distance with an assumed negligence which is really remarkable. Ours is really a constructive alliance rather than an old-world love-affair; I am the unicorn who lays his narwhale-horn in the pure virgin's lap, as in medieval tapestries.

6 August 1967

Dearest Idries:

David Ascoli of Cassell has sent me page proofs of the *Rubaiyyat*. I have corrected them as best I can, including Omar's preface, but I cannot check the bibliography at the end. Omar told Ascoli that he's going to Italy, and will be *incommunicado* for at least a month. From which I guess he will place Anna and Mina with her sister there, and then go to Jerusalem, Amman, Bagdad, Damascus; possibly also to Delhi and even Moscow? I told Ascoli merely that it is no good holding the proofs for him, and that you would doubtless make yourself responsible for the proper spelling of the names in the Bibliography. I gave him your address and telephone number. He is apparently most eager to learn about the Sufi background of the poem.

— I have made a few refinements on the translation, for euphony, and was delighted to find that the original of *rubaiyya* 110 is

Though pearls in praise of God I never strung

which is 1,000,000 times better than:

Though verse in praise of God I never penned.

Each time I read the poem, the more it impresses me. How he must have suffered!

— And how well he conveys, in the first part, the shallow, carefree spirit of his youth; which intensifies the turmoil of the second and the nobility of the third!

— I have asked David Ascoli to check with Michael Horniman (of Watt's) the copyright attribution for the fly leaf, and (if he does not know of Omar's Trust for the Regiment) to ask you whether it should figure in the copyright attribution. (Originally Omar and I agreed on going 50/50; but when I heard that he was giving his share to the Regiment Fund, I told him that I would take a third and let the remaining $16^2/_3$rd % go to the Fund too.)

. . . .

Anyhow, I am feeling very well, despite the huge amount of work entailed by constant visits from friends, mostly young undergraduates and that sort of thing. And also feeling very blessed: and protected against the assaults of the World, Flesh and Devil by those whom I love — especially the Shahs with whom I seem to commune even when no letters pass between us; and friends like Sonja, and Selwyn Jepson, and John Benson Brooks the American musician with whom I always lodge in NY. And, now that Aemilia has disappeared for some years at least and broken the bridge between us, there is Juli – who is here now with her family, and who is like a raindrop reflecting a whole countryside[40] and utterly to be trusted – the more so because she has never had any *histoire d'amour* of any importance, and defiantly keeps her virginal magic.

– I haven't written any poems for some weeks; which is a pleasant change, because it means a relief from the fearful tension of that Aemilia period. If poems come again it will be with a difference.

Báraka Basháḋ   Robert

Love to Juan and Kashfi and Saraita and the twins.

In January 1968, James Reeves sent Graves a copy of his *Collected Poems*, also a book, which he co-edited with S. Haldane, and which they had privately printed at their own cost, of poems by Trumbull Stickney (1874–1904), a neglected American poet 'rediscovered' by them.

4 January 1967 [*sic*]

Dearest James:

It was very good of you to send me the two books. Yours (as goes without saying) I love and admire wholeheartedly. As I read them again, my pulse stirs and quickens: especially to the earlier ones.

Trumbull Stickney – I wish I could share your enthusiasm but I am a generation older than you and mine was one when we first spat out all the poetical language of the late 19th century (which no more corresponded with contemporary speech than Virgil's did in *his* day) and the inertia of the contemporary metres. I have tried hard to read him and hear him as you do; but only occasionally does he come through as himself – e.g. 'Leave him now Quiet by the Way'. It is the *sameness* of the literary language that troubles me; if only he could have gone back to borrowings from the 17th or 16th centuries. I am sorry – I am not 'one who can hear'. If you get out of pocket, I'll willingly help: but beyond saying that he was well ahead of his generation of American poets, I am dumb.

. . . .

I'm glad Day-Lewis is poet-laureate. Nice man and now people will have someone, not me, to send their manuscripts to, for commendation.

I go on writing poems. There'll be a 1965–68 collection out in the Summer. They stand up, some of them, I think . . . Everyone else is fine, including Catherine whom I saw in Australia two months ago.[41]

I spend at least half my time these days on housework: I *like* it.

Much love to you all   Robert

Cecil Day-Lewis, a long-standing friend of Graves, had been appointed Poet Laureate at the New Year. Graves was not disappointed at not having received the Laureateship but was angered by comments in *The Times* suggesting the reasons why he had not been chosen, and made his anger clear in a letter to the editor (published on 12 January).

7 January 1968

Sir,

– In a *Times* article of January 2 it was suggested that I had been a candidate for the Poet Laureateship but that Mr Day-Lewis's choice was a more fortunate one because my 'periodic identification with the hippier end of the poetic spectrum' would have brought me enemies had the choice fallen on me; besides, I live in Majorca!

May I please correct this statement? It is true that I first made my home here in 1929, 30 years before it became famous as the holiday-making Hippies' 'Island of Love', living mainly on a First World War disability pension. It is not, however, true that I was a candidate for the still unreformed Laureateship.

As for the enemies whom my appointment might have brought me, had I been a candidate, that opens a wide realm of conjecture. It is true that I am co-founder with my daughter and son-in-law of the Indigo Jazz Club at Palma and that my appearance with my friends Spike Milligan and Annie Ross on a Poetry and Jazz television show – she sang my 'Mend Them Fences' – may have shocked the very same members of the Establishment who have since complained that I deny Omar Khayaam to have been a

Hippy. And it is true that the Haight Street 'Flower Children' of San Francisco who have used my *White Goddess* as a text-book for their *Ferialia* may have been shocked by my address on Post-Classical Science at the Massachusetts Institute of Technology.

And the London School of Economics authorities who a few years ago invited me to deliver their annual address – for which I chose the subject *Mammon* – may have since regretted my writings about hallucinatory drugs in modern life and primitive religion. In fact, I have probably made enemies all the way up and down the spectrum from infra-red to ultra-violet but at least I remain a loyal subject of Her Majesty the Queen (see my poem to that effect published in my *Collected Poems*, 1955, Doubleday, NY); and have congratulated my friend Cecil Day-Lewis on his appointment with: *Laurum qui meruit ferat*.[42]

One small and very English point remains. At the age of 72, when every Englishman is deemed to be drawing an old age pension even if he in fact has not yet applied for one, is not this a bar to being granted a new office of profit under the Crown – even if its original value of some £5000 in modern money has fallen to, I believe, £87 minus tax?

Yours faithfully,   Robert Graves

Graves had also written about the Laureate's 'profit' in *The White Goddess* (1948):

Wine is the poet's proper drink, as Ben Jonson knew well when he asked for his fee as Poet Laureate to be paid in sack. The base Colley Cibber [1671–1757 – actor and playwright whose appointment as Laureate in 1730 greatly angered Fielding and Pope] asked for a cash payment in lieu of wine, and no Poet Laureate since has been poet enough to demand a return to the old system of payment.

Graves wrote again to Reeves about the Laureateship, again making a mistake in the date.

16 January 1969 [*sic*]

Dearest James:

Jenny Lee[43] was trying to make the Laureateship an honorary five-year appointment divorced from Court nonsense. She ran up against the Prince Consort, or the Lord Chamberlain, or Prince

Charles, or somebody. Since I had already supported the reform
in Australia, on TV and in the Press, I wasn't invited, thank
goodness. (Beryl is overjoyed.)

Stickney is certainly very good indeed when he breaks away; but
he seems to have died before the wind of fashion changed, or
he'd have been a Georgian no doubt. So you and I don't disagree,
really, because a book of the few *intenser* poems would have been
too short to publish, so it's all or nothing.

Yes: Cecil is Established even by the fact of being a converted
Communist – I like him and his wife very much indeed
considering the position they occupy in the *grande monde*. She's
M. Balcon's daughter.[44]

Much love   Robert

Love to the family – dearest Stella hasn't written for months.

– I find myself writing nothing but *Songs*, of obsessional
perfectionalism; though the other day there *was* an ordinary poem
about neighbours in a semi-detached house, and how much got
overheard and suspected.[45]

On 6 December 1967 Graves had written to Shah, after receiving
his *Tales of the Dervishes*:

The *Dervish* book delights me and I am honoured by your
allowing me to praise it . . . The story of the 'Candy in the River',
which you once told me and which I didn't realize you would be
using yourself, I have made the basis of a children's story which
will be published next spring. It varies a good deal but I hope
Saraita will like it as well as either; and I know you'll forgive me
for the borrowing.

It seems from his reply, however, that Shah was not at all pleased
by Graves's 'unauthorized' use of the story (which was published in
1968 by Cassell under the title *The Poor Boy Who Followed His
Star*, with illustrations by Alice Meyer-Wallace) but told Graves to
'forget' it.

26 February 1968

Dearest Idries:

Nobody *can* forget any incident in their history; it's always there
for good or bad (as you know from your hypnotic experiences).

And the wise thing to do is to discover why the incident happened, rather than forget it – because the *why* is educative. I explained in my letter why I didn't mention the story earlier; I also explained why you should feel no reason to apologize to Cape[46] for my unauthorized act: Cape, being legally minded, would object only if I had infringed their copyright. So my intention in writing about 'money, public domain, damages, etc.' was not because I thought *you* cared a dam (small [   ] coin) about these matters, but because Cape might. At all events, the source of the story is now being printed with due acknowledgements on the jacket of the book, which will go to lots of homes and booksellers, so that Cape should feel more than happy about it. They are not competing with 'Juveniles'.

– My original fault was keeping the book a secret, for Saraita; my second fault was mistaking your letter (which was written with uncharacteristic asperity) for a lack of confidence in my judgement on the publishing situation. Whereas you were only worried . . .

– Having confessed to both faults, I shall now *not* forget the occasion because it constitutes a warning. Searching my heart for any previous occasion of misunderstanding between us, I find only one, also concerned with publishing; and that was writing the introduction to *The Sufis* (with your help) under the impression that you would at any rate let me proof-read the book for you. I confess that I felt hurt for not having my help accepted; and that obviously accounts for my own asperity, in the last letter I sent you, about crediting Sufi tradition with two pre-Moslem Christian stories. Forgive me! I think you underrated my readiness to help you as a friend, and freely and anonymously, as I help scores of other writers whom I do not value a one thousandth part of my love for you and yours.

   Báraka Basháoup   Robert

In July 1968, Graves was made an Adoptive Son of Deyá (the only one ever), an honour which pleased him greatly. He was also invited to read a poem at the Cultural Olympics in Mexico City. He had read a poem at the 1924 Olympics and won a bronze medal for 'At the Games'; this was published in *English Life* (May 1924), but Graves had forgotten its publication and had no copy, so wrote to Karl Gay, who as Curator of the Poetry Collection at Buffalo was in charge of Graves's manuscripts, among which he hoped to find a copy. Gay had received the money due to him and was now thoroughly reconciled with Graves – as was Margot, who with her daughter Daisy was one of the many visitors to Deyá that summer and who now resumed her former place as a close friend of the whole family.

27 July 1968

Dearest Karl:

Being made *Hijo Adoptivo de Deyá* today with all the trimmings – the Civil-Governor, Captain-General, etc., etc. You'd have a laugh.

– There'll be speeches in the school room and sherry for all natives. This is the last mayor of Deyá[47] (Valenti) because population has sunk to 318 and 500 at least are needed for a mayor.

– Can you help me, learned Sir; is there a draft or typescript among Robert Graves's early verse of a poem about two sportsmen called Maurice (one French, one English), which won the Bronze medal at Paris in 1924 at the Olympic Games, for a poem about sport?

I'm invited to Mexico by the Olympic Committee and cannot prove that such a poem ever existed. I'll be seeing Jimmy Metcalf there; he has beaten out the great copper cauldron for the Olympic fire. His wife, Pilar, is now Mexico's leading actress.

Margot is here, very collected, very busy, thoroughly reformed and generally beloved, along with my god-daughter Daisy, a very bright kid. Sends you and Rene her love.

As I do, and everyone else. So sorry about your sinus and Julie's teaching problem.

Wm's Felipe is exactly like me, and Lucia's Natalia is exactly unlike me.

Abrazos   Robert

In August, Graves wrote an essay (for *Playboy*, later republished in *Difficult Questions, Easy Answers*) on 'Genius'. Shah promised to send him his own notes on the subject which, however, arrived too late. Graves thought Shah's notes 'not at all characteristic' of him, but he answered Shah 'politely' and extended the essay in the letter

270

by giving his own personal opinions and prejudices on several famous geniuses, whom Shah had mentioned in his notes.

6 September 1968

Dearest Idries:

Your notes on genius, for which I am very grateful, came the day after my deadline for sending my piece off.

The main difference between your view and mine is that I go (as always) to the original meaning of a word. In Latin *genius* is the creative generative male power born in a man which acts as his conscience, oracle, protector and sense of love and honour. Hence the Latin words: *generous*, *genial* and *genuine* – as well as progenitor and genitals. The Romans later borrowed the idea of an *evil genius* from the Greeks after their conquest of Greece and other neighbours. It confused them. The Greeks had built-in opposites called evil genius κακοδαιμων and good genius αγαθοδαιμων. The Christians followed suit. A real Roman was said to *defraud his genius* if he acted without love, justice, restraint or decency; and, unless he suddenly changed for the better, was called a *lost man*. Since God is Love, there can be no evil genius.

– Genius in its modern sense (first coined by Henry Fielding in *Tom Jones*[48] 1740 [*sic*]) implies a way of thinking in the fifth dimension which allows a control of time as easy as that of space in our dimension. It is probably a regression to a pre-hominoid way of thought. In that dimension one can communicate with past and future and go straight to the answer, then go back and build a bridge between it and the present. Or one can go back in time to discover ancient secrets – analepsis as opposed to prolepsis – which is an experience that has happened to me, even.

But it seems that this power is reserved for people who have refused to be brain-washed or educated in logic and who have kept their *Genius* in the Roman sense; and keep to the path of truth and love.

Therefore I cannot call Napoleon, Alexander the Great, Pericles, or Hitler a genius because they all ended shamefully and ruined their own countries.

Nor can I give the title of genius to anyone who depresses one, or from whom one shrinks as from a boring intruder into one's private room.

And sickness denies genius, no health comes from unhealth; Shakespeare was noble, loving and wise, and clean despite being in Show Business.

– I could never love Michaelangelo, though granting him great mathematic gifts. He was a bully and turned from women – *genius* involves male procreation – to boys. He leaves me cold. Toulouse-Lautrec conquered his deformity somehow; lived with disgusting people but never lost his sense of love and nobility. Victor Hugo had immense talents but was no poet. (Think of a meeting between him and Rumi;[49] wouldn't you have blushed on Rumi's behalf?)

– Napoleon fought his Italian campaign on blue-prints given him by his teacher at St Cyr. He had the art of winning men's admiration; but not in the real way of genius such as characterized real pre-fire-arm heroes such as Belisarius or Scipio Africanus, by personal example. Napoleon was not *a man of the sword* he was a lost artilleryman, who even cheated his washerwoman. War ceased to be war when those two cannon were fired at Crécy. Napoleon should have died at Moscow.

I admire Jesus, not for his genius (because he never preached a single original text), but his always laying down the last cent and wholly without ambition. *Ambition* is contrary to *genius*. Genius goes straight to the point; *ambition* originally implied a cadging for votes, but soon came to mean going round by the backstairs to secure an office or favours. 'I am the Vine, ye are the branches' is a Pauline change from 'God is the vine, we are the branches.' As you know as a Moslem, Issa never equated himself with God. Were it not for the renegade Paul, Jesus would long be forgotten. Paul was ambition personified.

Music. I must be too sensitive; I can't bear the smell of inherited syphilis in Beethoven's 'great storms'. My favourite musician happens to be the same as Shakespeare's: *John Dowland*. His songs are sorrowful but heal the soul by their sweetness and courage.

G. B. Shaw was unpardonably vain. Humility and a sense of humour are part of genius. Shaw had wit, but no humour (which means being able to laugh at yourself and at the razor edge dividing true from false). I avoided him carefully; as I also did Yeats when young.

Tolstoy was pretty good, but wholly without taste (I have visited

272

his house) and a domestic tyrant. I prefer Chekov and Gogol; Dostoieffsky [*sic*] was an honest man (again the syphilitic taint however) whose works have depressed more young people in England and Russia than any other novelist from the first beginnings. *Genius* does not depress.

Augustine was false-hearted, a liar, and has done more harm to Xtianity than any other writer since the Roman Church was founded. On the other hand his fellow citizen of Madaura, Apuleius, was a genius whose *Golden Ass* is worthy of use in Sufi training.

– There are degrees of genius of course and one shouldn't confuse traditional craft, however lovely, with fifth-dimensional thought. The question of *genius* in women is extremely interesting; but too long for this letter. Suffice to say that a woman *parturiates*,[50] does not *engender*, so she has no *generative* genius; but comes (the Romans said) directly under the power of that extremely complex Moon-Goddess Juno Lucina. But they too can think fifth-dimensionally; Kashfi for one.

In short, dearest Idries, I seem to be in the foolish situation of criticizing you for being too generous with the word *genius*; foolish because you yourself have all the earmarks of genius, as Omar also has; so must know more about fifth dimensional and fourth dimensional thought than I can claim to know.

But I stand on the principle that a real word never loses its central meaning; and *genius* and *ambition* are instances. As for *talent*; this came from a complete Greek misunderstanding of Issa's Jewish parable about the Jew who rightly refused to put his money to interest, against the Law of Moses (and of Islam), and buried it until his master returned. But *talent* in Greek originally meant a doubtful oscillation of the scales when large weights of silver were being weighed. *Genius* implies *certainty*; *talent* still implies experiment and also doubt. This is how poets think: in the Irish-Sufic tradition.

A very pleasant young man from Montana is here; educated at the Sufi centre in Holland.

– I think I told you I have exchanged letters with your splendid father.

Much love to everyone   Robert

Don't trouble to answer. One day we'll meet and talk.
Mozart knew and foreknew and loved and made people feel healed.
Bach nobody can say anything against, either. – He lulls –
Wagner however was an exhibitionist.

At the Olympic Games Graves won the gold medal with his poem (written in Spanish) 'Antorcha y Corona, 1968', though under somewhat unusual circumstances, as he explained to Shah. He was also asked by Cecil Day-Lewis to accept the Queen's Gold Medal for Poetry.

4 November 1968

Dearest Idries
Thank you so much for the books.[51] I wished we lived closer and could read each other's proofs.
My mother's favourite story was about two visitors who visited the King's Garden. One noticed weeds growing even in the flower beds; the other, flowers growing even on the rubbish heap.
Your flowers are many and varied; but (for instance) I wouldn't have allowed you to weedily misquote Carlyle who qualified that definition of genius[52] with a '*first of all*' and then proceeded further (*Frederick the Great* IV, iii, 1).
– My works are full of weeds, mostly for lack of an enormous library or leisure to visit one.
– But if one reads the newspapers, how extravagantly *wrong* every news item is which one can check *oneself* from having been present!
– I have quoted somewhere Butler's remark to Festing Jones who said: 'But, Butler, even *God* can't change History.' 'No, Jones: only historians can do that.'
Much love and congratulations   Robert

Funny situation: I have been asked by the poet laureate to accept the Queen's Medal for a book of verse in order to give the award more distinction! Also I was given the Olympic Gold Medal for saving the Cultural Committee's face by improvising a small, very small, stage-army of poets to form the great 'Reunion of Poets' advertised. I was the only one whom they had invited (of my two companions one was a Puerto Rican interloper, the other a

274

Mexican who was rebelling against the Mexican poetic boycott of the Reunion!). It was well deserved I think especially as the audience had to be hauled in from the Olympic City Restaurant, no public announcement having been possible. About 60 in all!

N.B. About answering fools with silence . . .[53] Solomon says 'Answer a fool according to his folly lest he be wise in his own conceits' (i.e. concepts), Proverbs 26,5. Though *also* Solomon says: 'Answer *not* a fool according to his folly, lest thou also be like unto him.' Proverbs 26,4, which shows Solomon was a Sufi in his *apparent* self-contradiction.

It is extraordinary what power a woman can exert over a man merely by *being*, not even seeing him, not even being witty in her letters or sending him gifts. So long of course as her act of being is pure and consistent.

In fact, I am thoroughly blessed these days, and my power of work has doubled.

– Well, you saw her briefly at Amina Soraya's name-giving.

To Terence Hards

26 November or so

Dearest Terry:

That you have no news except the countryside is very good news. I have almost too much: my life has become so complicated with all my six surviving children (*and* their children) being dependent on me for support one way or another. Still, it keeps me working. And gives me an excuse for going places – such as the Olympic Games where they gave me a Gold Medal, and Australia whence I repatriated a grand-daughter (a nuclear physicist) and where I filled Sydney Town Hall. Also Hungary and Russia. The excuse is that I become a 'world figure' which sends up the value of my *manuscripts* – a main source of money – and thus enables me to drop food into the wide open beaks. Needless to say, I remain myself so don't get alarmed. Besides you I know of only one poet in England who knows what it is to be a poet: his name is David Sutton,[54] he lives at Wokingham, I have never met him but once talked to him on the phone. He has a terrible stammer and a cockney voice but writes like an angel, in the same tradition as you and I. He is about 25, married, and has taken on some ordinary job in rejection of a College fellowship.

On the 6th I dash to London to grab the Queen's gold medal – have been begged to accept it and give it a bit of *class*. It's an excuse for coming to London and going on to Oslo to cheer up my god-daughter (same heathen sort as Clodia) Juli who is dancing there – the only dark head in a flaxen wilderness – and incidentally to be cheered up myself.

I am writing occasional poems; and a book about the nature of love;[55] and occasional learned articles (at $1 or 50 cents a word) for *Playboy*, etc. *Playboy* publish the best and most serious articles in the US, as a cover for their slick nudes and dirty jokes. I can always reprint my pieces in plain covers; so who cares?

. . . .

Love to Clodialind and Rosia and Selma and all.
And to yourself   Robert

The stone you gave me is the centre piece in my work-room; stands under the figure of a bronze 17th century Nepalese Goddess. I anoint it with oil, as She requires, every now and then.

My closest friends are the two Afghan SHAH brothers, Omar and Idries: both of them now disguised as English country squires in large estates – one at Godalming; one at Langton Green, Kent.

Graves, now in his seventy-fourth year, began to suffer regular bouts of ill-health. Despite this, however, he continued to write a great number of poems and to travel extensively.

To Ruth Fainlight

13 January 1969

Dearest Ruth:

Can't get well – these last few months I've been sort of dragging around – stomach, head, throat – and my undefeatable spirit is still undefeatable but going through a sort of Black Period: weighing up the extent to which the forces of Evil have slowly pressed their conquests. Such a huge Bang it will have to be, before we are in the clear again; and by then so many crafts and magics will have been lost. It all started with the dethronement of women . . .

– Writing real English is on the way out except as a curiosity –

like the hand-thrown pots or hand-woven satins that very rich people buy, the people who have been foremost in destroying handicrafts – but there are still a few people who write and read poems, even, for the right reasons. ¿A?

Beryl comes back a week from today – I'll go into a clinic for a check-up first, if I can find a room free.

The weather here has been a succession of violent siroccos, stripping the orange trees and alternating with heavy clouds.

Haven't yet got your book. If it gets as rude a reception as my last, that will make two of us. But 'shabby, peeling, Georgian stucco' (*Listener*) is hard to beat. The joke being that it has absolutely no effect on the sales.

– Julie writes long and regularly which is, really, what matters most to me, and I have made about 100 lbs of marmalade – want some? Come and collect it.

Much love to you and Alan and the kids

Robert

I would have written earlier if you had put your *address on the letter* (English wise) and not on the envelope which we English always use for spills or for lighting our pipes. Economical.

12 February 1969

Dearest Ruth:

I can't remember posting a letter thanking you for the poems, a lot of which I did not know before. There are some very good ones there, but I find myself wondering whether you don't regard them too much as *work*. For me only prose is work; I mean in writing. Poetry is getting something out of the way. The dark, anonymous poem suddenly comes into my mind and I scratch its first two lines down, and then gradually get it into shape . . .

Christina Rossetti used to scribble her poems on the awkward wash-table in her bedroom while Dante Gabriel wrote his on a great Georgian desk.[56] Which lasted of the two? When I find a poem coming on I often take a spade and dig until I can hold no more in my mind; and then have to write it down.

Have written several unsatisfactory poems in about 12 drafts each, lately; stomach trouble. When I'm well again, I don't suppose more than one or two of them will stand up; my trouble is that I know too much of the *craft* of poetry, so that even non-

poems read beautifully. But O how *bored* I can be, reading them
a month later!

By the way surely:

'I circle, rat trapped deep within a pit'

isn't better really than

'I circle like a rat trapped in a pit'

is it? And I don't know what the wires in his neck are, because
I'm not told; and the two *necks* are confusing. Or not to you?

– I like the 'Wide-Eyed' poem but from my own experience
would have written the last line: Blind love, blind wide-eyed
jealousy.

It is very cold here – not English cold, but Majorcan cold – and
I continue on my cruelly Spartan diet and try not to be cross.
Most of the hippie-trash have been directed to leave the village.

Lots of love to you all   Robert

Have been digging and tidying the garden at the Tower – probably
the first time in fifty years. It's almost indecent now in its suburban
neatness. And Doña Leonora has promised to have a *matanza*[57]
for her stinking pig on the terrace above any day now.

To Idries Shah

7 May 1969

Dearest Idries:

Many thanks for the *Secret Garden*,[58] which is admirable in itself
but unfortunately translated into English verse at a period on the
other side of the great 1911 watershed, when poets were still bound
to a liturgical diction and vocabulary which now reads phoney
and hypocritical, however honest the material.

Arabic still, I gather, remains close to Classical Arabic; English,
because of an almost total breakdown in Bible reading, has
broken all ties with the Elizabethan period and even with the
Victorian. My own father's poems (apart from his Irish peasant
songs) are wholly unreadable today, and he wrote well, for his
period.

Language is a great problem for contemporary religious or
philosophical societies – we had some Rudolph Steiners along
yesterday – oh dear! – and is so important for direct conveyance
of truth.

To recognize the words with *báraka* and get rid of the academic and scientific ones is a task that the original Sufis probably did not need to face. It's something they must face now – and without going 'hippy' like some Protestant modernists.

I have been invited to Russia to take part in the Pushkin Celebrations. On Beryl's advice I have refused, saying that though I love Russia and admire Pushkin, my arrival would be misunderstood by many of my fellow-writers as an approval of the recent arrest and deportation to Labour Camps of Russian writers, on charges of which the libertarian Pushkin would hardly have approved. A pity! If it had been a non-Government invitation what fun it would have been!

Love to you all   Robert

Wm and I and Elena think we have the right house for you. He will write. The Edwardses[59] are good people and he has a peculiarly penetrative mind.

Graves made several trips to Eastern Europe during these years; his favourite Iron Curtain country is Hungary which he greatly enjoyed visiting and where he established several firm friendships among poets and printers. In May 1970, he went to Budapest for the second time, accompanied by his daughter Catherine, where he addressed a congress of Hungarian poets and established the Robert Graves Prize or 'Foundation', awarded annually for what the judges choose as the best poem (though poems specifically written for competitions are excluded) of that year (see pages 316–17, n. 60). In his 'Address to the Poets' in 1970, which is reprinted in *Difficult Questions, Easy Answers*, and in a photographic album of Hungary, he gave the main reason for his love of the country: 'There are, I believe, only three countries in Europe where the name of Poet is everywhere honoured rather than ridiculed ... [Ireland, Wales and Hungary] ... I am Irish by birth, Welsh by adoption, and Hungary has always brought me good luck, I suppose also because of its outstanding poetic tradition.'

To James Reeves

15 May 1970

Dearest James:

Just back from a Poets' Conference in Hungary – great fun. As in Wales everyone there is a sort of poet, including the big Party Boss[60] who had all my books ready for me to sign. Odd, eh?

– You may be right, but I never begat a brat in drink so I don't know.[61]

Here's a local poem:

In a stiff lump triangular
Our budding Buddha meditates.
Gates of Nirvana stand ajar,
He stares unwinking at the gates.
Brown rice his food,* water his drink –
Hey, stop that meditation!
                    Think!

*by the way Indian peasants *never* eat brown rice as mad Indianists suggest.

Lucia is having another 'brat', so is Wm's wife Elena. I hear Yancy has borne one to her beer-baron. I expect dear Stella will follow suit . . . I find it hard to stop writing poems, and get on with serious prose. New collection out in two or three months.[62]

Lots of love from us all   – Robert

Publication of Graves's and Omar Ali-Shah's translation of the *Rubaiyyat* of Omar Khayaam caused enormous controversy, to the extent that they were accused of forgery. Their attacks on Fitzgerald, English Persicologists and their claim that the two main manuscripts, the Chester Beatty and the Cambridge University Library manuscripts, were late copies, and the proud insistence that the hitherto unheard-of Shah family manuscript and the Shahs' Sufic interpretation of it were incontrovertibly authoritative, engendered a great deal of resentment among classical Persian scholars and admirers of Fitzgerald. Several attacks on the Shahs, and on Graves's abetment of or 'deception' by them, appeared in the press. Both Shahs kept silent during the controversy and so, uncharacteristically, did Graves – for he had up till then only repeated what the Shahs had told him and, moreover, he had never seen the actual manuscript, which was being kept by 'Guardians of the Tradition' in Afghanistan. Graves now asked the Shahs to produce the manuscript, but Idries, in a letter of 30 October, refused on the unconvincing (to Graves) grounds that if people were intent on proving the manuscript a forgery it would be impossible or anyway fruitless to stop them; such excellent forgeries are produced in Iran, he wrote, and radio-carbon dating does not work on ancient parchments from which the writing has been washed off and a new text written on with 'inert inks'. He maintained that the only way of proving a forgery is by internal textual evidence (and, anyway, Omar Ali-Shah had already stated in his introduction that all the verses 'occur in one or more of the earlier mss. housed in libraries throughout the world', so that it could be claimed he had made only a collation from these various manuscripts). Idries Shah wrote, in the same letter, that under the circumstances it seemed quite obvious to him that if the production of a manuscript would only produce the reaction that it was a forgery, 'it is high time that we realized that the hyaenas who are making so much noise are intent only on opposition, destructiveness and carrying on a campaign when, let's face it, nobody is really listening.' He went on to say that his father, Ikbar Ali-Shah, the head of the Shah family and author of various books, was so infuriated by the behaviour of the 'hyaenas', he would have nothing to do with the controversy. This was not strictly true as he did in fact write to Graves, from his home in Morocco, saying that the manuscript should be produced; Graves forwarded the letter to Omar Ali-Shah, unfortunately without taking a copy, because Shah never received it and a few days later the father died in a car crash. Idries Shah finished his letter: 'The manuscript, as you know, is not in my possession. If it were, I would have no hesitation at all in refusing to show it to anyone under any circumstances at any time whatever.'

Unfortunately, Omar Ali-Shah has not preserved the letters Graves wrote to him, and Idries Shah has mislaid almost all letters from Graves written after 1968, when the controversy began. However, for once Graves kept a copy of one of his personal letters, in answer to Idries Shah's letter mentioned above.

11 November 1970

Dearest Idries:

You and I are bound, not only by close bounds [*sic*] of personal friendship, but by having the same displayed eagle as a family crest, which suggests a Crusader–Saracen friendship dating from the twelfth century. And you and I first met and recognized each other in Palma when you were disguising yourself as a secretary of an old fraudulent witch-doctor.

Since then I have also made a very close alliance with Omar and his family, and in both cases I knew and valued the wife before I met the husband. This brings me to a matter of family honour: the Jan Fishan Khan *Omar Khayaam* manuscript. Its publication in translation by Omar and myself has done me a great deal of harm, especially from continually renewed attacks on my reputation in the powerful *Sunday Times* and in leading American newspapers, where Dr Arberry's[63] pupils have tried to prove that this ms. is a forgery. I am content to suffer if necessary, but I should not have accepted the task so cheerfully, in hospital three years ago, had I known that I was putting my head into a trap from which the Shahs were unable to extricate me and I still do not believe this to be true. Moreover Omar was given full permission by your father to undertake this work.

Nor do I believe that the use of infra-red rays would be unable to reveal that the Cambridge University and the Chester Beatty *Rubaiyyat* mss., which deceived Professor Arberry, were modern forgeries. Or that the obvious ancientness of the parchment of the Jan Fishan Khan mss. – which our enemies either date from the 1890s or deny to exist – plus an infra-ray test to prove that it is not a palimpsest, would not reveal its genuineness.

This letter of yours, by the way, completely contradicts two previous ones on the same subject, promising to produce this ms. from Afghanistan, where the Guardians of the Tradition would allow you to borrow it for a while, as the senior member of the family to whom the Sultan gave it in 1153. The trouble is that what is now publicly considered to be my gross deception by the Shah brothers has cast doubt on all my historical writings. This smudge can be shown to have reduced the royalties drawn from these that keep my family alive. I have recently had to support, wholly or partly, about a dozen of them. So your decision, for reasons of family pride, not to submit the manuscript to scrutiny under any circumstances seems difficult to reconcile with either our personal or family friendship – especially as this would be to injure the family of the Prophet – may his name be praised!

I am sending a copy of this letter to Omar whom I unfortunately missed last time in London as I also missed you; but I expect to be along at the close of this month.

Báraka bashad   Robert

By the way John Nicholson who deceived Jan Fishan Khan, and paid for it with his life, was no ancestor of mine but only of my first wife.

Shah replied with a brief, abrupt, businesslike letter, thanking Graves for his 'most interesting letter of November 11th' and saying only that he looked forward to discussing 'these and other matters when you come to England shortly'.

The manuscript was not produced, and when in 1978 persuasive evidence was produced to suggest that the Cambridge manuscript was a forgery, both Shahs remained silent and Graves was too ill to renew the controversy. However, Graves valued Shah and his friendship with him, so remained loyal, if unconvinced of Shah's rightness in withholding the manuscript, and they have continued to be good friends.

In 1969 Graves had experienced another 'professional' disappointment in his dealings with an old friend. Gordon Wasson had continued his investigations into the identity of soma and, although he remained convinced that it was a mushroom, after a close study of the Sanskrit Rig-Veda hymns, the Mahabharata, and the Brahmanas, and other historical and mycological evidence, he came to the conclusion that it could not have been the *Stropharia* mushroom as he had originally postulated, but was the white-spotted scarlet *Amanita muscaria*, or fly agaric, a hallucinogenic mushroom found under birch trees in the north and under pine trees below the fortieth parallel. In *Soma: Divine Mushroom of Immortality* (1969) Wasson produced his argument on the identity of soma without, however, mentioning Graves's part in the investigation. In a review of Wasson's book in the *Atlantic Monthly* (reprinted as 'The Two Births of Dionysus' in *Difficult Questions, Easy Answers*), Graves made clear what this had been: his identification, in 'Centaur's Food' (first published in the *Atlantic Monthly*, August 1957; reprinted in *Food for Centaurs*, Doubleday, New York, 1960), of ambrosia, the Greek equivalent of soma, as a hallucinogenic mushroom; his suggestion in the same essay that Nero's 'mushrooms are the food of the Gods' joke about the death of Claudius really referred to an ancient proverb and taboo on *Amanita muscaria*, which must have been reserved only for divine consumption; also, in conversation, Wasson had consulted Graves about a Rig-Veda text that did not seem to refer to *Amanita muscaria*, but 'I reassured him that he was thinking scientifically, not poetically, and that for me this text clinched his argument . . . ' Graves was deeply hurt by the absence of his name in the book and wrote in the review:

I make no claim to be a scholar. I get, record and pass on news and intuitions; but any mention of my work in academic books is so suspect as to detract from their sales value and general acceptance. Since, science-wise (as the Americans say), I do not exist, I have nothing against Wasson for failing to recall our speculations about soma at the time that I wrote my piece about Ambrosia . . . or for recording that his identification of soma with *Amanita muscaria* was forced on him, to his own great surprise, by a recent reading of Vedic literature!

The review, otherwise, was a very generous one and in it Graves came to his own, highly reasonable (judging from the evidence in Wasson's book) conclusion that fly agaric ceased to be used as soma in India first 'because its acquisition from the High Himalayas became difficult, but then because the *Stropharia* was a more effective hallucinogen'.

Wasson saw the review and wrote to Graves, thanking him for his praise and answering the charge of not mentioning Graves's name because it was unacceptable to the scholarly establishment:

I know that you know that there is nothing to this. We haven't seen much of each other since I went to the Orient . . . I had forgotten the conversation you mention, though your account of it brought it back to me, but like you I have also forgotten the occasion for it. Please forgive me if I failed to give you credit for the continuing debt that I owe to you. My whole book is an attack on the Vedic Establishment. [21 November 1969]

He also said that his omission of 'Centaur's Food' was not 'deliberate and intentional'; he hadn't mentioned the Greeks at all, not liking to make war on two fronts at once, but was 'reserving it' for the future when he would point out that ambrosia is cognate, according to linguists, with '*amrîta*, the Vedic word for "soma" in its loftiest aspects' (see page 158). To this Graves answered, 'Complete peace between me and you on the soma plane!' As with Shah, he valued Wasson too much as a friend to bear any grudge, and maintained his occasional correspondence with him.

No date

My dear Gordon:

There will always be additions to this subject, but I am very pleased when I can contribute any possibly new material to the Wasson Collection, where it will be in safe hands.

– The bloke who wrote enclosed letter to my neighbour Bill Ellis is named Harry Keith. Yes, I *was* a little surprised by your omission of my name in the Soma–Ambrosia context, especially as my *Food for Centaurs* was still around and dated 1960. But you explained that it had slipped out of the preface in error, so I hope it slips back again when you publish your enlarged popular edition of that splendid book.

I am writing little but poetry these days; soon my new translation of the Song of Songs will appear, with lithographs by Hans Erni. It will cost three or four hundred dollars but will eventually go into a popular edition. My most important (in the popular sense) contribution to literature has been my financing, re-Englishing and intervention in *Without Hardware*[64] my daughter Catherine Dalton's terrifying book about Nuclear World Politics and the murders it has involved, beginning with my son-in-law Dr Cliff Dalton, inventor of the Nuclear Fast-Breeder and founder of Dounray Nuclear Centre. It is called *Without Hardware* and she has printed it herself on a linotype machine in Canberra. I am also trying to get it published in England, Holland and USA. This week should see a big show-down in the Australian Parliament where Labour is asking searching questions about the murders from their Liberal rivals . . .

Did you ever take up my suggestion that Triptolemus took to India (and elsewhere) *not* the discovery of grain (already old hat) but (in his serpent-drawn chariot) the news of a substitute for the *Amanita muscaria*, namely the cow-dung *Stropharia*? So that

when the possessors of the birch-forests on the High Pyrenees
raised their prices for Soma, the Indians had a substitute which
cost them nothing. Which was perhaps why India so sadly declined
in honour and now possesses only a single small temple?

Affectionately always, and love to Masha and her husband.

The bond that occurs between people who have together entered
Tlalócan[65] is very strong. Jerry Robbins and I are planning a
ballet together. He sought me out in London at a poetry reading.

Yours always   Robert

By now Graves, who was in his late seventies, was feeling constantly
unwell: 'can't get my health back properly since that operation', he
wrote to Karl Gay; the operation, on his nose, necessitated his
being put under general anaesthetic for several hours and, although
successful, led to a virus infection and general ill health, the worst
symptom of which was the loss of his short-term memory (while his
long-term memory could on occasions be horrifyingly clear, as when
he recalled his experiences in France during the First World War).

In February 1972, Ruth Fainlight sent Graves a copy of her latest
volume of poetry.

28 February 1972

Dearest Ruth:

Thank you and Alan very much for the book. Your hand with
verse is a great deal steadier than it used to be . . .

Me, I'm deplorably old-fashioned and when pornographic terms
invade the field of poetry I feel insulted somehow.

My poetic morality dates from the very early Middle Ages, not
from the Franco-American revolution of the early 1920s. The odd
thing is that I (my poems) am now coming into fashion, even in
the States. Perhaps that will happen to you too.

Love to everyone   – Robert –

After a while he recovered the stability of his health but his memory
and concentration continued to fail and he therefore·gave up his
correspondence and all other writing, except occasional poetry, and
even that ceased after publication of his final volume, *At the Gate*,
in 1974. In that year James Reeves paid his last visit to Deyá, about

which he wrote in the *Malahat Review*, no. 35, a celebratory issue for Graves's eightieth birthday:

However long Deyá lasts – and it still looks solid and permanent – Robert will always be ambling back and forth among the olives, the shut cool houses, the antique terraces. He will never be, however, what his whole life has been, a protest against becoming – a ghost.

'Summary of Critical Principles' from *The Nazarene Gospel Restored*

In Matthew 23, 1–3, Jesus orders his Nazarene followers to obey the religious authority of the Pharisees. It is, therefore, only reasonable to check the Gospel accounts of his teaching against the two Talmuds and the Mishnah, which provide full information about the tenets held by the Pharisees during his lifetime. Like them, he regarded the Mosaic Law as immutable (Matthew 5, 18) and avoided all contact with ritually unclean Gentiles (Matthew 10, 5, and 15, 24). Close scrutiny of his sayings proves him to have been well versed in the oral and written Law, in the prophets and in the later Apocalyptics; thus it is most unlikely that he either misquoted or interpreted these in a heterodox sense. Since Pharisaic teaching was mainly delivered in the form of *midrashim*, or Scriptural commentaries, it may be assumed that so was Jesus's; thus the meaning, context and original wording of many of his 'hard sayings' can usually be restored by finding the Biblical or apocryphal texts to which they refer.

No Aramaic Gospel survives, or is likely ever to have existed in manuscript; not because the Apostles were unlettered, but because the Pharisees of the first and early second centuries, whose religious discussions were held in Aramaic, refrained from writing down even the more important pronouncements of their sages. There is evidence to show that at least some of Jesus's disciples were men of high education, and that they carefully memorized his sayings, or 'Oracles', though arranging them in Pharisaic style under subject-headings, not in chronological order. A generation later, these 'Oracles' were surreptitiously jotted down and translated by Greek-speaking converts. Several Greek lives of Jesus, published towards the end of the first century for the various Gentile Churches in Egypt, Syria, Asia Minor and Greece, were based on such collections of Oracles.

291

According to Luke 1, 1–4, the handling of this pirated material varied greatly. An unbridgeable gulf now separated the original Church of Jerusalem from the Gentile Churches, which did not even agree among themselves on doctrinal questions; thus the evangelists, having only a scanty knowledge of Jewish institutions, made many mistakes in reporting Jesus's acts and sayings, and frequently contradicted one another. Not before the mid-second century were Matthew, Mark and Luke collated, and some clumsy attempts made to reconcile their divergencies.

The Gentile Christians were anxious, for political as well as doctrinal reasons, to dissociate themselves from the Jews; but especially from the Pharisees, who continued to be the spiritual leaders of Jewry after Bar Cochba's revolt had failed in AD 132. Thus the evangelists falsely represented Jesus as having himself quarrelled with the Pharisees, annulled the Law of Moses, and kept on friendly terms with the Romans. Though hesitating to suppress any large part of the original Apostolic tradition, they nevertheless disguised its true meaning by ingenious omissions or interpolations, and by wholesale rearrangement. Wanton fictions, however, are rare; if, therefore, a saying or event does not fit its Canonical context, even after critical restoration of the passage in question, a lacuna can usually be found elsewhere into which it fits exactly.

Before the Nazarene tradition can be restored, it must first be decided whether each Gospel passage under scrutiny tallies with accepted historical fact. If not, the reason must be sought for its misplacement, distortion or invention; and this is more often found in ecclesiastical politics than in scribal error, and never in original misreporting. After those passages that betray the greatest editorial ineptitude have been closely examined, several techniques of textual manipulation can be detected and isolated, familiarity with which becomes an aid in the detection of more skilful changes. References to Jesus in Jewish or Classical literature, though meagre, are valuable to investigators, once the anti-Christian bias has been discounted; and so, of course, are suppressed Gospel passages surviving in Patristic literature and elsewhere.

Catholic Christianity combines the Aramaic Apostolic tradition with Paul's heretical teaching – a 'free' variety of Judaism – and with extraneous and alien religious theory derived largely from Alexandrian Gnostic philosophy by way of the Gospel according to St John. This Gospel, though embodying valuable material omitted from the Synoptics, is textually the most corrupt in the Canon, and was not accepted as genuine by the Catholics until towards the end of the second century.

Most Catholic views on Jesus's identity and life must be discounted. He was set apart from his contemporaries because John the Baptist had acclaimed him as the Saviour of his nation; was crowned King with all the ancient rites; ceremonially reborn from a Levite virgin, and made an honorary High Priest, though physically descended from the royal House of David. Thereafter, as the King–Messiah, he had to follow a rule of conduct laid down by the Prophets and hagiographers; and since the precise details of this rule are known, the truth of the Gospel narratives can be tested by it.

Jesus expected the present world to end during his lifetime in a series of catastrophes known as the 'Pangs of the Messiah'. The Kingdom of Heaven, which would then be inaugurated and last for a thousand years, with Jerusalem for its capital, was to be a heaven on earth, peopled partly by resurrected saints, partly by a few living saints who would not die until the world ended. True to his Pharisaic principles, Jesus declined to perform miracles in proof of his divine authority (Mark 8, 12), and apart from a few faith cures, the accounts of which have been greatly exaggerated and for which he gave all credit to God, was content to foretell the wonders of the coming Kingdom. Yet certain of his acts that conveyed a moral lesson have been misreported as miracles, to rival those reputedly performed by Apollonius of Tyana. The appearance of angels in the Gospel narrative – except where they are inspired human messengers, or dream visitants – formed no part of the original Apostolic tradition, which will have been as free from supernatural embellishments as the Talmudic accounts of first-century sages.

Jesus never identified himself with God, or even with the transcendental Son of Man. His title 'Son of God' was an ancient religious one, acquired at the Coronation. He preached that only devout Jews, who kept the spirit as well as the letter of the Law, could qualify for the Kingdom of Heaven; Gentiles who had not accepted circumcision and the yoke of the Law were excluded. In his view, the imminence of the Pangs was manifested by many signs of the times, and all who desired salvation must therefore cease to live a normal life, observe strict chastity and avoid every kind of pollution. He made the statutory round of his dominions, and by preaching as he went and sending out chosen missionaries, gave his whole people the chance to repent and be saved: and presently decided that the time had come to offer himself as a royal sacrifice for them. The manner of the sacrifice had been laid down in the last chapters of Zechariah, which deal with the 'Worthless Shepherd'. Only by careful examination of these can Jesus's actions during Passion Week be intelligibly reconstructed.

Though our restoration of the Nazarene Gospel may not be correct in every detail, it is at least free from the historical objections to which the Canonical Gospels are exposed. We hold that Jesus, a well-documented personage of the first century, can be understood only in terms of his contemporary background, and are at pains to emphasize what the Church has been at pains to suppress: that he neither preached to the Gentiles, nor encouraged his apostles to do so, nor showed any concern for their fate; and that he hourly expected the literal fulfilment of eschatological prophecies. We hold also that he officially died on the Cross; but afterwards, when he recovered from his deathlike coma, and found that the Kingdom of Heaven had not come, it was gradually borne in upon him that his sacrifice had been premature. He therefore tried to expiate his error by self-exile from Palestine, intending to return only when the 'Day of the Lord' finally dawned. The Apostles continued the missionary work in obedience to his parting orders. Later, their expectation that he would triumphantly reappear became a dogma with the Gentile Churches; but he was then believed to be seated in Heaven on the right hand of God, rather than wandering somewhere in the far East among the Jews of the Dispersal, a penitent and branded fugitive.

NOTES

Part One

1. Gelat's son.

2. *Laura and Francisca*, a long poem by Laura Riding (published by the Seizin Press) about Mallorca and her relationship with Francisca, a young village girl who used to go to play at Canelluñ.

3. The doctor had denounced Graves as a foreign spy in the early thirties.

4. The cove.

5. Rope-soled shoes.

6. These were published as *The Common Asphodel* by Cassell in September 1949; this book was not published in the USA because of objections raised by Laura Riding about republication of their early collaborative essays (see page 60).

7. The Crown Albion hand press used by Graves and Riding was sold to a priest for 500 pesetas; it is now in the Imprenta Mossèn Alcover in Palma de Mallorca. For a detailed account of the press, see Hugh Ford's 'The Seizin Press' in the *Private Library*, autumn 1972; also an article by James Moran in *Black Art*, vol. 2, 1963.

8. The *Nation* did not publish the poem; the only poem Graves has published about the Bass Rock (see page 30) is 'Single Fare', which appeared in 1929.

9. San Juan, the patron saint of Deyá, whose day (24 June) is the village's fiesta. *Ensaimadas* are a sweet, whorled pastry, a speciality of Mallorca.

10. Red mullet.

11. Before leaving England Graves saw the early reviews of what remains his best single volume of poetry, *Poems 1938–45*; these first reviews were favourable (see *In Broken Images*, p. 344), but the *New Statesman* review which reached him at Deyá was openly hostile.

12. Hamish Hamilton, the publisher, for whom Hodge was doing editorial and other work at this time.

13. This story, an early version of 'Está en su Casa', was subsequently rejected by *Cosmopolitan*.

14. This is the text, often referred to by Graves, forbidding the treasurers

to accept money immorally earned; in *The Nazarene Gospel Restored* Graves cites the text from Deuteronomy 23, 18:

(275) It was told unto Jesus by James, his brother according to the spirit:

'There was brought unto the Treasury the hire of an harlot and with it the Chief Rulers have builded a chamber of easement for the High Priest, against the Day of Atonement when he abideth in the Temple.'

Wherefore James asked him: 'Master, what sayest thou? Is it not written: "Thou shalt not bring the hire of an harlot into the House of the Lord"?'

Jesus answered and said: 'Yea, and shall a High Priest which fasteth on the Day of Atonement have need of a chamber of easement? Verily, that which was gained in filth, is spent upon a work of filth.

'Therefore did Micah preach against the Temple which was in Samaria, saying of the golden adornment that hanged there, the hire of harlots: "She gathered it from the hire of harlots, and unto such it will return again."

'And he prophesied, saying: "This evil is incurable; it is also come unto Judah." '

15. See Appendix for Graves's revised opinions, as stated in *The Nazarene Gospel Restored*.

16. Graves's friend Len Lye (see *In Broken Images*) had just left his South African wife Jane while they were in the process of leaving England to live in America.

17. Betty and Ricardo Sicre; see page 49.

18. Graves's translation (published 1950) was for E. V. Rieu's Penguin Classics series. Previously *The Golden Ass* was best known in the early Elizabethan translation of William Adlington.

19. T. S. Matthews's father was a bishop.

20. Sam Graves, the youngest of Graves's children from his marriage to Nancy Nicholson, who became an architect.

21. Catherine Nicholson, the third child of his marriage to Nancy Nicholson; she was married to Clifford Dalton, the nuclear scientist, after whose death she wrote *Without Hardware* (Nicholson Prints and Publishing, Canberra, Australia, 1970); see pages 285–6 and note.

22. *Fibre*, a novel by Barry Sullivan, recommended to Graves by Liddell Hart.

23. When Karl Gay joined the Pioneer Corps in England in 1940 he had to change his name from Karl Goldschmidt; the name he chose was Kenneth Gay, but he has always been called Karl by Graves and his other friends.

24. Ramon Llull (1233–1316), Catalan poet, theologian, mystic and missionary, who studied and taught Arabic in order to convert the Arabs to Christianity.

25. Sir Thomas Browne (1605–82), physician and scholar; his works include *Religio Medici*, *Hydriotaphia*, *Urn Burial*, *Garden of Cyrus* and *Christian Morals*.

26. 'The Song of Amergin', an ancient Celtic calendar alphabet found,

according to Graves in *The White Goddess*, in several 'purposely garbled' Irish and Welsh texts and which 'briefly summarizes the prime poetic myth'. Graves 'tentatively restored' both the poem and the myth in *The White Goddess.*

27. Although Canellun and the land surrounding it was paid for by Graves, the deeds were in Riding's name – as they were for Ca'n Torrent, the house next door, which had mostly been paid for by Norman Cameron. After their break-up in 1939 Riding said that she would transfer the ownership of both houses to Graves, forgetting, however, that in 1936 she had legally given Gelat power of attorney over the properties. Riding now, therefore, sent Gelat a document instructing him to 'sell' Graves the properties, though stating that no money was to change hands. This was, however, not legally acceptable and although Graves's ownership of the houses was finally established, the land (a considerable amount) remained in Gelat's name. Graves trusted Gelat implicitly, but found some years after Gelat's death in 1949 that he had passed the land on to his son, who regarded it as his own property. There was nothing Graves could do about this and he subsequently repurchased about half the land from the Gelat family.

28. The 'Spirit of the Year'.

29. *The Perennial Philosophy* (1946) by Aldous Huxley (1894–1963). See *The White Goddess* (rev. edn, 1952), p. 483.

30. Eliot agreed and the book was published as a single volume.

31. Graves's half-brother, Richard Graves, a diplomat, who had been in Cairo when Graves went there as Professor of English Literature in 1925; he remained Mayor of Jerusalem until the British (who after the First World War had gained a mandate over Palestine) withdrew in May 1948.

32. Douglas Glass, the photographer, and his wife Jane.

33. For Puig, the name of the hill around which the houses of Deyá are built.

34. Alexander Clifford, journalist, husband of Graves's daughter Jenny. The letters they exchanged between Russia and America, and their general impressions of both countries gained during these visits, were published as a book, *The Sickle and the Stars.*

35. Archie Gittes, a painter and antique dealer, his wife Cicely, a musician, and their children lived in Palma at this time.

36. George Schwarz, a German neighbour of Graves in Deyá. In 1936 Graves and Riding translated and published (as a Seizin Press book) his memoir, *Almost Forgotten Germany.*

37. For Graves's theory on the Holy Trinity, see *The White Goddess* (rev. edn, 1952), pp. 468–9, and *The Nazarene Gospel Restored.*

38. 'A good Jewish word for an immensely long tedious hair-splitting tract.' See page 61.

39. To know everything is to forgive everything.

40. Sicre wrote a novel about his war experiences, called *The Tap on the Left Shoulder*, in which he was assisted by Graves.

41. William Le Queux wrote 'mystery and spy stories with loose and improbable plots, and such scandalous revelations as *Love Affairs of the Kaiser's Sons*; he went on writing until 1927' (from *The Long Week-End*, Graves and Hodge, 1943).

42. A reference to disturbances after the United Nations announcement of the partition of Palestine and of Jerusalem being placed under UN trusteeship. Graves had not been to Jerusalem, though perhaps he had mentioned the possibility of visiting his brother Richard there.

43. William had a serious accident on his bicycle in August 1947, badly injuring his foot. Graves had to take him to Barcelona for treatment, and it was there that he wrote most of *Seven Days in New Crete*.

44. Raphael Patai, anthropologist, folklorist and Biblical scholar; Director of the Palestine Institute of Folklore and Ethnology in Jerusalem, then, after he moved to America, Director of Research at the Theodor Herzl Institute in New York. He has lectured in several universities and written many books. Graves began a correspondence with him after reading *Man and Temple*, and they later collaborated on *Hebrew Myths: The Book of Genesis* (1964).

45. 'Oh, I have messed myself.' Seneca's wordplay (see page 55) was in combining two verbs, *concacare*, to defecate, and *concavare*, to hollow out, in Claudius's stutter.

46. '. . . meadow mushrooms are the safest; don't trust any other sort' (Horace, *Satires*, II iv 20).

47. 'What's all the fuss? Oh, it's *you*, Mr Lizard . . . /Gobbling fungi as an audience pleaser./What's the best I can suggest/To cram into your gut and gizzard?/The mushroom that got Claudius Caesar' (Martial, *Epigrams*, I xx).

48. 'On the point of death Claudius blurted out his last words: "Oh! I think I've m-m-messed mys-s-self!" '

49. A short narrative ballad by the poet Sir Henry Newbolt (1862–1938); Newbolt wrote some Kiplingesque poems and was for a while considered to be better than Kipling, but his reputation soon declined and he is now rarely read. He was knighted in 1915 and made a Companion of Honour in 1922.

50. Sir William Robertson-Nicoll (1851–1923), editor (*Bookman, The Expositor*) and author of numerous theological and critical works.

51. Alfred Noyes (1880–1958), poet and critic; perhaps now best remembered for his ballad 'The Highwayman'.

52. G. S. Fraser. See page 312, note 67. Fraser was neither Canadian nor at Oxford.

53. Graves receives cuttings of all mentions of his name in the British press, due to an arrangement he made with Joshua Podro, who supplied Graves with the press cuttings in return for a copy of each book that Graves wrote. Podro's sons continue the arrangement.

54. Stephen Spender (born 1909), poet, critic, translator, co-editor (*Horizon, Encounter*) and academic. Graves refers to him in other letters by the nickname 'Stainless Stephen Stainforth'.

55. J. L. Garvin (1868–1947), editor of the Sunday *Observer* until 1942, and author of a *Life of Joseph Chamberlain* (3 vols., 1932–34).

56. Reeves suffered from glaucoma and over the years his eyes worsened until in 1952 he lost his sight almost completely. When that happened he retired from teaching, taught himself to touch-type, organized people to read to him and continued to be extremely prolific as a poet and as an educational editor/author/anthologist.

57. Graves's literary agent, A. P. Watt Ltd (at that time managed by A. S. Watt).

58. Dorothy and Montague Simmons, English friends of Graves and Riding in the thirties. Dorothy Simmons, an artist, made a portrait bust of Graves in the thirties which was purchased by the University of Buffalo in 1968.

59. Schuyler Brinckerhoff Jackson, who married Laura Riding after her break with Graves and set up a citrus farm with her in Florida. He worked with Riding on the *Dictionary of Exact Meanings*, later retitled *Rational Meaning: A New Foundation for the Definition of Words*, until his death in 1969, when the book was still incomplete. (Riding finished it alone but it is still unpublished.)

60. George Ivanovitch Gurdjieff (1872–1950), a Caucasian Greek thinker, teacher and writer, who taught his 'System' (a philosophical-psychological programme of 'spiritual discipline' for 'awakening' man) first in Moscow, then in Europe and America. His books include *Beelzebub's Tales to his Grandson, Meetings with Remarkable Men*, and *Life is Real Only Then, When 'I Am'*. Graves never made a close study of his work (Riding told Tom Matthews that she thought Gurdjieff 'wicked'), despite his later enthusiasm for the teachings of Idries Shah. Shah's beliefs are considerably different to Gurdjieff's but he 'inherited' the Gurdjieff tradition in at least one sense: in 1936 J. G. Bennett, one of Gurdjieff's chief pupils, and other members of the English-based Gurdjieff group, met Shah and 'after two years of intensive study Bennet and his colleagues were convinced that Idries Shah had a most significant contribution to make to the Betterment of mankind in the present critical phase of human development . . . ' (from *Systematics*, the Institute's journal). They then gave

Coombe Springs, a large country estate near London where they had established their Institute, to Shah, who established there his Society for Understanding Fundamental Ideas (SUFI).

61. Katherine Mansfield (pseudonym of Kathleen Mansfield Beauchamp, 1888–1923), New Zealand short-story writer who moved to London in 1903 and married the critic John Middleton Murry in 1918. In 1917 she developed tuberculosis and six years later died at Gurdjieff's Institute for the Harmonious Development of Man, which was then set in the Château du Prieuré near Fontainebleau.

62. Margaret Russell was nurse to Graves's children in the twenties and again in 1941.

63. M. J. Tambimuttu, editor of *Poetry London*.

64. This miscellany was published as *Occupation: Writer* (Creative Age Press, New York, 1950).

65. *The Islands of Unwisdom* (Doubleday, New York, 1949; published as *The Isles of Unwisdom* in Britain).

66. Joän Junyer, Catalan painter and friend of Graves since the early thirties.

67. *The Poet's World*, an anthology of English poetry for schools edited by James Reeves (Heinemann, 1948).

68. Lucie Aldridge (*née* Brown) and her husband John Aldridge (born 1905), landscape painter and illustrator. For Graves's letters to him, see *In Broken Images*. In 1968 he did a portrait of Graves, now on permanent exhibition at the National Portrait Gallery in London. Aldridge was not a portrait painter, Graves wrote to Gay at the time, 'but he found my face an interesting landscape'.

69. Jacob Bronowski, mathematician, scientist and author of *William Blake: A Man Without a Mask*. He lived in Ca'n Torrent in the thirties but he and Graves argued and he returned to England. Bronowski was a good friend of Reeves both before and after his sojourn in Deyá.

70. Eileen Garrett, the owner of Creative Age Press, Graves's American publisher at that time.

71. Ricardo Sicre's novel, *The Tap on the Left Shoulder*.

72. The Tonga novel was never written.

73. Norman Cameron, Scottish poet and translator of Rimbaud, who lived in Deyá from 1931 to 1932.

74. Professor Lancelot Hogben (1895–1975), zoologist, physiologist, linguist and author. In *The White Goddess* Graves quotes from his 'The New Authoritarianism' (Conway Memorial Lecture, 1949) and says that as a scientist he is exceptional in having 'sufficient knowledge of history and the humanities to be able to view science objectively.'

75. The *Dictionary of Exact Meanings*. See note 59 above.

76. A scheme to restore a ruined eighteenth-century farmhouse on Jackson's farm in Pennsylvania.

77. See note 14 above.

78. See Appendix.

79. Sir Desmond MacCarthy (1877–1952), critic and literary journalist, at that time a weekly contributor to the *Sunday Times*.

80. *The Reader Over Your Shoulder: A Handbook for Writers of English Prose*, by Graves and Alan Hodge (Jonathan Cape, 1943).

81. The preliminary title of *The Nazarene Gospel Restored*, it remained as the title of one of the introductory chapters.

82. Angharad, Lynette Roberts's daughter, Graves's god-daughter.

83. In *The Nazarene Gospel Restored* Graves tried to justify the discrepancies between the two books by pointing out that the narrator of *King Jesus*, Agabus, a first-century AD Alexandrian scholar, had made no claim to be an authority on Pharisaic law, believed in the supernatural and 'relied in part on already falsified texts, so that his view does not correspond with ours on many points, particularly on the question of the Nativity.'

Later, he tried to suppress *King Jesus* because of his revised opinions (see page 191).

84. Morley Kennedy, one of Eliot's fellow directors at Faber.

85. James Thurber (1894–1961), American comic writer and cartoonist. *The Cocktail Party*, Eliot's three-act verse comedy, was first performed at the Edinburgh Festival in 1949.

86. For Graves's friendship and then argument with Eliot in the twenties, see *In Broken Images*.

87. *The Long Week-End: A Social History of Great Britain 1918–1939*, by Graves and Alan Hodge (Faber and Faber Ltd).

88. *Goliath and David* (1916) and *Treasure Box* (1919), both printed by the Chiswick Press.

89. *Over the Brazier* (1916), published by Harold Monro at the Poetry Bookshop.

90. 'Peeping Tom'.

91. *Green Chartreuse*.

92. A nursery rhyme Reeves included in his anthology, *The Merry Go-Round, A Collection of Rhymes and Poems for Children* (Heinemann, 1955).

93. Georges Simenon (born 1903), French novelist famous for his 'Maigret' books.

94. *The Black Italian*. They often discussed Jepson's series characters in their letters as if they were real people, e.g. Eve Gill, Ordinary Smith, Commodore Rupert Gill . . .

95. *The Hungry Spider* (Doubleday, New York, 1950).

96. The American edition, which was published in February 1950, over a year before the English edition.

97. Oscar Williams (1900–1964), American poet and compiler of numerous anthologies.

98. In 1955 Graves published his theory on the 'Hebrew Creation Myth' in *Adam's Rib*.

99. i.e. the London Library.

100. Guillermo Mesquida, seventeenth-century Majorcan painter, one of whose paintings, *Bodegon de Octubre* ('October Still-Life') hangs in Graves's dining room. Wasson's interest in the picture was that it shows the large *rubellon* mushroom, considered a delicacy in Catalonia. (It is not usually eaten in England, where it is known as the orange or saffron milk cap; its botanical name is *Lactarius deliciosus*.)

101. Graves sent Wasson an oil-lamp wick to demonstrate the mushroom form of the shadow it throws, thus suggesting a reason for etymological links in various languages between 'wick' and 'mushroom'.

102. Graves had been visited by an American professor of ancient history who believed that olive oil was extracted from the leaves of the tree.

103. *Mulcaster Market: Three Plays for Young Players*, by James Reeves (Heinemann, 1951).

104. 'Queen Mother to New Queen', published in *Poems and Satires* (Cassell, 1951).

105. Joseph Severn (1793–1879), painter and friend of Keats, whom he accompanied to Italy in 1820.

106. W. S. Merwin, American poet and translator.

107. Dr Paul Schmiedel, Professor of New Testament Exegesis at Zürich, who wrote the 'Gospels' entry in the *Encyclopaedia Biblica*.

108. See Appendix.

109. Exodus 24:

8. And Moses took the blood and sprinkled it on the people, and said, Behold the blood of the Covenant which the Lord hath made with you, concerning all these words.
9. Then went up Moses and Aaron, Nadab and Abihu, and seventy of the Elders of Israel:
10. And they saw the God of Israel: and there was under his feet, as it were a paved work of a sapphire stone, and as it were the body of heaven in his clearness.
11. And upon the Nobles of the Children of Israel he laid not his hand: also they saw God, and did eat and drink.

110. Graves's essay on 'Loving Mad Tom' (a 'Bedlamite' verse of the seventeenth century) was first published in 1927, reprinted in *The Common Asphodel* (1949).

111. This was in proportion to the amount of work each did on the book.

112. Part III was in fact published by itself, by Cassell in 1955, but in a small edition of only 756.

113. In Toledo.

114. *Man Friday: An Introduction to English Composition and Grammar*, by James Reeves (Heinemann, 1939).

115. *Enriquillo*, by the Dominican novelist Manuel de Jesús Galván, translated by Robert and Beryl Graves as *The Cross and the Sword* (Indiana University Press, 1955) for the UNESCO 'Collection of Representative Works: Latin American Series'.

116. Jay MacPherson, whose first book of poetry, *Nineteen Poems*, Graves published under the Seizin Press imprint in June 1952.

117. John Hayward, scholar, editor and anthologist. He shared a flat with Eliot before Eliot's second marriage.

Part Two

1. The articles were 'Mother Goose's Lost Goslings' for the *Hudson Review* and 'The Future of Western Religion' for *Nine*. The article in *History Today* was about *The Nazarene Gospel Restored*.

2. Pedro Antonio de Alarcón (1833–91), Spanish novelist, best known for his story 'The Three-Cornered Hat' which was made into a famous ballet, with music by Manuel de Falla. Graves's translation, *The Infant with the Globe*, was published in 1955 by the Trianon Press.

3. Diana Graves, the actress.

4. Alexander Clifford died in March of the following year (an obituary of him by Graves appeared in *The Times* on 28 March). Some time after, Jenny married again, to Patrick Crosse of Reuter's.

5. *Poems and Satires* (Cassell, 1951).

6. Wendy Toye, a friend of Jenny Nicholson since they had worked together as Cochrane's Young Ladies; she later became a well-known producer and director of West End musicals and plays.

7. *The Speaking Oak: An Anthology of English Poetry and Prose* (for schools), edited by James Reeves (Heinemann, 1951).

8. This was never written.

9. Beryl Graves's part of the letter.

10. *The Wandering Moon: Poems for Children*, by James Reeves, illustrated by Edward Ardizzone (Heinemann, 1950).

11. 'Old Crabbed Men' was published in *The Password and Other Poems* (1952). 'The voyage' seems to refer to an early version of 'Old and Young', published in *The Talking Skull* (1958) (in which 'moonlight' remains unchanged).

12. *Adam's Rib*. The illustrations were originally to have been done by

Judith, but in the end they were done (as wood engravings) by James Metcalf.

13. Benito Pérez Galdós (1843–1920), Spanish novelist.

14. Brendan Bracken (1901–58), politician (Minister of Information, 1941–45; First Lord of the Admiralty, 1945), publisher and newspaper proprietor.

15. *Poems 1953*. Judith had ceased to be Graves's Muse earlier in the year; he was to be without any Muse until 1959.

16. Graves wrote many of his letters on versos of old manuscripts and typescripts; on the back of this letter is the first page of Chapter 38 of *The Greek Myths*, 'Deucalion's Flood'.

17. W. H. Auden (1907–73), whose poetry Graves thought 'synthetic' and whom he accused of plagiarizing from Laura Riding (see *In Broken Images*, p. 263). There was a brief correspondence with Auden after Graves succeeded him as Professor of Poetry at Oxford in 1961; Auden wrote congratulating Graves and recommending the Fellow of Jesus College who had 'ghosted' the 'Oratio Creweiana' for him (Graves, however, could write his own).

18. Vachel Lindsay (1879–1931), American poet, who gave famous dramatic recitals of his poetry. Graves arranged for him to read at Oxford in 1920.

19. Gerard Manley Hopkins (1844–89), English poet and Jesuit priest. Reeves's edition of Hopkins's poems (Heinemann) had recently been published. Graves had written about him in *A Survey of Modernist Poetry* (with Laura Riding, 1927) – see page 194.

20. Desmond Flower, author and Graves's editor at Cassell.

21. *The Collected Poems of Norman Cameron* was published, with an introduction by Graves, by the Hogarth Press in 1957.

22. 'To the Queen'.

23. 'Poetically' alive, that is.

24. Ken McCormick, a director of Doubleday.

25. George Macaulay Trevelyan (1896–1962), historian who was appointed Regius Professor of Modern History at Cambridge in 1927 and who was later Master of Trinity College until his retirement in 1951. His well-known books include *Blenheim* (1930), *The Peace and the Protestant Succession* (1934), and *English Social History* (1942). His Clark Lectures were published in 1954.

26. Nothing seems to have come of this.

27. See page 145.

28. Field Marshal General Edmund Allenby (1861–1936). Philip Perceval Graves (1876–1953), journalist (famous for his part in the exposure of the Protocols of the Elders of Zion) and author of various books, including the mammoth *Hutchinson Quarterly Record of the War: Third Quarter*

to the Twenty-fourth Quarter. Robin Buxton, T.E.L.'s banker, who helped finance *Seven Pillars of Wisdom.* David Hogarth, archaeologist, Keeper of the Ashmolean Museum Oxford (1908), writer of travel books on the Middle East; he greatly influenced Lawrence at Oxford. Vyvyan Richards, writer and printer (he taught Graves and Riding how to print); a friend of Lawrence, in 1936 he published *A Portrait of T.E.L.* George Lord Lloyd MP, High Commissioner of Egypt, author of *Egypt Since Cromer.* Sergeant Pugh, who knew Lawrence in the RAF.

29. During the interview (in 1918) George V offered T.E.L. the OM, which he refused, and the King replied, 'Then I suppose it will have to go to Foch.' (Ferdinand Foch, who in 1918 became Marshal of France and Supreme Generalissimo of the Allied Armies on the Western Front, mounted the final offensives against the Germans that led them to request an armistice in November 1918.) Lord Stamfordham was King George's secretary.

30. 'S.A.' – to whom Lawrence dedicated *Seven Pillars of Wisdom.* Graves claimed that the initials stood for *Son Altesse* ('Her Majesty'), a term used by troubadours to describe their loves (T.E.L. had immersed himself, Graves said, in French medieval poetry).

31. Lowell Thomas, author of *With Lawrence in Arabia* (Century, New York, 1924).

32. Raymond Savage, literary agent who had at one time acted for both Graves and Liddell Hart, and who was also the literary agent for the Lawrence Estate.

33. Lawrence was the illegitimate son of Sir Thomas Chapman, an unhappily married Irish baronet who went to live in France with the daughter of a Scottish engineer; in France they lived as man and wife, under the name of 'Lawrence', until Chapman's death.

34. G. A. Henty (1832–1902), writer of adventure stories for boys, such as *Under Drake's Flag, A Tale of Venice* and *With Roberts to Pretoria,* and novels, the best known of which is *Colonel Thorndyke's Secret.*

35. *T. E. Lawrence to his Biographer R. G.* Graves, however, was not asked to reissue the book, a commercial edition of which did not appear until 1963. It originally had to be published as a limited edition because of copyright objections by Professor A. W. Lawrence (see *In Broken Images,* pp. 269 ff.).

36. i.e. in the Thames; Lawrence said that the first draft of the book was lost 'while changing trains in Reading in December, 1919', implying that the bag containing it was stolen at Reading station. Graves, however, suspected (from other comments by Lawrence) that the 'loss' of the book was deliberate and that Lawrence had thrown it into the river.

37. Eric Kennington (1888–1960), portrait painter and sculptor. A friend of Graves since the First World War, he used him as a model for the *Intellectual Soldier* in the 47th Division Memorial Statue in Battersea Park.

He was also a close friend of Lawrence and was most vociferous in attacking the Aldington book. For Graves's earlier friendship with him, see *In Broken Images*.

38. Willis Wing, Graves's literary agent in New York at this time.

39. Viking Press had commissioned the US hardback edition of *The Greek Myths*.

40. See page 135.

41. Billy Graham, American demagogic evangelist.

42. B. W. Huebsch, managing director of Viking Press.

43. *Poems of John Clare*, ed. J. W. Tibble (2 vols., 1935). This was not a complete edition of the poems. Tibble also wrote *John Clare: His Life and Poetry* (1956).

44. Lady Kathleen Liddell Hart, B. L. H.'s wife.

45. Colonel John Buchan (1875–1940), novelist and imperial statesman. During the First World War he was an intelligence officer and later Director of Information. His books include *The Thirty-Nine Steps* (1915), *Mr Standfast* (1919) and *Huntingtower* (1922). *Greenmantle* was published in 1916. In 1935 Buchan became Governor General of Canada and his biography of George V, *The King's Grace*, was published.

46. Cecil Day-Lewis (1904–72), poet, critic and, under the pseudonym of Nicholas Blake, detective story writer. Poet Laureate, 1968–72 (see page 266).

47. For the compost.

48. This was for Graves's translation of George Sand's *Un Hiver à Majorque* (1841). Sand (pseudonym of Amandine Aurore-Lucie Dupin, 1804–76) had spent several months in Valldemosa, the village nearest to Deyá in Mallorca, with Frédéric Chopin; she described the disastrous nature of their stay and their intense dislike of Majorca and Majorcans in this book. Graves wrote a 'historical introduction' to the translation, and added a 'Refutation of George Sand' by José Quadrado as an epilogue.

49. Stevie Smith (1905–71), poet and novelist. *Collected Poems* (1975).

50. The Reverend C. H. Dodd (1884–1973), theologian, and from 1950 to 1965 General Director, New Translation of The Bible. Author of numerous books about the Bible.

51. See page 24.

52. Tania Jepson's partner in the bookshop business.

53. Siegfried Sassoon (1886–1967), Graves's close war-time friend who argued with him after publication of *Goodbye to All That* in 1929 (see *In Broken Images* for their extensive correspondence). When Graves was Clark Lecturer in Cambridge they met accidentally in King's College Chapel, and afterwards Sassoon wrote that on seeing Graves again 'all the years and misunderstandings' had melted away. His 'recently printed verse'

was *The Tasking*, printed by Geoffrey Keynes in a private edition of 100 copies.

54. Graves took part in the radio programme 'Thomas Hardy – by his Friends', broadcast on the BBC Home Service on 20 February 1955.

55. A radio talk by Savage about his first meeting with Graves.

56. The 'Whitaker Negroes' were a group of American Negroes suffering from a hereditary lack of sweat glands and living in almost total isolation in a swamp by the Mississippi. Graves first heard the story from Will Price (see note 58 below), and after broadcasting about it in August 1953 received a letter from an English doctor reporting a case of the same disease in Liverpool. He also received a letter from an English woman who was going off on a tour of the Southern States and who intended to find the Whitaker Negroes – which she did; on 1 February 1955, she wrote to Graves giving an account of her findings. Graves wrote up the account, including Mrs Otto Lobstein's letter, for *Encounter* (later republished in his *Collected Short Stories*).

57. F. W. Bateson (1901–78), literary critic and academic; founder and co-editor (with Stephen de R. Wall) of *Essays in Criticism*.

58. Will Price, largely unsuccessful Hollywood scriptwriter, who met Graves in 1952 and who worked with him on various projects: a film script based on an *Arabian Nights* story (called *The World's Delight*), a film version of *I, Claudius* and the TV *Arabian Nights* 'spectacular' for NBC mentioned here – none of which was realized.

59. *Battle for the Mind: A Physiology of Conversion and Brain-Washing*, by William Sargant (Heinemann, 1957). As well as 'Englishing' the book, Graves contributed a chapter called 'Brain-Washing in Ancient Times'. He also 'Englished' Sargant's autobiography, *The Unquiet Mind*.

60. Gretl, Norman Cameron's wife (she later married John Aldridge). Alan Hodge had undertaken to prepare Cameron's *Collected Poems* for publication; they finally appeared in June 1957 (published by the Hogarth Press), with an introduction by Graves.

61. Roberto Rossellini, the Italian film director. Graves had met Rossellini and Ingrid Bergman while visiting Jenny in Rome in 1954. Not long after they considered making *Homer's Daughter*, they split up (though later reunited) and Rossellini never made the film.

62. *Mushrooms, Russia and History* was published in a limited edition, at $125 a copy.

63. Speaking between ourselves.

64. Wasson had described strong, highly coloured 'Daedalic' visions which suggested to Graves that one main use of the hallucinogenic mushroom may have been to inspire the smith (using the word in its widest meaning as 'craftsman in the visual arts'). Hence the reference to the smith-gods Wieland, Hephaestus, Daedalus and Talos.

65. F. J. Child, *The English and Scottish Popular Ballads* (5 vols., 1882–98).

66. See page 260.

67. Two of Reeves's children.

68. Of the mushroom-eating ceremony in Mexico, which took place in total darkness.

69. The *curandera*.

70. *Esclatasangs*: Mallorquín for *rubellons*. See Part One, note 100.

71. Peggy Glanville-Hicks, an Australian composer, finished *Nausicaa* in 1959; it had its premiere at the Festival of Athens, which Graves attended. He wrote the libretto, with the help of Alastair Reid (see Martin Seymour-Smith, *Robert Graves: His Life and Work*, p. 499).

72. *The Critical Sense: An Introduction to Practical Criticism*, by James Reeves.

73. Mount Holyoke College, Massachusetts. Graves gave three lectures there: 'Legitimate Criticism of Poetry', 'The White Goddess' and 'Diseases of Scholarship, Clinically Considered'.

74. Sir Anthony Eden, Prime Minister, 1955–56. This refers to the Suez crisis which culminated in the Franco-British attack and occupation of the Canal Zone on 31 October, under Eden's orders. Reeves at first supported Eden but later admitted he had made an error of judgement.

75. Alastair Reid (born 1926), Scottish poet, translator and journalist (*New Yorker*). He first met Graves in the summer of 1954 and soon became one of his closest friends. He collaborated with Graves on the libretto of *Nausicaa* (though later asked that his name not be included in the credits), helped him by doing 'rough work' on the Suetonius translation, and about this time was working with Graves on a screenplay based on *The White Goddess* (see page 310, note 38).

76. 'Adepts'.

77. 'Mushroom'.

78. King Jaime of Spain (1213–76), who conquered Mallorca in 1229.

79. Arturo Toscanini (1867–1957), the Italian conductor.

80. *Colmado:* grocery shop.

81. Graves wrote up this episode in his story 'A Bicycle in Majorca'.

82. Vincent Korda, a Hungarian, who with his brothers Alexander and Zoltan ran London Films Ltd. Alexander Korda had bought the film rights of *I, Claudius* in 1934 (see *In Broken Images*, pp. 241 ff.).

Part Three

1. A selection of Graves's poems, read by him: *Robert Graves*, Argo 191.

2. 'Around the Mountain'.

3. 'The Viscountess and the Short-Haired Girl', reprinted in *Collected Short Stories.*

4. *Five Pens in Hand* (Doubleday, New York, 1958).

5. Alston Anderson, born in 1924 in Panama (of Jamaican parents); his first and only book, *Lover Man* (Cassell, 1959), was a collection of short stories, with a foreword by Graves. Sir Arthur Bliss (1891–1975), English composer. Brendan Gill (born 1914), film critic, novelist, short-story writer and playwright; a regular contributor to the *New Yorker*.

6. Reeves had adapted Cervantes' *Don Quixote* for children.

7. Graves had been invited to compile a 'guest anthology' of poems for an issue of *New Writing* (December 1958) and write an introduction to it. His selection consisted of poems by Reeves, Matthews, Reid, Hards, Seymour-Smith, Sally Chilver and Marnie Pomeroy, an American friend.

8. Graves's father, Alfred Perceval Graves (1846–1931) was an inspector of schools in Ireland until 1910 and thereafter in England. He was secretary and president of the Irish Literary Society, editor of Everyman's Irish Library and also of many collections of Irish literature and music. His own poems, in *Father O'Flynn and Other Ballads* (1889) and *The Irish Poems of Alfred Perceval Graves* (1908), are still popular in Ireland.

9. For Graves's historical theories on *The Tempest* see *The Common Asphodel* (1949).

10. *Don Quixote del Mar*, a yacht on which Alastair Reid was sailing, with some friends.

11. Dr F. R. Leavis (1895–1978), Cambridge literary critic and educationist; one of the founders of *Scrutiny*, which he edited from 1932 until it ceased publication in 1953. Fellow of Downing College, Cambridge. His many and highly influential books include *New Bearings on English Poetry* (1932), *Revaluation* (1936), *The Great Tradition* (1948), *D. H. Lawrence: Novelist* (1955), *Dickens the Novelist* (1970), *The Living Principle: English as a Discipline of Thought* (1975).

12. For Graves's letters to Alun Lewis, see *In Broken Images.*

13. Tyrone Guthrie, English actor, director and producer.

14. *Listen*, LPV2. Recorded in London, 28 April 1959.

15. In fact it was Huw Wheldon of the 'Monitor' programme who came to interview Graves.

16. Monk Gibbon (born 1896), Irish poet (*Collected Poems*, 1951) and author of numerous prose works, including *Mount Ida* (1948) and *Inglorious Soldier* (1968).

17. *A Short History of English Poetry 1340–1940*, by James Reeves (Heinemann, 1961). *A History of English Poetry*, by W. J. Courthorpe (6 vols., Macmillan, 1895–1910).

18. The letter was written on paper printed with Sally Chilver's London address.

19. Small hot-air balloons.

20. The dog.

21. For an account of Milton's essays in favour of divorce (1634–35), see Graves's *Wife to Mr Milton*.

22. Oscar Wilde.

23. Edmund Blunden (1896–1974), poet and critic. For his friendship and correspondence with Graves, see *In Broken Images*.

24. Charles Hamilton Sorley (1895–1915), who was one of the first war poets to realize the true nature of the war and the one whom Graves himself admired most, although his output was slight and by the time he was killed he had still not had enough time for his style to mature. See *In Broken Images*, pp. 39 ff.

25. Charles Doughty (1843–1926), author of *Travels in Arabia Deserta* (1888), *Dawn in Britain* (1906), a 30,000-line epic poem, and *Adam Cast Forth: A Sacred Drama* (1908).

26. Jerome Robbins, American choreographer.

27. This discussion with Jung did not take place, however.

28. Alastair Reid's son.

29. Esteban Frances, a Spanish friend of Graves, then living in New York. Cindy, alias Aemelia Laraçuen, see pages 233 ff.

30. In the end Graves's help on the film was minimal, though he did help Peter O'Toole, who was finally cast as Lawrence, in his characterization. The script of the film was by Robert Bolt.

31. 'A woman, when she is in labour, hath sorrow, because her hour is come: but as soon as she is delivered of the child, she remembreth no more the anguish, for joy that a man is born into the world.' Ruth Fainlight's son Nimrod was just about to be born.

32. Richard Hughes (1900–1976), novelist and poet; long-standing friend of Graves. Best known for his novels *A High Wind in Jamaica*, *The Fox in the Attic* and *The Wooden Shepherdess*.

33. See Graves's story 'Old Papa Johnson'.

34. *The Penny Fiddle*, poems for children by Graves, illustrated by Edward Ardizzone, a friend of Reeves (Cassell, 1960).

35. Raymond Mortimer (1895–1980), literary editor of the *New Statesman*.

36. Sturge Moore (1870–1944), poet and historian; a close friend of Yeats. *Selected Poems* (1934).

37. This sentence was omitted by the *Observer* when printing the letter.

38. Graves first had the idea for a film based on *The White Goddess* in 1954 and had been working at it with Alastair Reid. The idea seemed 'crazy', he wrote to Savage, 'but it isn't really and may easily come off. After all it's all really about men, women and love on a high emotional not to say magic level.' William Morris, the Hollywood film agent, was

interested in the project but he failed to find a producer for it. (The idea
for a film based on *The White Goddess* has recently been revived.)

39. Terence (185–159 BC). Graves's edition of *The Comedies of Terence*
was published by Doubleday in 1962.

40. Sir Edmund Gosse (1849–1928), writer, poet and notoriously conser-
vative, inaccurate yet nevertheless influential critic, who after the war wrote
a weekly article on current books for the *Sunday Times*.

41. '11. A word fitly spoken is like apples of gold in pictures of silver.
'12. As an ear-ring of gold, and an ornament of fine gold, so is a wise
reprover upon an obedient ear.'

42. Sir John Betjeman (born 1906), Poet Laureate. His *Collected Poems*
had been an enormous success in 1958.

43. Anne Lye, Len Lye's second wife.

44. On 22 January the *Observer* had published a series of twenty-one
poems by Graves, which were republished in book form in May (*More
Poems*, Cassell, 1961) – 'finishing' the Margot episode, as Graves then
thought.

45. *The More Deserving Cases: Eighteen Reconsidered Poems* (Marlborough College Press, 1962).

46. Lucia later changed her mind and read Spanish at St Anne's College,
Oxford – while Graves was Professor of Poetry.

47. First Baron Hankey (1877–1963), Imperial statesman; member of
the War Cabinet from 1916 to 1918. Author of various books on war and
diplomacy.

48. Jan Mayen Island, north of Iceland. Presumably the disaster was
connected with oil-drilling.

49. David Graves (born 1920), Graves's eldest son, was killed in the
Second World War, in 1943.

50. Liss in Hampshire, where Jepson lives.

51. Published as *The Siege and Fall of Troy* (Cassell, 1962).

52. This film was not made, however.

53. Zulfikar Ghose (born 1935), Pakistani novelist, poet, critic and sports
journalist (writing in English). Associate Professor in English, University of
Texas at Austin, since 1969.

54. John Freeman (1880–1929), poet who worked as the secretary of
a large insurance organization; *Collected Poems* (1928). Edward Shanks
(1892–1953), poet and literary journalist.

55. Where Lucia and Stella Reeves were sharing a flat.

56. Len Lye's daughter.

57. In one of several attacks on Shah by academics, L. P. Elwell-Sutton
(Reader in Persian at the University of Edinburgh and author of several
books on Persia) wrote in 1975 that this claim (based on the 'Sayed'
part of Shah's name) by Graves, an attempt to 'upgrade' Shah's 'rather

undistinguished lineage', was 'a rather unfortunate gaffe, since all the three sons of the Prophet died in infancy'.

58. This is in connection with Rig-Veda texts stating that the urine of the priest who had taken soma was also potent. When Indra, the God of soma, was once asked by some followers for soma, he offered them his urine.

59. Kingsley Amis (born 1922), poet and novelist: with Sillitoe and Wain part of the 'Angry Young Man' generation.

60. The poem ends:

To learn impossibility from you
Is to be reconciled ungrudgingly
To yet another of the kinds of love,
The kind of love by which the loser wins.

61. 'Demigods' was the title (and subject) of one of the poems Reeves sent.

63. See page 224.

64. James Reeves disapproved of Bedales as a choice of school for Tomás.

65. Sir Walter Ralegh (*c.* 1552–1618), Elizabethan poet.

66. Richard Tottel (died 1594), publisher, printer and bookseller; editor of the famous *Tottel's Miscellany*, perhaps the first anthology of English poetry. It included poems mainly by Sir Thomas Wyatt (1503–42) and Henry Howard, Earl of Surrey (1517–47). (Tottel put titles to many of the poems.)

67. G. S. Fraser (1915–81), poet and critic; author of *The Modern Writer and his World* (1953), and *Vision and Rhetoric* (1959), both of which reprint studies of Graves. He wrote several reviews and essays on Graves's work, including 'The Reputation of Robert Graves' in *Shenandoah*, winter 1962.

The 'birthday poem', written to Margot, was 'Name Day':

Tears of delight that on my name-day
She gave me nothing, and in return
Accepted every gift I heaped upon her –
Call me the richest poet alive!

68. Brian Guinness (born 1905), Baron Moyne, Vice-Chairman of Arthur Guinness & Son, Dublin; novelist, poet and short-story writer.

69. The words and melody of 'Fain Would I Change That Note' have been attributed to Sir Tobias Hume, Elizabethan lutanist and soldier of fortune.

Part Four

1. One of the Oxford lectures.

2. Ralph Jacobs, a New York schoolteacher and friend of both Graves and Cindy.

3. Christopher Hill, historian and biographer; Master of Balliol College, Oxford, 1965–78.

4. Isla Cameron, the folksinger, a close friend of Graves.

5. Sir Laurence Olivier, the actor, and Kenneth Tynan (1927–1980), the theatre critic, who became literary manager of the National Theatre in 1963. *Much Ado About Nothing*, with Graves's textual changes, was performed at the National Theatre in 1965.

6. Dr William Waldren, American archaeologist, who lives in Deyá with his wife Jackie and their daughters. Waldren was a close friend of Graves during these years, and together they established a library (which was later closed down) and an archaeological museum at Deyá. Waldren still runs the museum as part of the Deyá Archaeological Museum and Research Centre.

7. The Indigo, a jazz night club established by Graves with his daughter Lucia and her husband Ramón Farrán, a Catalan jazz musician.

8. It came from T. S. Matthews.

9. Omar Ali-Shah, Idries's brother, who later collaborated with Graves on a new translation of the *Rubaiyyat* of Omar Khayaam (see pages 253 ff.)

10. This was never finished, though Graves did later translate the Song of Songs (Collins, 1973).

11. It was not.

12. For many years it has been Graves's custom to celebrate his birthday by writing a play – a loosely knit farce acted by members of the family and close friends, and staged at an open-air theatre built on Graves's land by his great-nephew Simon Gough, for an audience of Deyá friends. The play referred to here is 'The Lighthouse'.

13. Jackson was engaged in a long-term study of Doughty's use of language in *Arabia Deserta* (see page 310, note 25).

14. Allen Tate (1899–1981), American poet and a member of the Fugitive group. For an account of his relationship with Laura Riding, see Martin Seymour-Smith, *Robert Graves: His Life and Work*.

15. Edna O'Brien, Irish novelist and short-story writer, friend of both the Sillitoe and Graves families. Her books include *Girls in Their Married Bliss*, *A Pagan Place* and *The Love Object*.

16. *La Luna de los Perros* by Ramón J. Sender (born 1902), Spanish novelist (who later became an American citizen), whose books include *Mr*

Witt among the Rebels and *Requiem for a Spanish Peasant*. Graves's translation, *Dogs Watch the Moon*, is unpublished.

17. A 'lost one'.

18. Robert Jones, Elizabethan anthologist and poet; author of *The Muses' Garden of Delights* (1610).

19. Padraic Colum (1881–1972), Irish poet, playwright and prose writer; edited *An Anthology of Irish Verse* (1948).

20. W. Y. Tyrell, minor British poet.

21. A collection of letters and manuscripts was sold to Southern Illinois University at Carbondale.

22. Graham Greene (born 1904), novelist and dramatist. T. H. White (1906–64), novelist, best known for his Arthurian tetralogy *The Once and Future King* (1958) and for *The Goshawk* (1951).

23. See Graves's poem 'My Ghost'.

24. From 'Pride of Love':

> I face impossible feats at your command,
> Resentful at the tears of love you shed
> For the faith-hearted sick who flock to you;
> But since all love lies wholly in the giving,
> Weep on: your tears are true,
> Nor can despair provoke me to self-pity
> Where pride alone is due.

25. John Benson Brooks, a New York musician and friend of Graves. See page 265.

26. Fred H. Higginson, American academic and Graves's bibliographer (*A Bibliography of the Works of Robert Graves*, Nicholas Vane, 1966).

27. San Juan de la Cruz (1542–91), Spanish poet and mystic. Graves's introductory essay, *A lo Divino*, was to the revised edition (1968) of John Frederich Nims's translation (Grove Press Inc., New York).

28. The index of *The Sufis* was published separately.

29. *The Madness of Suibne*: a ninth-century Irish prose tale, incorporating a sequence of dramatic poems, about the tragedy of Suibne Geilt, the poet–king of Dal Araidhe. This magical and 'impossible' tale conceals a true one, according to Graves in *The White Goddess*:

That of the poet obsessed by the Hag of the Mill, another name for the White Goddess. He calls her 'the woman white with flour' just as the Greeks called her 'Alphito, Goddess of the Barley Flour'. This poet quarrels with both the Church and the bards of the Academic Establishment, and is outlawed by them. He loses touch with his more practical wife, once his Muse; and though, pitying such misery, she admits to a still unextinguished love for him he can no longer reach her. He trusts nobody, not even his best friend, and enjoys no companionship but that of the blackbirds, the stags, the larks, the badgers, the little foxes, and the wild trees. Towards the end of his tale Suibne has lost even the Hag of the Mill, who snaps her neckbone in leaping along with him; which means, I suppose, that he breaks down as a poet under the strain of loneliness. In his extremity Suibne returns to Eorann [his wife]; but her heart has gone dead by now, and she sends him coldly away.

This must be, Graves wrote, 'the most ruthless and bitter description in all European literature of an obsessed poet's predicament'.

30. Niccolo Tucci (born 1908, in Italy), American novelist, journalist and friend of Graves (who wrote the blurb to the English edition of his book *Before My Time*, 1962). His other books include *Unfinished Funeral* (1964) and *Gili Atlantidi* (1968), his autobiography.

31. Ava Gardner, the film star, had visited Graves (she is a friend of the Sicres) in 1956; he wrote an account of the visit in 'A Toast to Ava Gardner'. They corresponded occasionally but the visit Graves mentions here was cancelled and she has not visited Deyá since 1956.

31A. Graves was misinformed. Joyce never had a psychiatrist and did not die in a catatonic trance.

32. The Sillitoes made various trips to the Soviet Union, as did Beryl Graves (Graves accompanied her there in 1968).

33. *Baleares*, one of the local newspapers in the Balearic Islands.

34. Sir Francis Chichester, the first round-the-world solo yachtsman.

35. Ted Hughes (born 1930), poet.

36. Ca'n Quet, a small hotel in Deyá, which William and Elena Graves were running at that time.

37. Graves took part in the Memorial Service for John Masefield at Westminster Abbey on 20 June 1967.

38. Called 'The Individual Strikes Again', this is unpublished.

39. The King of Afghanistan, with whom it appears the Shahs were in close contact.

40. Graves's poem, 'Dew-drop and Diamond', describes the different qualities of the two muses:

The difference between you and her
(Whom I to you did once prefer)
Is clear enough to settle:
She like a diamond shone, but you
Shine like an early drop of dew
Poised on a red-rose petal.

The dew-drop carries in its eye
Mountain and forest, sea and sky,
With every change of weather;
Contrariwise, a diamond splits
The prospect into idle bits
That none can piece together.

41. Graves visited Australia, to see Catherine and to lecture, in October 1967.

42. 'Let he who deserves the laurel wear it.'

43. In a letter of 16 July 1970 to the Sillitoes, Graves wrote:

Yes, the Labour Govt had some good people in it. I will even grant you Jenny Lee, whom I remember in 1929 writing a hysterical outburst of a foul review of *Goodbye to All That*. However under a Labour Govt it eventually became an 'A' level requirement, and she settled down to be an elder stateswoman.

44. Jill Balcon, actress and broadcaster; daughter of Michael Balcon, the film producer.

45. 'Semi-Detached', in *Collected Poems 1975*.

46. The publishing firm of Jonathan Cape Ltd. For Graves's letters to Jonathan Cape, the founder and chairman of the company, who died in 1960, see *In Broken Images*.

47. Deyá in fact has retained its right to have a mayor.

48. 'By the wonderful force of genius only, without the least assistance of learning' (*Tom Jones*, 1749, xiv, i).

49. Jalâl al-Dîn, known as Rumi (of Rum, Asia Minor) (1207–73), the greatest of the Sufi poets (author of the *Mathnari*) and founder of the Merlevi order (the 'Dancing Dervishes'). See *The Way of the Sufi* (1968), by Idries Shah.

50. Parturiate: to bring forth young, to bear fruit.

51. Three recently published books by Shah: *Reflections* (Zenith Books, London), *The Way of the Sufi* and *Caravan of Dreams* (both published by Octagon Press, London).

52. 'Genius is one per cent inspiration and ninety-nine per cent perspiration.'

53. In *Reflections* Shah commented on the proverb, 'The answer to a fool is silence,' saying that 'any other answer would have the same effect in the long run'.

54. David Sutton's first book of poems, *Out on a Limb*, was published by Rapp and Whiting in 1969, with a short foreword by Graves.

55. This was never finished.

56. Christina Rossetti (1830–94) and her brother Dante Gabriel Rossetti (1828–82) were part of the Pre-Raphaelite Movement.

57. A pig-killing.

58. *The Secret Garden* of Hahmud Shabistari, translated by Johnson Pasha (Octagon Press).

59. Robert and Margaret Edwards, friends of Shah, who had bought a house in Deyá.

60. George Aczél, Deputy Prime Minister and Minister for Culture. With

Graves's friend, the poet and translator Gábor Devesceri, Aczél used to judge the poems for the Robert Graves Prize.

61. Referring to a poem Reeves had sent Graves, called 'One Propriety'.

62. *Poems 1968–70* (Cassell, 1970).

63. A. J. Arberry, classical Persian scholar and translator, author of various books including *Classical Persian Literature* (1958) and a translation of the *Rubaiyyat, Omar Khayaam, A New Version Based upon Recent Discoveries* (1952). The 'recent discoveries' were two manuscripts bought in the East by Arberry and resold, to the Chester Beatty Library and to the Cambridge University Library, in Britain.

64. *Without Hardware*, by C. R. Dalton (Nicholson Prints and Publishing, Canberra, Australia, 1970). During the Second World War Catherine had married Dr Clifford Dalton (1916–61), a New Zealand Rhodes Scholar, whose career at Oxford was interrupted by the war, during which he served as a Research Officer of the RAF. In 1947, Dalton was appointed the first head of the Fast-Breeder Reactor Division at Harwell, Berkshire, after he had written a seminal paper on fast-breeder reactors, the first of which was built, to his design and under his guidance, at Dounray in Scotland. In 1955, Dalton was appointed Chief Engineer of the Australian Atomic Energy Commission's new research establishment at Lucas Heights near Sydney. In 1961, Dalton died, under mysterious circumstances directly connected, Catherine claims in her book, with the top-secret work he was engaged on. A family friend, Dr Gilbert Bogle, the laser expert, offered to help her investigate the death, but in 1963 he was murdered. Catherine then suffered a series of severe harassments due to her continued investigation of her husband's death and other, related, 'cases of treason' in Australia – the results of which she published in *Without Hardware*.

65. Tlalócan, the Mexican Eden Graves 'entered' on eating the psilocybe mushroom; see 'The Universal Paradise' in *Difficult Questions, Easy Answers*.

Index

Abercrombie, Lascelles, 187, 212

Aczél, George, 281, 316–17 (n. 60)

Alarcón, Pedro Antonio de, 102, 121, 303 (n. 2)

Aldington, Richard, 47, 122–3, 124, 125–6, 132–3, 140, 142

Aldridge (*née* Brown), Lucie, 59, 300 (n. 68)

Ali Shah, Ikbar, 281

Ali-Shah, Omar (Mo), 18, 238, 243, 253–4, 260, 263, 273, 276, 280–83, 313 (n. 9), 317 (n. 63)

Allan, Mary, 241

Allenby, Edmund Henry, Viscount, 123, 304 (n. 28)

Alswang, Ralph, 180, 181

Amis, Kingsley, 219, 312 (n. 59)

Anderson, Alston, 174, 188, 309 (n. 5)

Arberry, Dr A. J., 283, 317 (n. 63)

Ardizzone, Edward, 192, 310 (n. 34)

Ascoli, David, 264

Auden, W. H., 113, 116, 200, 304 (n. 17)

Balcon, Jill, 268, 316 (n. 44)

Balcon, Michael, 269, 316 (n. 44)

Bateson, F. W., 144, 307 (n. 57)

Beaumont, Agnes, 85

Beaumont, Hugh, 184, 185

Beerbohm, Max, 102, 141

Bennett, J. G., 132, 299 (n. 60)

Benton, Senator, 183

Bergman, Ingrid, 145, 174, 307 (n. 61)

Betjeman, Sir John, 200, 311 (n. 42)

Blau, Tom, 212

Bliss, Sir Arthur, 174, 309 (n. 5)

Blunden, Edmund, 187, 252, 310 (n. 23)

Bogle, Dr Gilbert, 317 (n. 64)

Boland, Brigid, 171

Bolt, Robert, 310 (n. 30)

Bracken, Brendan, 14, 111, 304 (n. 14)

Brando, Marlon, 191

Bridges, Robert, 114

Bronowski, Jacob, 59, 300 (n. 69)

Brooke, Rupert, 187

Brooks, John Benson, 256, 265, 314 (n. 25)

Buchan, Colonel John, 134, 250, 306 (n. 45)

Butler, Samuel, 118, 119

Buxton, Robin, 123, 305 (n. 28)

Cameron (later Aldridge), Gretl, 145, 307 (n. 60)

Cameron, Isla, 232, 262, 313 (n. 4)

Cameron, Norman, 14, 60, 114, 115, 166, 297 (n. 27), 300 (n. 73), 307 (n. 60)

Campbell, Roy, 173

Cape, Jonathan, 61, 133, 269, 316 (n. 46)

Carnarvon, Lady, 172, 173

Carroll, Lewis, 121

Cassell, 81, 98, 104, 112, 113, 124, 125, 140, 141, 172, 264, 268, 303 (n. 112), 304 (n. 20)

Chapman, Sir Thomas, 305 (n. 33)

Chertoff, Mordecai, 45, 46

Chichester, Sir Francis, 261, 315 (n. 34)

Child, F. J., 150, 308 (n. 65)

Chilver, Sally, 58, 60, 183, 203, 235, 253, 255, 309 (nn. 7, 18)

Chopin, Frédéric, 136, 143, 306 (n. 48)

Churchill, Sir Winston, 133, 134, 136–7

Clare, John, 96, 117, 131, 306 (n. 43)

Clifford, Alexander, 44, 102, 297 (n. 34)

Clifford (*née* Nicholson, later Crosse), Jenny, 17, 71, 79, 102, 124, 125, 154, 162, 171, 172, 177, 178, 181, 182, 188, 190, 208, 236, 237, 239, 303 (nn. 4, 6)

Cohen, Alexander, 177–82 *passim*, 247

Cohen, E. E., 45

Coleridge, Samuel T., 88, 146, 147, 152, 177, 178, 200, 258

Collins, 124, 125, 126–7

Colum, Padraic, 250, 314 (n. 19)

Cook, A. B., 107–8

Cornford, F., 187

Coward, Sir Noel, 114

Cox, Geoffrey, 205

Crosse, Patrick, 116, 124, 173, 303 (n. 4)

Cummings, E. E., 161

Index

Dahlberg, Edward, 209, 210
Dalton, Catherine, *see* Nicholson
Dalton, Dr Cliff, 285, 317 (n. 64)
Davie, Donald, 144
Davies, W. H., 24, 187, 212, 225
Davy, Charles, 197
Day-Lewis, Cecil, 136, 150, 266, 267, 268, 274, 306 (n. 46)
de la Mare, Walter, 187, 212
Devesceri, Gábor, 317 (n. 60)
Dickie, James, 257
Dodd, Rev. C. H., 139–40, 306 (n. 50)
Doubleday, 98, 118, 124–8 *passim*, 131, 140, 141, 156–7, 162, 175, 192, 197, 200, 214, 234, 240, 241
Doughty, Charles, 187, 310 (n. 25)
Duncan, Ronald, 82

Eastwood, Berwyn and Margaret, 58
Eden, Sir Anthony (later Lord Avon), 157
Edwards, Robert and Margaret, 279, 316 (n. 59)
Eliot, T. S., 13, 36–7, 40–43 *passim*, 47, 51, 52, 58, 73–8 *passim*, 94–5, 97–8, 209, 297 (n. 30), 301 (n. 86)
Ellis, Bill, 285
Elwell-Sutton, L. P., 311 (n. 57)
Engler, Dr, 190–91
Epstein, Dr, 74
Erni, Hans, 285

Faber and Faber, 74, 75, 97–8, 110, 119, 142
Fainlight, Ruth, 13, 137, 191–2, 245, 248, 258–60, 276–8, 286, 310 (n. 31)
Farrán, Ramón, 239, 259, 313 (n. 7)
Farrar Straus, 94–5, 98, 103, 104, 107
Festing-Jones, Henry, 118, 274

Fielding, Henry, 271, 316 (n. 48)
Fishan Khan, Jan, 282, 283
Fitzgerald, Edward, 254, 261, 280
Fitzgerald, Scott, 116
Flecker, James Elroy, 187, 192
Flower, Desmond, 114, 304 (n. 20)
Flynn, Erroll, 202
Foch, Marshal Ferdinand, 305 (n. 29)
Frances, Esteban, 189, 196, 310 (n. 29)
Fraser, G. S., 57, 222, 299 (n. 52), 312 (n. 67)
Freeman, John, 212, 311 (n. 54)
Freud, Sigmund, 190, 262
Frost, Robert, 161, 188, 191, 222
Fuad, King, 193

Galdós, Benito Pérez, 107, 304 (n. 13)
Galván, Manuel de Jesús, 96, 138, 142, 303 (n. 115)
Gardner, Ava, 259, 315 (n. 31)
Gardner, Dr Gerald, 214
Garrett, Eileen, 59–60, 61, 300 (n. 70)
Garrod, Miss, 86
Garvin, J. L., 57, 199, 299 (n. 55)
Gay, Karl and Rene, 13, 23, 27, 29, 37, 40–46 *passim*, 56, 58, 59–60, 70, 115–17, 132, 144, 160, 163, 173, 184–5, 187–9, 197, 232, 246–8, 251, 252–3, 269–70, 286, 296 (n. 23)
Gelat, Juan (father, son, grandson), 23, 26, 28, 35, 59, 115, 172, 297 (n. 27)
genius, defined by R.G., 271–4, 316 (nn. 48, 52)
George V, King, 123, 216, 305 (n. 29)
Georgian Poetry, 187, 192, 211–12
Ghose, Zulfikar, 211, 311 (n. 53)
Gibbon, Monk, 180, 194, 309 (n. 16)

Gill, Brendan, 102, 174, 309 (n. 5)
Gittes, Archie and Cicely, 44, 297 (n. 35)
Glanville, Janet, *see* Seymour-Smith
Glanville-Hicks, Peggy, 155, 308 (n. 71)
Glass, Douglas and Jane, 44, 297 (n. 32)
Gosse, Sir Edmund, 199, 311 (n. 40)
Gough, Simon, 313 (n. 12)
Graham, Billy, 128, 131, 306 (n. 41)
Graves, Alfred Perceval, 176, 278, 309 (n. 8)
Graves, Beryl, 17, 23, 28, 29, 30, 33, 34, 44, 46, 50, 59, 67, 71–2, 83, 89, 93, 94, 96, 102, 112–13, 117, 118, 124, 139, 144, 146, 150, 160, 165, 173, 183, 184, 187, 188, 190, 191, 196, 200, 202, 211, 219, 220, 232, 234, 242, 243, 249, 251, 261, 277, 279
Graves, Clarissa, 113
Graves, David, 206, 311 (n. 49)
Graves, Diana, 102, 177, 303 (n. 3)
Graves, Elena, 280, 315 (n. 36)
Graves, John, 59
Graves, Juan, 23, 26, 33, 35, 50, 59, 116, 124, 139, 160, 165, 171, 179, 183, 204, 210, 223, 239
Graves (later Farrán), Lucia, 23, 25, 26, 33, 50, 93, 124, 139, 154, 156, 171, 183, 187, 202–11 *passim*, 222, 239, 250, 253, 259, 280, 311 (n. 46), 313 (n. 7)
Graves, Philip Perceval, 123, 133, 304 (n. 28)
Graves, Richard, 44, 50, 297 (n. 31), 298 (n. 42)
Graves, Sam, 35, 296 (n. 20)
Graves, Tomás, 113, 114, 124, 154, 172, 174, 176, 183, 187, 190, 202, 204, 210, 212, 220, 223, 259
Graves, William, 23, 25, 33, 50, 59, 93, 101, 120, 124, 134, 139, 171, 173, 175,

Index

183, 202, 203, 204, 207,
210, 212, 222, 238, 244,
259, 270, 298 (n. 43)
Greene, Graham, 253, 314
(n. 22)
Greta, 96, 97, 115
Guinness, Alec, 162, 171,
175, 183, 184, 185
Guinness, Bryan, Baron
Moyne, 224, 312 (n. 68)
Gurdjieff, George Ivanovich,
58, 299 (n. 60)
Guthrie, Tyrone, 178, 179,
181, 309 (n. 13)

Haig, Douglas, first Earl,
204–5
Haldane, S., 266
Hamilton, Hamish, 14, 58,
60, 61, 62, 295 (n. 12)
Hammond, John, 256
Hamon, Jake, 207
Hankey, Lord, 205, 311
(n. 47)
Hards, Terence, 13, 150,
204, 260, 275, 309 (n. 7)
Hardy, Thomas, 142, 187,
307 (n. 54)
Hart, Captain Sir Basil
Liddell, 13–14, 36, 122,
132–4, 136, 166–7,
204–5, 296 (n. 22)
Hart, Lady Kathleen Liddell,
133, 166, 306 (n. 44)
Hawking, Eileen, 83
Haymon, Mark, 139
Hayward, John, 98
Heim, Professor Roger, 16,
155, 216
Heinemann, William, 61, 83,
105, 144, 177
Hemingway, Ernest, 116,
173
Henty, G. A., 125, 305
(n. 34)
Higginson, Fred, 256, 314
(n. 26)
Hill, Christopher, 232, 313
(n. 3)
Hodgart, M. J. C., 135
Hodge, Alan, 13, 27–9, 31,
39, 42, 60–62, 67–8, 106,
145, 150, 301 (nn. 80,
87), 307 (n. 60)
Hodgson, Ralph, 187, 192
Hofmann, Professor Albert,
196, 213, 216

Hogarth, David, 123, 305
(n. 28)
Hogben, Professor Lancelot,
60
Hokusai, 120
Hopkins, Gerard Manley,
114–15, 193, 194, 199,
304 (n. 19)
Horne, Lena, 180
Horniman, Michael, 264
Horvat, Leslie, 175
Housman, A. E., 187
Huebsch, B. W., 128, 306
(n. 42)
Hughes, Richard, 192
Hughes, Ted, 16, 262, 315
(n. 35)
Hume, Sir Tobias, 225, 250,
312 (n. 69)
Huxley, Aldous, 42, 297
(n. 29)

Jackson, Schuyler
Brinckerhoff, 14, 58, 61,
196, 206, 244, 299
(n. 59), 313 (n. 13)
Jacobs, Ralph, 243, 247, 313
(n. 2)
Jalāl al-Dîn (Rumi), 272,
316 (n. 49)
James, William, 116
Jepson, Selwyn and Tania,
14, 79–82, 101–3,
118–22, 125–9, 131,
140–41, 143, 162,
180–81, 185, 207, 209,
233, 244–5, 252, 254, 256,
265, 301 (n. 94)
Joyce, James, 116, 259–60,
262
Jung, Carl Gustav, 109, 110,
127, 154, 188, 190
Junyer, Joän, 59, 300 (n. 66)

Kahn, Robert, 182
Kedourie, Elie, 137
Keith, Harry, 285
Kennedy, Morley, 74, 301
(n. 84)
Kennington, Eric, 126, 127,
305 (n. 37)
Kipling, Rudyard, 56
Korda, Alexander, 171, 308
(n. 82)
Korda, Vincent, 162, 171,
308 (n. 82)
Kubler, Otto, 67

Lacey, Mrs, 182
Laraçuen, Aemelia (Cindy),
see Muses
Laughton, Charles, 171
Lawrence, Professor, A. W.
(Arnie), 123, 124, 133,
184–5, 305 (n. 35)
Lawrence, D. H., 126
Lawrence, Mrs (mother of
T. E.), 126, 132
Lawrence, Sam, 174
Lawrence, T. E., 111, 122–4,
126, 129, 132–4, 136–7,
140, 142, 184, 186, 191,
305 (nn. 29–37 passim)
Lean, David, 184, 185
Leavis, F. R., 177, 200
Lee, Jenny, 267, 316 (n. 43)
Lewis, Alun, 177, 309
(n. 12)
Lindsay, Vachel, 114, 304
(n. 18)
Lloyd, George Lord, 305
(n. 28)
Llull, Ramon, 37, 296
(n. 24)
Lobstein, Mrs Otto
('Whitaker Negroes'), 307
(n. 56)
Lowell, Robert, 161
Luce, Henry, 195
Luckner, Count von, 144
Lye, Anne, 202, 311 (n. 43)
Lye, Jane and Len, 33, 58,
189, 296 (n. 16)
Lye, Yancy, 212, 311 (n. 56)

MacCarthy, Sir Desmond,
67, 301 (n. 79)
McCormick, Ken, 119, 121,
125–31 passim, 140, 157,
200
McNab, Jess, 188, 190
MacPherson, Jay, 96–7, 303
(n. 116)
Magnani, Anna, 162
Mandersteig, Hans, 145
Mansfield, Katherine, 58,
300 (n. 61)
Marin, Louis, 241
Marples, A. Ernest, 189
Masefield, John, 187, 261,
315 (n. 37)
Matthews, Julie, 31, 33–6
Matthews, Tom, 13, 14, 27,
31–3, 41, 115, 145, 195–6,
204, 206, 236, 243–4, 296

(n. 19), 309 (n. 7), 313 (n. 8)
Merrill, George, 144, 153
Mesquida, Guillermo, 86, 302 (n. 100)
Metcalf, James and Pilar, 140, 184, 238, 270, 303–4 (n. 12)
Meyer-Wallace, Alice, 268
Milligan, Spike, 266
Monro, Harold, 187, 301 (n. 89)
Moore, George, 31, 32
Moore, Sturge, 195, 310 (n. 36)
Morgenstein, Charles, 213
Morley, Frank, 110–11
Morris, William, 197, 202, 221, 310 (n. 38)
Mortimer, Raymond, 194–5, 310 (n. 35)
Murrow, Ed, 188
Murry, John Middleton, 300 (n. 61)
Muses (R.G.'s), 82, 83, 224–5, 231–2; Judith, 82, 102, 103, 260, 304 (n. 15); Margot, 201, 206, 212, 218–20, 223–7, 231–3, 248–9, 258–9, 311 (n. 44), 312 (n. 67); Cindy (Emile, Aemilia), 83, 189, 227, 232–43 *passim*, 245–50, 254–5, 256, 257, 258, 262, 263, 265, 310 (n. 29), 331 (n. 2); Julie, 257–8, 259, 263, 265, 276, 277, 315 (n. 40)

Napoleon, 272
Nazarene Gospel Restored, The, 36, 62 ff., 80 ff., 94–8 *passim*, 104, 106–7, 124, 134–43 *passim*, 241, 291–4, 301 (nn. 81, 83)
Newbolt, Sir Henry, 56, 298 (n. 49)
Nicholson (later Ðalton), Catherine, 36, 266, 279, 285, 296 (n. 21), 316 (n. 41), 317 (n. 64)
Nicholson, Jenny, *see* Clifford, Jenny
Nicholson, John, 283
Nicholson, Nancy, 23, 36, 71, 72, 152

Noyes, Alfred, 56, 298 (n. 51)

O'Brien, Edna, 246, 313 (n. 15)
O'Toole, Peter, 310 (n. 30)
Olivier, Sir (later Lord) Laurence, 234, 313 (n. 5)
Owen, Wilfred, 187

Palmer, Dr, 155–6
Parkinson, Cyril Northcote, 253
Patai, Raphael, 18, 51, 65, 66, 74, 171, 191, 202, 298 (n. 44)
Penguin Books, 101; Classics, 102, 104, 121, 124, 127, 128, 142, 154
Pescadora, Juana, 26
Podro, David, 50
Podro, Fanny, 91
Podro, Joshua, 14–15, 17, 27, 44–6, 50–51, 62–72 *passim*, 74–8 *passim*, 90–91, 95, 97, 98, 106, 124, 126, 128, 134, 135, 151, 154, 189, 299 (n. 53)
Pomeroy, Marnie, 309 (n. 7)
Potter, J. G. F., 199
Pound, Ezra, 194, 195
Price, Will, 144, 171, 307 (nn. 56, 58)
Priestley, J. B., 193
Pugh, Sergeant, 123, 305 (n. 28)
Pushkin, Alexandr, 279

Quennell, Peter, 14
Queux, William Le, 49, 298 (n. 41)

Ralegh, Sir Walter, 222, 312 (n. 65)
Ramsbottom, John, 54
Ransom, John Crowe, 161–2
Rattigan, Terence, 184, 185
Read, Sir Herbert, 38, 111, 144, 154, 209, 210
Reeves, Ethel, 79, 156
Reeves, Gareth, 152, 308 (n. 67)
Reeves, James and Mary, 15, 23–7, 56–9, 78–9, 82, 88–9, 96–7, 112–15, 117–18, 131–2, 135–6, 139–40, 144, 150, 152,

156, 163, 166, 173–80 *passim*, 186–7, 192–3, 200–203, 208, 211–15, 218–22, 225–7, 250, 253, 255–6, 265–6, 280, 286–7, 299 (n. 56), 300 (n. 69), 308 (n. 74), 309 (nn. 6, 7, 17)
Reeves, Stella, 152, 208, 211, 212, 219, 225, 251, 253, 268, 280, 311 (n. 55)
Reid, Alastair, 51, 155, 157, 162, 172, 174, 177, 178, 188, 201, 212, 219, 220, 308 (n. 75), 309 (nn. 7, 10), 310 (nn. 28, 38)
Rhys, Keidrych, 37, 71
Richards, Arnold, 123
Richards, Vyvyan, 123, 305 (n. 28)
Riding, Laura, 13, 14, 15, 23, 24, 27, 29, 42, 58, 60, 61, 103, 161, 173, 187, 196, 204, 206, 207, 244, 295 (nn. 2, 6, 7), 297 (n. 27), 299 (nn. 59, 60), 304 (n. 17), 305 (n. 28)
Rieu, E. V., 130, 150
Robbins, Jerome, 188, 190, 197, 202, 286, 310 (n. 26)
Roberts, Angharad, 72, 301 (n. 82)
Roberts (later Rhys), Lynette, 13, 15, 37, 71–2, 87–8, 301 (n. 82)
Robertson-Nicoll, Sir William, 56, 298 (n. 50)
Roe, T. W. C., 252
Rosenberg, Isaac, 187
Rosentingl, Arnaldo and Ruth, 50
Ross, Annie, 266
Rossellini, Roberto, 145, 174, 307 (n. 61)
Rossetti, Christina and Dante Gabriel, 278, 316 (n. 56)
Russell, Margaret, 58, 300 (n. 62)

Salote, Queen of Tonga, 118
San Juan de la Cruz, 257, 314 (n. 27)
Sand, George, 136, 138, 143, 306 (n. 48)
Sargant, William, 145, 307 (n. 59)

Index

Sassoon, Siegfried, 118, 142,
154, 187, 252, 306
(n. 53)
Savage, Derek, 15, 37–40,
83–5, 89–90, 92–3,
103–4, 110–11, 141–2,
153–4, 186, 307 (n. 55)
Savage, Raymond, 123, 305
(n. 32)
Schmiedel, Dr Paul, 90–91,
302 (n. 107)
Schon, Bob, 211
Schwarz, George, 44, 297
(n. 36)
Searle, Ronald, 175, 176
Sender, Ramón J., 246, 313
(n. 16)
Severn, Joseph, 89, 302
(n. 105)
Seymour-Smith, Frank, 29
Seymour-Smith (*née*
Glanville), Janet, 93, 101,
102, 112, 113, 159,
209–11
Seymour-Smith, Martin, 15,
29–30, 60, 88, 93, 101,
103, 112, 150, 159, 175,
203–4
Shabistari, Hahmud, 278,
316 (n. 58)
Shah, Idries, 15–16, 18, 83,
213–16, 218, 222–4,
232–43 *passim*, 249,
253–4, 257, 263, 264–5,
268–9, 270–75, 276,
278–9, 280–83, 299
(n. 60), 311 (n. 57)
Shanks, Edward, 212, 311
(n. 54)
Sharp, Cecil J., 175
Shaw, G. B., 272
Sicre, Betty and Ricardo, 33,
48, 49, 152–3, 155, 178,
183, 188, 296 (n. 17), 298
(n. 40), 300 (n. 71)
Sillitoe, Allan, 16, 137–8,
175, 182–3, 191–2,
245–6, 248, 259, 261, 315
(n. 32), 316 (n. 43)

Simenon, Georges, 80, 301
(n. 93)
Simmons, Dorothy and
Montague, 58, 299 (n. 58)
Simon, George and Joanna,
16, 47–50, 257
Simon, Helena, 48, 49
Skelton, John, 194, 195
Smith, Janet Adam, 78
Smith, Stevie, 138, 306
(n. 49)
Somers, Sir George, 176–7
Sorley, Charles Hamilton,
187, 310 (n. 24)
Spender, Humphrey, 96
Spender, Stephen, 57, 96,
174, 299 (n. 54)
Spiegel, Sam, 184, 185, 188,
191
Squire, J. C., 187
Stalin, Josef, 94
Stamfordham, Lord, 123,
126, 305 (n. 29)
Starkie, Enid, 200
Stevenson, Adlai, 183
Stickney, Trumbull, 265,
268
Suibne Geilt, 257, 314–15
(n. 29)
Sullivan, Barry, 36, 296
(n. 22)
Sutton, David, 275–6

Tambimuttu, M. J., 58, 300
(n. 63)
Tate, Allen, 244, 313 (n. 14)
Tennyson, Alfred, Lord, 109
Thomas, Edward, 187
Thomas, Lowell, 123, 133,
305 (n. 31)
Thurber, James, 75, 145,
301 (n. 85)
Toscanini, Arturo, 160, 308
(n. 79)
Tottel, Richard, 222, 312
(n. 66)
Toye, Wendy, 103, 141, 207,
303 (n. 6)

Trevelyan, George
Macaulay, 120, 304 (n. 25)
Trotsky, Leon, 94
Tucci, Niccolo, 259, 315
(n. 30)
Tynan, Kenneth, 234, 313
(n. 5)
Tyrell, W. Y., 250

Viking Press, 127, 131, 306
(nn. 39, 42)

Wain, John, 16, 193–5,
197–200
Waldren, Jackie and Dr
William, 236, 241, 313
(n. 6)
Walter, John, 138–9
Warner Bros., 120–21
Wasson, R. Gordon, 16,
52–6, 75, 85–7, 93–4,
107–10, 121, 138–9,
145–9, 152, 155–9
passim, 163, 174, 187–91
passim, 196, 213,
215–16, 227–8, 233,
283–6, 302 (nn. 100,
101), 307 (n. 64)
Wasson, Dr Valentina, 16,
52, 107, 108, 165, 187
Watt, A. S. and W. P., 57,
62, 95, 105, 119, 120–21,
121–2, 123–4, 129, 185,
299 (n. 57)
Wheldon, Huw, 309 (n. 15)
White, T. H., 253, 314
(n. 22)
Wilde, Oscar, 67, 187
Williams, Oscar, 84, 302
(n. 97)
Wing, Willis, 127, 182, 306
(n. 38)
Woodward, David, 205
Wyllie, Philip, 188

Yeats, W. B., 24, 180, 194–5
Youngstein, Max, 162

Zeitlin, Dr Solomon, 36

COLOPHON

The incorrect pagination of the front matter has been adhered to in this edition in order to maintain the accuracy of the index. The text of this book was set in Sabon, a typeface designed by Jan Tschichold (1902–1974). Early in his career, he was influenced by the classic Italian Renaissance types. The front matter was set in Bembo, a typeface designed by Aldus Manutius and Francesco Griffo in the early 16th century.

Composed by Books, Deatsville, Alabama.

The book was printed by Princeton University Press, Lawrenceville, New Jersey on acid free paper.

This is part of a series of Robert Graves books. Other titles in the series include IN BROKEN IMAGES: Selected Correspondence (1914–1946); THE GREEK MYTHS; THE HEBREW MYTHS; THE NAZARENE GOSPEL RESTORED; and POEMS ABOUT WAR.